A HISTORY OF

THE HORSHAM
COUNTY CRICKET FESTIVAL

1908-2007

Robin Martin-Jenkins. Christopher Martin-Jenkins' son Robin is a product of Horsham CC's colts system (and thus a 'Dewdrop').
He once scored two centuries in the same day for Horsham Under-13s.
His career best bowling performance (7-51 v. Leicestershire) came at Horsham in 2002.

To my very good friend Peter Morgan, who has been a greater influence on my sporting life than he will ever know.

A HISTORY OF   *David Boorman.*

THE HORSHAM
COUNTY CRICKET FESTIVAL
1908-2007

by

DAVID BOORMAN

ROGER HEAVENS
2008

Also by David Boorman

A HISTORY OF NUTHURST CRICKET CLUB 1830-2004.

Other *Roger Heavens* publications

Limited Edition Exact Facsimiles:
Volumes I to XV of "Scores and Biographies" by Arthur Haygarth
Henry Bentley's "Book of Cricket", with a new preface by David Rayvern Allen
John Lillywhite's Cricketers' Companion 1865
Fresh Light on 18th Century Cricket by G. B. Buckley
Fresh Light on Pre-Victorian Cricket by G. B. Buckley

Volume XVI "Scores and Biographies" by Arthur Haygarth
Indexes to Scores and Biographies Volumes I to XVI
Hambledon: The Men and the Myths by John Goulstone
Arthur Haygarth Remembered

First Published July 2008

British Library Cataloguing-in-Publication Data
A Catalogue record for this book is available from
The British Library

ISBN 978 1 900592 50 5

Edited by Roger Packham

Published by Roger Heavens
2 Lowfields, Little Eversden, Cambridge, CB23 1HJ, England
www.booksoncricket.net

Typeset and printed by E. & E. Plumridge Ltd.,
Linton, Cambridge, England

CONTENTS

LIST OF ILLUSTRATIONS

FRONTISPIECE: Robin Martin-Jenkins. Christopher Martin-Jenkins' son Robin is a product of Horsham CC's colts system (and thus a 'Dewdrop'). He once scored two centuries in the same day for Horsham Under-13s. His career best bowling performance (7-51 v. Leicestershire) came at Horsham in 2002.

Between pages 80 and 81

1. George Cox's swan-song. Eighty years on his match return of 17-106 is still the only occasion a Sussex player has taken 17 wickets in a match.

2. Educated at Collyer's Grammar School when it was situated at the bottom of The Causeway, the bespectacled Tim Killick (4 matches) made his debut for Horsham CC in 1892. In 1894 he took six wickets and scored an unbeaten century against Brighton Teachers. A talented amateur musician, he was much in demand at local concerts.

3. George Pearce (4 matches). Very much a local boy, George's family ran a butcher's shop in East Street. His mother helped run the whist drives during the Carnival.

4. The legendary Ranji's only appearance at Horsham was a disappointment – he was described as being 'slow between the wickets'.

5. The 1932 Carnival was a great success. On a deliciously warm evening, huge crowds thronged the streets and festivities culminated in a flying display in which a car was flour-bombed. This reportedly had 'the greatest effect on the emotions of the spectators.'

6. Sussex at Horsham, 1913. Left to right: Back row: WH Edwards (scorer), RR Relf, AE Relf, PGH Fender, JH Vincett, GR Cox, J Vine. Middle Row: P Cartwright, HL Wilson, HP Chaplin (capt), NJ Holloway, AH Lang. On grass: VWC Jupp.

7. Yet more Festival rain in 1946 as Field Marshal Montgomery inspects the Sussex and Glamorgan troops on the first day of peacetime cricket in Horsham. To 'Monty's' right are Sussex players Jack Nye, Jim Cornford, Harry Parks, John Langridge, Jack Oakes and Billy Griffith, while behind Griffith are Hugh Bartlett and Jim Langridge. On his immediate left is Glamorgan skipper John Clay. When play did get under way, Sussex were bowled out twice in under four hours. Their first innings total of 35 is the lowest first-class score ever made on the ground.

8. The opening day attendance for the Surrey game in 1931 is believed to be a ground record. Despite a century from Duleepsinhji the Notts match was to end controversially.

9. A view taken in the 1960s showing Joker Oakes' cottage at its best.

10. A bleak opening day view of the 1935 Festival. Inspecting the rain-sodden pitch are (left to right): Maurice Tate, G.B. Cuthbertson and A.W. Snowden of Northants, Alfred Oakes, Arthur Gilligan, Alan Melville and Sussex CCC secretary Lance Knowles. Rain completely ruined both matches.

11. With 12 appearances Surrey have visited Horsham more often than any other county. In 1912 Razor Smith's match figures of 11-132 ensured that the spoils went to the visitors. Sussex wicket-keeper AH Lang (pictured) was among those killed in the Great War.

12. A view from Denne Hill during the match against Cambridge University in 1971. This game was awarded to Horsham as part of the town club's bi-centennial celebrations.

13. John Barclay (4 matches) scored a century against Sri Lanka at Horsham in 1979. In July 1971 the 'local squash club player' was assisting Horsham CC in a league match against Hastings. Barclay's great-uncle played on the ground in 1889.

14. Tony Pigott (8 matches) enjoyed a love-hate relationship with Horsham. A playing member of Horsham CC, three of Sussex's five most expensive bowling analyses in one-day cricket have his name alongside them.

15. By contrast, another of Horsham's favourite sons, Old Collyerian Paul Parker (6 matches) has a remarkable one-day record at Cricket Field Road averaging over 70. Another 'Dewdrop', Parker is one of only two Sussex players to have made a first-class and one-day century on the ground. With Allan Green he holds the Sussex record 2nd wicket stand in first-class matches at Horsham.

Between pages 176 and 177

16. Here in 1898 there is no trace of the present-day Cricket Field Road, while the pavilion – presented to the club by the Lucas family of Warnham Court in 1878 – is situated by the railway close to the Barrackfield crossing.

17. By the 1930s it is much more recognisable.

18. The legendary Jack Hobbs played six times at Horsham between 1909 and 1934. In 1912 he and his veteran partner Tom Hayward put on 50 in the first half hour.

19. Charlie Oakes (20 matches). Born in the groundsman's cottage in 1912, he made a century for Horsham CC at the age of 16. Made his County debut at Horsham in 1935. Three years later (v Surrey) made his only century on his father's wicket. Lived to be 95.

20. At the age of 20 Charlie's brother Jack (11 matches) scored 157 for Horsham against Christ's Hospital. A lively, ebullient character he and fellow local boy George Cox hold the County's record 6th wicket partnership on the ground.

21. Only Maurice Tate has taken more career wickets for Sussex than Warnham's George Cox senior (22 matches) and only Tate and Jim Cornford have taken

more at Horsham. Yet George's 9/50 in 'Cox's match' in 1926 is not the best individual performance on the ground.

22. Old George's son young George (27 matches) made 50 centuries for Sussex but only one of them on his home ground – and he was 41 years old when he managed that. Yet only the Langridge brothers, Ted Bowley and Jim Parks senior have scored more runs at Horsham than George Cox junior.

23. The Oxford University attack at the 1912 Festival was described as being so ineffective as to positively invite punishment, Sussex winning by an innings and plenty.

24. A contemporary matchday view looking towards the tennis courts and St Mary's Church.

25. Action from the first morning's play against Worcestershire in 2001. Michael Yardy has just been dismissed and Murray Goodwin defends watchfully against Andy Bichel. Non-striker is Bas Zuiderent. The scoreboard fell victim to arsonists in February 2003.

26. The much sought-after Festival programmes were produced between 1931 and 1956 by local journalist Bob Green. That for 1939 proudly boasts 'the present ground provides a rural charm unequalled in the country. That is what we in Horsham think and our visitors invariably agree with us.'

27. Carl Hopkinson plays club cricket for Horsham CC and made a half-century in his one County appearance to date at Cricket Field Road.

28. John Dew never played County cricket on his home turf but as Horsham CC captain for 10 seasons and club president for over 40 more, he has probably spent more hours on the ground than most. He is now 88 and a former GP in the town.

29. Another playing member of Horsham CC, reserve wicket keeper Andrew Hodd also scored a half-century on his only first-class innings on the ground, helping skipper Chris Adams put on 158 for the 5th wicket v Durham in 2007.

30. Yet another 'Dewdrop', Chris Nash has been playing cricket at Horsham since the age of seven. He too made a half-century on his only first-class appearance to date on home soil.

31. One from the archives. Serried ranks of scholars from Christ's Hospital watch attentively as Surrey's first innings draws to a close in 1909. 'Shrimp' Leveson Gower is the 'last man 34'.

32. Oh dear! Durham's opening bat Mark Stoneman is comprehensively bowled by Rana Naved-ul-Hasan in the second over of his side's second innings in 2007. It was Stoneman's first-class debut.

FOREWORD
by Christopher Martin-Jenkins

It may be that I have played my last game at Horsham, but I very much hope not. If the revered old club's equally revered old president, John Dew, could take over the gloves when nearer eighty than seventy and whip off the bails to make a brilliant stumping off the bowling of one of his promising colts, I can still come in one Thursday to squirt a few through gully; perhaps, when facing the church, even to cream a drive all along the ground into that prickly hedge at extra cover, or to pull a long-hop into the wall of the Pavilion, simultaneously thereby bruising the ball and a fast bowler's pride.

Memories of Cricket Field Road do not go nearly so far back for me as they do for John and one or two others who still savour the pleasures of this lovely expanse of turf between the wooded slopes of Denne Hill and the curling, timeless spire of St. Mary's. I first came here to play for Cranleigh Cricket Club in the summers after leaving my school in Wiltshire in the early 1960s.

For a young club cricketer it always was and always will be a special place to play cricket, not big enough to be daunting but still with the feel of an important ground, one where the County plays. That in itself gives it a cachet enjoyed by very few clubs in Sussex. Hove, of course, is Sussex's true home but, with respect to Worthing (not what it used to be) and smaller grounds of character such as Middleton, only the old Priory Ground at Hastings and the Saffrons at Eastbourne had a similar stature to Horsham in those days. In recent times, despite the handsome new ground at Hastings, none has quite compared with Horsham.

The pitch 40 years ago was, as it usually still is, a joy to bat on. It was always hard, with some pace and an even bounce. To take guard required a hefty smack with the corner of the bat's bottom in order to make any mark at all. The noise echoed back and you knew at once that the fiery Treadaway, pawing the ground about 42 yards away after taking his first wicket, would whistle through off the pitch. A bit of luck and couple of overs residence, however, and you were starting to enjoy it. A few off the middle and the afore-mentioned Doctor Dew was into his routine: ever courteous, ever enthusiastic, generous as a kind and affluent uncle; genuine as a granite boulder.

I should have made a hundred in one of those matches, but fell four short, caught and bowled off a leg-spinner whose name has slipped my mind. It was a happy chance that brought me back to Horsham Cricket Club when my wife and I moved to Sussex ten years later. Our sons, James and Robin, had the good fortune then to join the vast ranks of keen young school cricketers who got the chance to play on midweek evenings in the Colts sessions run by the Doctor and willing helpers such as Alan Dinsdale, Rod Olliphant-Callum, Neil Chartres and David Hudson. Their successors look after at least as many keen young cricketers today, including lots of girls.

The abundance of different teams has always been as important an element of Horsham cricket as the beauty of the surroundings and the excellence of the pitches, never better than they were in the 1980s under the especially devoted care of Jeg Francis. The proof of his quality and industry as a groundsman was that he got the square on the John Dew Ground as good as the main one. Successors such as Laurence Gosling and Roger Ward have maintained those high standards.

Just occasionally when my children were young I got a chance to watch an evening game on the John Dew ground involving one of my sons and great fun they always were, with the parents very much welcomed into the Horsham cricket family. Robin must wish that Sussex's opposition now could be quite so easily dominated as most of the opponents of Horsham Colts teams seemed to be when he and Philip Hudson, now a respected MCC coach, were learning the game.

There is no greater fun than playing cricket yourself, however, and it is matches mainly for the Thursday eleven that I remember most fondly. Again, there were always runs in abundance and fine cricketers too: talented old stagers like Ian Thwaites, Mark Upton, Richard Marshall, brothers Andy and Robin Beer, Howard Kasey, John Baker and that rubicund and loquacious stalwart of Cricket Field Road, the unique Paul Baker. Augmenting these less than fleet-footed athletes, generally speaking, were rising stars of the club: Bruce Pike and others who have followed, often to the fringes of the dressing-room at Hove, not least in recent seasons the highly promising Chris Nash and Will Beer, both on the Sussex staff.

The link between Horsham and Sussex County Cricket Club itself is symbiotic and important. It is symbolised by visits from the County side that now date back exactly 100 years. In 2007 the County's win over Durham here was crucial to the third Championship title in five years. It was largely the work of two of the great pillars of the Championship-winning side of the last few seasons, Chris Adams and Mushtaq Ahmed, but as usual there were also vital contributions from other members of a genuine team.

In the centenary year the Sussex week falls in the middle of summer, later in the season than has been the case in recent years, when rain has given a lot of extra work to the club's hard-working volunteers, the likes of Barry Peay, Richard Marshall and the late and lamented Mike Beckwith. Writing just before the event, the hope is for some balmy summer weather to attract the usual eager crowds to Cricket Field Road. It is a beautiful ground and a perfect setting for county cricket. Give me this broad green field, St. Mary's church, the river and the mellow trees every time in preference to the concrete stadiums where most contemporary international cricket is played.

May 2008

INTRODUCTION

I suppose that, as with all books, the first question is – why? Why bother recording for posterity the history of a relatively obscure cricket festival? Anyone who has read Grenville Simons *History of the Cheltenham Festival* (Wisteria Books, 2004); or Chris Westcott's *The History of Cricket at the Saffrons, Eastbourne* (Omnipress, 2000) will not need to ask.

For those who haven't, I can only echo Alan Lee's sentiments. In his series *The Good Ground Guide*, he concluded his feature on Horsham in 2001 with the words 'there are no stands at Horsham, little shelter and few public facilities. This, though, is a ground with soul and atmosphere, a ground to which people will still hurry after work to watch an hour's cricket in the evening sun. It is a reminder of what has been lost, and what county cricket must never completely surrender.' These sentiments are echoed by the distinguished author and broadcaster Christopher Martin-Jenkins, who referred in 2004 to 'the glorious turf below Denne Hill in Horsham, where I enjoyed such strictly rationed club cricket as I have been able to play in the last 25 years.' What is it about Horsham that can inspire such enthusiasm?

Horsham doesn't aspire to the soaring Gothic splendour of Cheltenham any more than it does the cathedral-like solemnity of Lord's, or the breeziness of other festival venues such as Scarborough. Its charms are of a more homely nature that reach deep into the English psyche. As George Plumptre put it in his *Homes Of Cricket* (1988) 'as much as any other place where county cricket is played, Horsham evokes an air of the village game.'

But the cricket festival in Horsham was never just about cricket. Up until the 1939-45 War, it took over the town in a way that can scarcely be imagined today. 'County Week' was without doubt the social highlight of Horsham's year. There were high society balls for the great and the good, popular-style dances for everybody else, amateur dramatics, carnivals, whist drives, processions, shop-window displays and (literally) all the fun of the fair. The town really was *en fête* – and proud to be so. War put a stop to all that, but ask anyone 'of a certain age' locally about the heyday of the cricket festival and you risk coming away with the impression that the cricket was more or less incidental. I am anxious to capture this broader context and ensure that this is not simply 'another book about cricket' – such was never my intention.

I have followed the simplest possible structure. After looking at a number of factors that came together to give birth to the Festival, I review each match chronologically and conclude by exploring briefly a number of related on and off the field 'topics'. As with city centre bus tours, this approach enables readers the freedom to hop on and hop off wherever they choose. Such rigidity has its limitations, but I am trusting the benefits will outweigh the deficiencies!

A *leitmotiv* running through the book is finance (or more often, the lack of). As will be seen, that particular wolf was – is – never far from the Horsham door. For many years, the Festival was taken away from the town and even today, the crown doesn't seem to sit easily... In 1988 Plumptre wrote somewhat apocalyptically that 'There was no match in 1986, however, and although Sussex did return again in 1987, one feels that Horsham's days as a ground for annual county championship cricket are over.'

This theme is explored a little further at Chapter 19, but even if it proves one day to be true, an astonishing array of world-class cricketers has graced the Cricket Field Road ground over the years. Setting to one side the many splendid Sussex cricketers on show, pre-War patrons would have thrilled to such talents as Les Ames, Wally Hammond, Jack Hobbs, Harold Larwood and Frank Woolley. And if you wanted to stage a six-a-side contest between domestic and overseas players from more recent times, how about Mike Atherton, Graham Gooch, Graeme Hick, Kevin Pietersen, Alec Stewart and Steve Harmison v. Imran Khan, Justin Langer, Majid Khan, Malcolm Marshall, Wasim Akram and Mark Waugh. Opening it up to One-day matches would net Vivian Richards, Joel Garner, Richard Hadlee, Michael Holding, Clive Lloyd, Clive Rice and Chris Cairns.

As Plumptre observed, 'those balmy times of the festival provide lots of memories'. So in answer to the question posed at the outset, this book is written partly to recapture some of those cricketing memories; partly to record what the Festival in its broader sense meant in the life of an engaging but intrinsically unremarkable little market town; and wholly to thank all those who have laboured so tirelessly to keep the flame of county cricket alight in Horsham when many more famous cricket Festivals – one thinks here of the likes of Hastings, Folkestone and Weston-super-Mare – are no more.

ACKNOWLEDGEMENTS

This is – quite deliberately – a local history, so I have concentrated on local rather than national sources. I spent countless hours interrogating the fertile pages of the *West Sussex County Times* down at Horsham's well-appointed library - so much so that those working there must have wondered whether I had been taken on the staff. Not only do I thank them for their patience and courtesy, but my gratitude extends to all those anonymous sports journalists at the *County Times* down the years who covered County Week so expansively.

When researching my earlier book *The Nutters* (a history of Nuthurst Cricket Club, 1830-2004), I remarked on not just the generosity of spirit shown to me by Roger Packham, but also his basic humanity. Yet again, Roger has given unstintingly of his time, knowledge, wisdom and encouragement – to say nothing of his meticulous proof-reading skills, which have saved me from all sorts of elementary grammatical and factual solecisms. All that said, the final responsibility for opinions aired, accuracy, etc rests squarely on my shoulders and I apologise in advance for any schoolboy or other howlers that may have managed to sneak in under cover of ignorance or momentary inattention.

Others without whose assistance this offering would be the poorer include Nicholas Sharp, whose collection of Sussex cricketana is truly astonishing. Most of the illustrations come from Nicholas' collection and he couldn't have been more generous in allowing me to use them. I am equally grateful too to others whose collections I have plundered – not least the late Cecil Cramp. He was a well-known local character and I was fortunate enough to spend many hours in conversation with him.

So much for the written word. To balance this, I wanted to talk to people who were (or had been) involved with the Festival. First port of call therefore was officials past and present of Horsham Cricket Club such as Barry Peay and the late Mike Beckwith. However, no reference to Horsham CC would be complete without John Dew. Of few people can it truly be said that they are a legend in their own lifetime. Dr Dew is one such and even now, in his late 80s, he remains as charming and courteous as ever.

Corporately, Horsham CC couldn't have been more helpful, allowing me unfettered access to their archives, even though you did have to be a contortionist to physically access them! However, it is little short of scandalous that such a big club with such rich traditions continues to await its first full history, particularly when some village clubs close by have already found their chroniclers. There is material aplenty – I know: I've seen it – and a fascinating tale to be told, so how about it someone?

I must also thank the commercial bravery of Roger Heavens in swallowing hard and consenting to publish this book. Only time will tell whether his judgment has been wonderfully vindicated or spectacularly misplaced.

My final thanks are due to my family. I said when I completed *The Nutters* that that was it. No more. Never again. Yet the ink was hardly dry when I was off again on another cricketing odyssey. What my wife Margaret must have thought of this I hardly dare enquire. But she knows how much it meant to me and without her forebearance this book would never have seen the light of day. Thanks too to my two children, Jack and Georgina, for their support even if they did think from time to time that 'the old man ought to get out more!'

Chapter 1

A FORTUNATE CONJUNCTION

It is a matter of record when Championship cricket was first played in Horsham, but *why* did it come to the town? And why in 1908? The answer to these questions is that a number of factors had to be in the right place at the right time. Before we plunge into a review of the games, let's look briefly at some of these, starting with:

County Cricket in Sussex

As West Sussex County Council archivist Timothy McCann's *Sussex Cricket in the Eighteenth century* (2004) reveals, there was an extensive and well established network of cricket in the county before 1800 and it was just a matter of time before a proper 'county' side emerged. The first match played under a Sussex banner appears to have taken place in September 1734 against Kent at Sevenoaks (though this again is debatable) and sporadic games continued throughout the 18th and early 19th centuries. A key year was 1839, when, following a meeting at Pegg's Hotel in Brighton, a more-or-less genuinely county-wide club in a form we might recognise today, was formed.

However, early fixtures were arranged in a somewhat random fashion. With association football becoming increasingly 'professional' (and popular) in the final quarter of the 19th century, it was clear that cricket's rather quaint, ad hoc way of doing things couldn't go on. In December 1889, the county secretaries met to decide which of their number should be designated as First-Class and came up with a list of eight – the powerful and largely professional Northern trio of Yorkshire, Lancashire and Nottinghamshire; and three socially well-connected Southern outfits, Surrey, Middlesex and Kent. The other two were Gloucestershire – home of the renowned Grace family – and Sussex. Without wishing to re-ignite another old cricketing debate, it is accepted by many that the County Championship as we know it today was first competed for in 1890. Surrey were the winners and, sad to relate, Sussex trailed in last, winning but one and losing 11 of their 16 matches. Although they were to spend more time looking up than down in this formative period, the golden years of CB Fry and KS Ranjitsinhji were only just around the corner.

By the turn of the 20th century, a pattern of outground cricket had already been established in the county with matches taking place at the comparatively new Saffrons ground at Eastbourne; the famous Central recreation ground at Hastings; and Priory Park Chichester.

Yet two of these three venues were well to the east of the county; and – if you include Hove – all four were on the coast, two of them at the geographical extremities of the county. Where were the inland venues? How were the cricketing appetites of the swelling population in the hinterland to be satisfied? If the powers-that-be at Hove wanted to tap into the increasing number of people living in the northern half of the county, they needed a major venue there.

Horsham Cricket Club

One obvious difficulty with this was that there weren't that many options. One such was Horsham. It was a prosperous and well established market town with a strong agricultural tradition. It had good rail connections to London. But what was Horsham's cricketing pedigree? Closer inspection reveals that cricket had already put down deep roots in the town. The first reference to the game locally came on 23 June 1772, when John Baker's diary mentions a game of cricket against Dorking at the Artillery Ground (Baker was a London lawyer who lived for a number of years in Park House, an elegant building that still stands close to the town centre).

Slightly earlier, the *Sussex Weekly Advertiser* refers to a match on Hurston Common on 5 August 1771 between 11 Gentlemen of Horsham and 22 Gentlemen of West Chiltington. This has been assumed by Horsham CC to mark their formation.

Many - but by no means all – major matches in the town at this time were played on the Artillery Ground, which was located very close to the current ground. However, in 1795/96, at the height of the Napoleonic war, a major army barracks sprang up across the Artillery Ground. Its loss was probably a material factor in the formation of the Denne Park Cricket Club. Matches in nearby Denne Park, where the fallow deer still roam free, were played on the level plateau north east of the House and visitors today will be easily able to imagine what an attractive sight it must have been: country house cricket in a gracious parkland setting. But as with any exposed setting there is a price to pay. Its charms would have been altogether less evident when the wind blew (anyone who has played cricket at, say, Petworth Park on an April afternoon, will have an idea what I mean). Other venues in the town were Horsham Common in North Parade, which was still in use in 1832; and Stanford's, or the New Ground, which was first used in 1825 and where Horsham CC were known to have played on their reformation in 1842. Even as late as the 1880s, venues that sound a little more *al fresco* were being pressed into service - 'a meadow near the Fountain Inn' (1881); 'Mrs Millyard's Meadow, North Street' (1884); 'a field by Spencer's Farm, North Parade' (1886); 'a suitable field...in the Wimblehurst Road' (1886); ' a meadow near the Worthing Road' (1882); and 'a meadow at the back of the [West Street] brewery' (1882) .

In 1851, Horsham CC moved back down the hill to a new ground leased to them the previous year by Edward Tredcroft Esq. In addition to leasing the land for the new ground, Tredcroft also contributed to the cost of laying down the playing surface. On 18 May 1851, Bell's Life in London reported that *'During the winter months a cricket club has been established in this town under the patronage of E Tredcroft Esq and other gentlemen which promises to be of permanent standing. Indeed the facilities afforded by this gentleman to the aspirants of the national game are not to be surpassed in any town in...Sussex. Within less than a quarter of a mile of the centre of town there are four acres of meadow ground, the property of Mr Tredcroft, enclosed for the amusement of all who choose to avail themselves of the advantages thus afforded them for practicing with bat and ball. About an acre in the centre of the piece enclosed has been well underlaid with chalk and efficiently turfed. Proximate to the ground are some delightful walks, possessing the advantage of being agreeably shaded from the sun by some tall elms irregularly dispersed about the extremities of the ground enclosed. The opening match of the club was played on Tuesday week, and notwithstanding the cold biting winds which prevailed...a goodly muster of spectators assembled'.*

Things progressed apace and by August, the ground was sufficiently well established for the Gentlemen of Sussex to play host to their counterparts from Surrey there. Of this match, the *Morning Herald* commented 'Notwithstanding that this gentleman has a beautiful cricket-ground in his own park, Mr Tredcroft, with a view to the greater encouragement of the game, expressed a wish that the present contest should be fought on what may be termed the borough, or town, ground as therefore the inhabitants would have a smaller distance to go to witness 'the doings''. It seems his confidence was not misplaced, for 'The inhabitants flocked to the ground in large numbers to gaze upon the proceedings'.

In 1854, the celebrated Nicholas Wanostrocht ('Felix') – who, with Alfred Mynn, Fuller Pilch and EG Wenman, was a pivotal figure in the all-conquering Kent side of the 1840s - played for the club against both Ifield and West Grinstead. In the 1860s, one of Horsham CCs more prominent players was Harry Charlwood. Known as 'the Hope of Sussex', he made three of Horsham CC's earliest known centuries and went on to play in the first ever Test match in Australia in 1877. An interesting glimpse at the travel arrangements of the time was afforded in August 1873, when the 'Horsham cricketers (were) borne in procession *a cheval* from East Grinstead.'

By now well-established in their new surroundings, a pavilion was given to the club in 1878 by the Lucas family of Warnham Court, who were to prove generous benefactors over the years, and who we will meet again shortly. A match inaugurating the new pavilion was held on July 15 & 16, which witnessed the club rattle up 534 against Priory Park Chichester, with the left-handed former county amateur Charles Sharp contributing 206. Another well-known player to represent the side around this time was Archdale Wickham from South Holmwood (near Dorking), a young clergyman who – clerical duties permitting – was to enjoy a long career keeping wicket for Somerset between 1891 and 1907. He played 19 times for Horsham CC between 1875 and 1878. 'Snickham' was quite a character. His preferred dress code was a pair of lightish-grey flannels, black cummerbund, pads of a distinct brownish hue with a thick black band at the top, and the whole *ensemble* topped off by a harlequin cap. No unnecessary bending for Archie. His legs were ramrod straight, with feet as far apart as it was possible to get them, and gloves resting on top of the pads. Yet he was by all accounts a top-class gloveman. He was behind the sticks at Bristol in May 1895 when WG Grace made his 100th hundred (only allowing four byes); and again at Taunton two months later when Archie MacLaren made his historic 424. Against Hampshire in 1899, he didn't let one bye through as the opposition hit up the little matter of 672/7. While vicar of Martock, he would drive to home games in a pony and trap and was said to try to unsettle batsmen by muttering Greek and Latin verses at them! An inveterate cards and billiards player, he was also alleged to have smeared butter on his opponent's cue ball!

The 1880s and 1890s were arguably Horsham CC's 'Golden Age'. They were solvent enough to employ a series of ground bowlers, the first of whom appears to be J Chilman (1881-84). These included men with county experience such as Richard Lowe (1891-92), who played briefly for Notts and Sussex and pre-Championship Glamorgan. Triple Cambridge Blue Philip Morton took 95 wickets at 9.1 in his solitary season (1885); while Nottingham-born Frank Guttridge (1890-1891) went on to play 49 matches for Sussex and in 1906 had the disquieting experience of reading his own obituary. What stands out for me is the number of outstanding county and international players who turned out both for and against the club around this time. It might be worthwhile pausing for a few moments and taking a closer look at this.

In May 1880, the legendary Cambridge University and Kent smiter CI ('Buns') Thornton scored 47 for Horsham against Esher in a match that also saw MP Lucas given out, hit the ball twice. In June, the top four in the visiting Harrow Wanderers batting line-up included ID Walker, AJ Webbe and AN Hornby. Walker captained Middlesex between 1873 and 1884, while Webbe succeeded him as Middlesex captain in 1885, remaining in post until 1898. Hornby had an even more distinguished pedigree – captain of Lancashire between 1880 and 1891 and again in 1897 and 1898. He captained England at both cricket and rugby union and was once famously described as 'small, truculent, bellicose, adventurous, rash and a poor runner between the wickets'. On 2/3 July, CT Studd (Middlesex & England) – who was to play a key role in the famous Ashes test at the Oval in 1882 - scored 69 for the MCC.

Not to be outdone, Horsham CC's side that season included no fewer than five Lucases, including AP ('Bunny') who also played for England; Archdale Wickham; and AG Steel (Lancashire & England). A barrister by profession, 21-year-old Steel was already regarded by many as the second most talented all-round cricketer in the land behind WG Grace. In September he was to represent England at the Oval, and indeed captained England to victory over Australia in all three Tests in 1886.

There was no respite in 1881. The MCC side in early July included two Test players – Kent's left-arm medium pacer George Hearne (who had match figures of 9-110) and Nottinghamshire's Wilf Flowers (9-102). For the record, Horsham CC still won! July was also remarkable for a *tour de force* from Studd, who scored 222 n/o and then took 5-41 as Horsham (387-5 dec) demolished Guildford by 221 runs. Studd reappeared later in the month for Warnham Court, settling for a more modest 65. CT Studd would have been 20 at this time, yet had already been capped by England whilst at Cambridge University. His career ended abruptly after the 1884 season when he gave up a gilded existence to become a missionary, serving – often in conditions of great hardship - in China, India and the Belgian Congo.

In 1882, it was the turn of SS Schultz to shine at Horsham, scoring 177 for the visiting Butterflies. He played one Test for England in 1878/9 and in later years changed his name to Storey on account of Schultz sounding too Germanic! On 20 June 1883, an even better-known name appeared at the ground – Surrey's WW Read. Walter Read was a very strong-minded individual, who played in 18 Tests, captaining the England side on two occasions. He was said to have made a Test century at the Oval in 1884 out of sheer temper when his captain (Lord Harris) sent him in too low down the batting order! But Read was a class act and on a Horsham wicket made slow and heavy by recent rain, he made 134 n/o out of Reigate Priory's 200/9 on a day when everybody else struggled simply to survive. In June 1885, 21-year-old Charles de Trafford opened the batting for Horsham against Ockley, making 0 in the first innings. De Trafford was brother-in-law to Tim O'Brien (see below) and subsequently captained Leicestershire between 1890 and 1906.

1888 saw the inauguration of the club's cricket week and 1889 was another bumper season, being remarkable for its heavy run-scoring in an era of heavy run-scoring. In July, Mr Oliver's XI included five 'Blues', among them, Gregor MacGregor, who was to play the first of his eight Tests in 1890 while an undergraduate at Cambridge. MacGregor captained Middlesex from 1899 until 1907 and was also a Scottish rugby union international. July also witnessed a match against the Free Foresters, in which the peppery Irishman Sir TC (Tim) O'Brien (Middlesex & England) played for Horsham CC. A big, powerfully built man, O'Brien played with little distinction in his five Tests but by way of compensation was to sire 10 children. Among the opposition ranks lurked his county colleague FGJ Ford ('six foot two of don't care'), who made 59 of his side's 486/5. Horsham got off lightly for the following season 'Stork' Ford took 191 off Sussex when playing for Cambridge University. By a bizarre twist, even Horsham's 21-year-old professional Charlie Mills went on to become a Test player. A journeyman performer (briefly) for Surrey in 1888, Mills emigrated to South Africa in the close season and played one not wholly unsuccessful Test for his adopted country against England in 1891/92.

In August 1892, the Eton Ramblers side included future Hampshire and England fast bowler Christopher Heseltine (who took nine wickets in the match); and Herbert Bainbridge, who was to captain Warwickshire between 1888 and 1902. The following July, AJL Hill scored 102 and 38 for Mr Oliver's XI. Another gifted all-round cricketer, Hill played for Cambridge University, Hampshire and England. At Cape Town on Lord Hawke's tour of 1895/96, he first scored 124 and then took 4-8 against South Africa. Coming in at No 7, 49-year-old ID Walker hit 135 n/o for the Old Harrovians in July 1893, while in early September, Essex and England's Walter Mead took 11 wickets in the match for one of Mr Lucas' various XIs. AG Steel re-appeared for the club against the MCC in 1893, returning match figures of 13-106. Against slightly less demanding opposition, 17 year old Tim Killick took

15-107 in the game against Littlehampton, also in 1893.

By the middle of the decade, Horsham CC was to acquire some potent players of their own to set against these visiting superstars. In 1894, George Cox and Killick were regular/semi-regular members of the eleven, and this certainly beefed up their attack. On 26 May, coming in at No 3, Killick hit 125 n/o against Brighton Teachers, having earlier taken 6-44. Having made his debut for Horsham CC in 1892, Killick was to take 124 wickets for the club in 1893; 107 (at 8.8) in 1894; and 71 (at 9.2) in 1895. Not to be outdone, 'old George' – not so old then of course - took 9-54 against Guildford in May and 8-19 (including the hat-trick) against Knepp Castle in July. In one match, these two were supplemented by Fred Tate. Undeterred, the Old Harrovians rolled into town in July 1895 with Somerset's fierce left-handed opening bat Herbert Hewett supporting 'old faithfuls' Walker and Webbe. Another peppery character, Hewett captained his county between 1891 and 1893, in which year he resigned abruptly because he felt his authority had been unwarrantably over-ruled during the Tour match against the Australians.

Horsham CC's attack in 1895 frequently consisted of Cox, Killick and the tearaway fast bowler, HV Hesketh-Prichard, who lived with his mother in Hurst Road. A fascinating and multi-faceted character, Hesketh-Prichard had come to the town (ostensibly) to study law. He made his debut against Ockley in May, taking 4-7 and went on to play intermittently for Hampshire. But again they had opponents worthy of their mettle. The Hon Ivo Bligh (Kent & England) scored 63 (retired) for the MCC in June, while a latter-day Kent captain – CJ (Pinkie) Burnup – was among the Old Malvernians ranks in August. Another frequent visitor with the Old Malvernians over the years was George Simpson-Hayward, best remembered perhaps for being the last of the old underarm lob bowlers – yet who was good enough to play for Worcestershire between 1899 and 1914 and in five Tests for England in South Africa in 1909/10, taking 23 comparatively inexpensive wickets on the matting.

By 1896 Killick had found his way into the county side but by way of replacement, Horsham CC were more often than not able to include Lincolnshire's Cyril Bland, who was qualifying for

Sussex. In August, Bland had match figures of 13-62 against Incogniti. In his single season, Bland scored 295 runs at 18.7 but more importantly took 75 wickets at 9.1 apiece. For much of the season the club attack was Bland, Hesketh-Prichard and Cox. Hesketh-Prichard took 51 wickets (at 15.3 apiece) in 1896 and 53 (at 8.5 each) in 1898. Among their more prominent opponents were the freshly-graduated Pelham Warner, who was to go on to captain both Middlesex and England but who, in 1896, featured in the Warnham Lodge lineup; and Kent's Sam Day, another Old Malvernian. A prominent footballer, Day played soccer for England and the famous amateur side Corinthians.

The following season (1897), current Surrey captain KJ Key assisted his side, Old Cliftonians, in racking up 463 in August; while back in June, Horsham's opening bat against the MCC was none other than Len Braund. Aged 22, Braund was a top quality *Golden Age* all-rounder who was then on Surrey's books but shortly moved down to Somerset, where he played from 1899 until 1920, winning 23 Test caps.

In 1898, Horsham CC won the single-season West Sussex Cricket League – and would have won the junior competition also had not Warnham controversially included George Cox in their side for the play-off match with Horsham 2nd XI at Warnham Lodge.

The continued expansion of the County Championship sounded the death-knell for many of these gilded amateurs touring with their old club or university sides during the summer vacation. The standard of club cricket on offer at Horsham CC in the new century was still high – it's just that there weren't so many household names on show. Hesketh-Prichard popped up for one match in June 1902, picking up 11-69 against Arbemarle. In June 1904, future Sussex captain CLA Smith turned out for nearby village side Roffey against Horsham, scoring 80 of his side's 126 and then capturing 9-33. The Old Malvernians continued for a while to swim against this tide of increasing professionalism. Their side in 1904 included not only old stalwarts such as Day (who scored a sparkling 129) and Simpson-Hayward, but also HDG ('Shrimp') Leveson Gower, who played for Surrey between 1895 and 1920, skippering the side between 1908 and 1910.

Leveson Gower also captained England in three Tests in South Africa in 1909/10.

So, in what shape was the town side in the immediate run-up to their ground being awarded county status? In brief, pretty good. Of the 26 first team matches played in 1907, 18 were won, 4 drawn, 3 lost and one abandoned. The *West Sussex County Times* was fairly dismissive of one of the defeats, sustained against the Christ's Hospital Masters, on the grounds that they 'can scarcely be considered as opponents, one half of the Horsham team being pitted against the other half, and as the masters...generally constitute the better half...they usually get the best of the game when playing against the remainder.'

The Tredcroft Family and Early County Cricket in Horsham

For those seeking a precedent, there was a history of county cricket locally - albeit fleeting to the point of near-invisibility - dating back to the 1850s. But behind these three matches lies a story of an historic landed family in financial turmoil.

The Tredcrofts were descended from the Rev'd Nathaniel Tredcroft, who was presented to the living of Horsham by none other than Oliver Cromwell. The family owned all the land between Manor House in the Causeway and Denne Park, plus the fine mansion of Warnham Court. But Edward Tredcroft never looked after his business affairs and was said by his cousin Charles to have been 'a very spoiled boy'. Born in 1828, Edward came into the family estates at the age of 18 on the death of his father in 1844. Unfortunately, he had also joined a 'fast' cavalry regiment and acquired all sorts of extravagant habits, which he financed by heavier and heavier borrowing. It wasn't long before he was fatally in hock to a rapacious local lawyer and money lender named Henry Padwick. The end came with frightening finality, and by 1854, the bulk of the Tredcroft estate (including the Barrack Field lands) were on the market with Plumer & Co, auctioneers and estate agents in the town. The story is told – I suspect apocryphally – that when matters came to a head, Padwick said to Edward Tredcroft 'Well now Sir, you and I must change places'; whereupon without so much as a by your leave, Edward coolly put on his hat and walked out of his handsome town house without a backward glance, never to return. Warnham Court was sold separately to Sir John Henry Pelly in 1855, around the time of the three matches we are about to look at.

At this time, Tredcroft would have been in his mid-20s and a distinctly useful cricketer, having honed his skills at Eton. A versatile performer, he was a dashing lower order right-hand bat; fast underarm bowler who could revert to bowling slow; noteworthy deep field; and more than passable wicket keeper who 'kept' (inter alia) for I Zingari. He took part in over 50 first-class matches in a career stretching from 1851 to 1865.

All three matches were against MCC and had markedly different outcomes. In August 1853, MCC won the toss and batted. They were indebted to a rapid 63 from Walter Fellows, coming in at No 8, for their 177 all out. John Wisden took 5-57 off 43 four-ball overs for Sussex and James Lillywhite 3-34 off 25. Sussex could only muster 96 in reply, the pocket-sized Wisden top scoring with 22. MCC's second innings of 98 all out left Sussex the task of scoring 179 for victory. At the end of the second day they were encouragingly placed at 83 for 2, but Pulborough born Edwin Napper's dismissal early on the third morning led to a total collapse - 100 all out, with only Tredcroft himself (28) making much of a fist against the redoubtable Nottinghamshire professional pairing of Jemmy Grundy and Tom Nixon, who between them took 16 wickets in the match. Fellows' dismissal in MCC's second innings caused something of a stir in that he was caught by Tredcroft, standing between the ropes of a marquee. It seems there was some debate as to whether he should be given out, which the batsman himself resolved by 'leaving the crease.'

This result was emphatically reversed the following year when MCC won comfortably despite being behind on first innings. Batting first Sussex were indebted to John Wisden for their 165 all out. Coming in at a parlous 76/6, his half century gave his side a workable total. He and Jemmy Dean then starred with the ball as MCC were dismissed at the close of the first day for 129 (Wisden 3/39, Dean 4/53). However, Sussex's batting broke down completely on the second day against Grundy (4/26) and Nixon (5/21 off 26.1 overs). For the second year in a row, these two took 16 wickets between them in the match, but the home side's 64 all out was an abject effort. Any thoughts they might have harboured of victory went out the window with an equally shoddy display in the field. In the face of frugal bowling once again from Wisden and Dean, MCC took 73.2 overs to make the 103 required (Walter Fellows 40 not out). One point of interest was a tremendous blow from MCC's Balfour, which travelled 111 yards from hit to pitch. MCC were 60/4 at the close of the second day and scored the remaining runs without further loss the following morning. With the match finishing so early, a single wicket contest was played in the afternoon.

This scoreline was reversed again in 1855, albeit in somewhat unsatisfactory circumstances. Sussex batted first and by close on the first day, had compiled 206 all out. Veteran keeper Tom Box, coming in at No 9, top scored with an unbeaten 40, but no fewer than nine of the side made it into double figures. MCC were then bowled out twice in a day by Wisden and Dean. First time round they could only muster 61 (all 10 wickets falling to catches), while their second effort (77 all out) was precious little better. Only Harry Royston (14 & 31) and Reginald Hankey (16 & 14) showed to advantage as Dean returned a match analysis of 14 for 77. But reports carried by *The Times* remarked pointedly that certain gentlemen who had promised to play for the MCC failed to do so.

Pinning down where these three matches were played has proved elusive. Received wisdom has it that they took place at Warnham, but the distinguished historian and researcher Roger Packham mounts a strong case for them being held on the new town ground.

Christ's Hospital School

Christ's Hospital was founded in 1553 as an educational establishment for poor children and orphans 'pregnant and apt to learning.' It was located in Newgate Street, in the heart of the City of London, and was based in the old buildings of the Greyfriars, a friary dissolved by Henry VIII in 1538. But by the late 19th Century, the school was cramped, hemmed-in and ripe for relocation.

In 1882, the Aylesbury Dairy Company bought a large area of land at Stammerham, in the Sussex Weald just outside Horsham, and went in for cattle breeding on a large scale. Unfortunately, they over-reached themselves, their investment in farm buildings being on such a scale that the enterprise went bankrupt, the position not being assisted by the murder of the managing director in Monte Carlo. They needed to sell.

Potentially, it was a union waiting to happen - the Stammerham lands were available at just the time Christ's Hospital was looking to relocate. And so it proved. Work commenced in 1893; the foundation stone was laid on 23 October 1897 by none other than the Prince of Wales; and work was completed in 1902. 'CH' even has its own railway station. Even today, over a century on, there is an impressive feel of 'grandeur in repose' at 'CH', where austere and towering buildings surround a vast quadrangle. It was said that this monumentally overpowering feel resulted from the Charity Commissioners discarding most of what they considered to be superfluous ornamentation. The School's distinctive uniform of long, belted dark blue coat, white neckband and yellow socks is still very much part of the Horsham scene today.

With its wealth, social cachet and impressive City and establishment connections – the school band still performs each year at the Mayor of the City of London's inauguration – Christ's Hospital was quite a 'catch' for the town and as we have just seen, its masters quickly formed the backbone of Horsham CC's 1st XI. These included men such as Edward Wright, who played a smattering of matches for Oxford University, Gloucestershire and Kent around the turn of the century. He was an assistant master at 'CH' for 35 years and assisted Horsham CC for many of them. Also HS (Harry) Goodwin, who also played intermittently for Gloucestershire in the 1880s in company with WG Grace. For many years, Mr Goodwin played a leading part in the amateur dramatics that underpinned county week and lived long enough to serve as Horsham CC president in 1951. Without wishing to over-egg the pudding, let's just say that the newly arrived Christ's Hospital connection wouldn't have done the town's chances of landing a county match any harm…

Time finally to look at two powerful local patrons whose lobbying and support was to prove so vital. For this, we must turn to the nearby village of Warnham.

Warnham Court – the Lucas Family

The Warnham Court estate passed into the hands of the Lucas family in 1865 and thus commenced an era of cricketing patronage that extended well into the 20th century. The wicket there was flawless, the gardens stunningly beautiful and at their zenith, the sumptuous country house festivals in July were said to rival Canterbury for grandeur.

Four Lucases were to play county cricket for Sussex - Charles Eric (1906 to 1908); his father Charles James (1880 to 1882), and uncles Morton Peto (1877 to 1890) and Frederick Murray (1880 to 1887). In one match against Derbyshire, a little bit of history was made when three of them - FM, CJ and MP – were in the starting lineup. In cricketing terms, perhaps the best-known (and most gifted) was FM. Fred Lucas was a hard hitting left-handed bat who on his day was quite irresistible – in 1882, he made a staggering 302 n/o for Horsham CC as they ran up over 500 runs in a single day against a gallant but hopelessly outgunned Storrington. Born in 1860, Fred played for Marlborough College, later going on to Cambridge. Never a very strong man, he suffered at various times in his tragically short life from scarlet fever and typhoid, before succumbing to choleraic diarrhoea while on a shooting holiday in India in November 1887. Fred was Sussex captain in 1883 when they beat the all-powerful Yorkshire side at Sheffield by three runs, but perhaps his most enduring achievement came on a joyous June day at Hove in 1885, when, in under seven hours at the crease, he compiled a magnificent 215 not out against Gloucestershire. This was the first-ever double century by a Sussex player in a Championship match and he never gave a chance until reaching 150. WG Grace was reportedly so impressed that he had the match ball mounted on a silver band and presented it to Fred, saying that it was the best innings by a left-hander he had ever seen. At close of play 'Everyone on the ground collected round the Pavilion shouting his name: and when he appeared, hats were thrown about, and cries were raised of 'Well done Horsham". In July 1880, he made three centuries in a week – 141 n/o for Warnham Court v. Horsham; 132 for Horsham v Northbrook; and 184 for Horsham v Rudgwick.

All four were members of an extended family of talented cricketing brothers and cousins who, in a series of challenge matches in the 1880s, proved themselves more than capable of holding their own with the powerful Horsham town side. In fact so bold was the Lucas clan that in 1880, CJ threw out a challenge to the county side itself – and received no response! To complete the set in first-class terms, there was Alfred George (CJ's brother), who turned out for the MCC. Contrary to some reports, the celebrated AP ("Bunny") Lucas, who played for Essex and England, was not a blood relative. He was, though, quite content to be wheeled out pretty much annually to help make up the Warnham Court numbers and took a particularly severe toll of the Horsham CC attack.

In the form of the Lucas family, a powerful local connection between the town and county club had been forged. Perhaps crucially, Charles J Lucas was Sussex CCC president in 1907, the year before county cricket came to Horsham; and was also president of Horsham CC for an unparalleled 29 seasons between 1900 and his death in 1928.

Strange to relate, a second and equally powerful influence was to be found at the other end of the same small village.

Warnham Lodge – Sir Henry Harben

The driving force up at Warnham Lodge was another remarkable cricketing squire, Sir Henry Harben. Born in August 1823 in Bloomsbury, Sir Henry came of old Sussex stock, his ancestors having been bankers in Lewes. A qualified surveyor, he switched professional horses in 1851 and became secretary of a struggling three year old assurance company known as the Prudential Mutual. He eventually rose to become president of what was by now the mighty Prudential Assurance Company. Henry Harben was reputedly responsible for introducing the practice of insurance cover to the working classes for amounts as low as one old penny per week, to be collected by a network of local agents. He was knighted in 1897 and became High Sheriff for Sussex in 1898. Harben was also a Governor of Christ's Hospital and was largely instrumental in the purchase of the lands at Stammerham mentioned earlier. He twice stood for Parliament (at Norwich and Cardiff) as a Conservative, neither time successfully.

However meritorious his public life, Sir Henry's main interest for us stems from his purchase late in life of Warnham Lodge. No great shakes as a cricketer himself (though his grandson was to play four games as a teenager for Sussex in 1919), he was an ardent cricket enthusiast. He expanded the estate and quickly set about developing a ground that was to boast one of the finest pitches in the county. His first groundsman in the late-1890s was a youngster from the village by the name of George Cox. Many years later, George was to recall how Sir Henry's generosity enabled him to receive coaching from top county professionals Walter Mead (the 'Essex Treasure') and Kent's Colin Blythe.

Warnham Lodge was run very much along traditional Victorian lines, with family prayers before breakfast. Mead was for several years Sir Henry's coach, a post subsequently filled by Joe Vine. George Cox was retained by Sir Henry during the winter months as, in later years was another local man, George Street. Sir Henry was a liberal benefactor in other ways. He met the entire cost of Cyril Bland's qualification for the county; and shortly afterwards defrayed half the cost when JEBBPQC Dwyer qualified. He also took a paternalistic interest in the doings of the village cricket club.

Cricketers and their guests were accommodated in a special wing of the house and found Sir Henry to be a lavish host. For breakfast during his legendary cricket Weeks, they had a choice of kidneys, ham, eggs (boiled and buttered), bacon, kippers, mushrooms and toast. After an equally vast lunch – specially conveyed to the ground from the house - a still more gargantuan dinner lay in wait in the evening. Among the poultry courses featuring on one typical Warnham Lodge menu were snipe, woodcock, partridge, pheasant, guinea fowl, and duck. Salmon, in season, was also served on huge platters, while sweets included huge gooseberries, succulent raspberries and nectarines, all gathered from the walled garden.

Sir Henry often acted as scorer in these matches and one of his more endearing traits was to present a five pound note to anyone making a century. On one occasion the gift was declined because the putative beneficiary declared, with some asperity, that he was not a professional!

Horsham CC received a terrible mauling at the hands of Warnham Lodge in 1898 in a match that gave rise to considerable disquiet within the club. The Lodge posted a formidable 364 all out, but it was the town club's reply that caused such angst - 25 all out and 13 all out, though in mitigation it should be pointed out that the home side's bowlers were Fred Geeson, who played 135 matches for Leicestershire and George Cox, by then three years into a Sussex career that was to extend from 1895 until 1928.

Such was Sir Henry's standing locally that an alternative date for the ill-fated 1911 county match had to be declined because it clashed with his cricket week! Sir Henry Harben died at Warnham Lodge in December 1911 at the age of 88, leaving an estate worth £398,000. Sadly, his magnificent house fell on hard times and was eventually demolished in 1960 but the attractive pavilion with its wonderful memories still remains. But to return to our story, Sir Henry was another vital piece in the jigsaw that was to bring county cricket to Horsham, for he was a long-standing vice president of Sussex CCC. Crucially, he was also president in 1901 and 1906.

In Conclusion

By the high summer of the Edwardian era all but one of these pieces were in place. The powers that be at Hove were looking for a cricketing outlet in the north of the county. Those responsible for cricket in the town were progressive and outward looking and the town club was strong, well-established and socially well connected. There were two powerful local patrons whose voices would be heard in the highest circles at the county ground.

All that was needed now was a catalyst to bring these disparate elements together. Step forward Arthur Campbell Oddie.

A full appreciation of Arthur Oddie will be found elsewhere but suffice it to say here that he was a man with a long held and almost Messianic vision – to bring sustainable county cricket to Horsham. Oddie was typical of many of his time and class. Public spirited almost to a fault, he would interest himself in just about everything that went on locally. A large and physically imposing man, he had a powerful, hard-driving yet essentially genial style and was one of those bluff, larger than life characters who it was impossible to say 'No' to. A former captain of Horsham CC, Oddie had been at the centre of cricketing activities in the town since the early 1880s and was another who possessed strong links with Sussex CCC. He wasn't at all shy of exploiting these links and was able to lobby and network as only insiders can. This relentlessly high-octane lifestyle was to result in his premature death, but there is little doubt in my mind that but for Arthur Oddie's vision, determination, charisma and barnstorming talents, Horsham cricket week would never have got off the ground in 1908 - and possibly never taken place at all. He was the final – and perhaps most vital - piece in the jigsaw.

Chapter 2

MATCHDAY

No spectator with any romance in his soul would dream of entering the ground via Cricket Field Road. The classic approach remains, as in 1908, down the 'lime-scented Causeway'; through the churchyard; across the wooden bridge; and up the grassy knoll past what was Joker Oakes' cottage. Indeed Cricket Field Road – or Cricket Approach as it was originally known – was not developed to the extent we see it today until the 1930s. As late as 1931, there were only five houses on one side and one on the other.

In 1933, 'The Parish Church, peaceful and solid...overlooked the wide expanse of emerald sward', while 'further along were the tall and stately trees giving the effect of a Constable painting from the press tent...Colour there was everywhere and it might well be that as the chimes of mid-day wafted across with a seed carrying breeze, a poet would have found inspiration for an English lyric about a lyrical game. Yes, cricket needs its ballads and the song of a troubadour would not have been out of place in such surroundings.'

Who too cannot fail to identify with the following description, penned in 1950 but still fresh today, when 'Horsham's long awaited, carefully planned County Cricket Week got off...to a colourful start. Visitors and town and country folk...mingled with shopping crowds in streets gay with bunting and flags...A sunny day with enough breeze to make the clouds here and there just seem to float along...the boundary ringed with deck chairs...a sea of faces...birds singing...the 'plock' of bat against ball...the lazy rustle of the oak leaves. That was Saturday on the lovely Horsham cricket ground...an idyllic scene...The sun shimmered on the roofs of the cars parked in their scores, it threw the big pavilion into sharp relief against the cool green of the new-mown grass. It shone warmly on the crowds...Businessmen watched the play in their shirt sleeves and braces and lost no dignity by it. So did the men who earn their living in village and farm by the sweat of their brows. Cricket has a common brotherhood...The gay dresses of their womenfolk provided colour upon colour, yet even the most exquisite ensemble got no more than passing glance and remark...for in this lovely corner of England the players held the stage and all else was merely the backdrop.'

There have been many changes to the ground in the century since 1908, yet paradoxically, it remains curiously unchanged, with an appeal that is both timeless and enduring. The only permanent structure remaining is the pavilion, which replaced one provided by the Lucas family in July 1878. The old structure was situated at the Denne Hill end of the ground, not far from the footbridge over the railway.

Just after the Great War, the club was offered an opportunity by the then owner Mr Eversfield, to purchase the freehold of the ground, plus the adjoining field on which is now situated the Dr Dew ground and nets. The sum sought was £2,500, which, after negotiation, was reduced to £2,000. The deal was completed in 1924 by means of a bank loan which was guaranteed personally by a small number of members. This was paid off in 1944, but did mean that there was little left in the kitty for essential maintenance. So parlous were the club's finances that by 1929, there was already serious discussion about selling off the 'Dr Dew' land. Mercifully this was not taken forward.

In 1923 there were calls at the club's AGM for new sightscreens. Before the Great War, the ground benefited from some very good screens provided by Sir Henry Harben but these were now 'neglected, falling to pieces and beyond repair.' Calls in 1926 by Cyril Hunt for a new scoreboard ('especially needed for the county games'), were also rejected on cost grounds. The following season Sir Home Gordon branded the pavilion 'primitive' and the seating 'uncomfortable'. By 1929 a new scoreboard was in place, yet it clearly failed to find universal acclaim: ('from the Press tent it is necessary to use field glasses if all the figures are to be distinguished therefore it must be really difficult to see from the pavilion').

This parsimonious, 'make do and mend' approach continued into the new decade. In August 1930, a quote was accepted from Messrs Holmes & Cooper of East Street to install electricity (and hot and cold showers) in the pavilion but this was paid for in large part by Horsham Rugby club, who had just entered into a seven-year lease to use part of the adjoining field. In 1932, Horsham CC's AGM heard that extensive repairs had been carried out to the pavilion which 'had become almost derelict.'

Perhaps in an attempt to persuade the county not to strip them of the Festival, a limited improvement programme took place during and after World War II. During the War, Alfred Oakes had filled in 'the once obnoxious dip in which an outfielder was almost concealed'; while in 1953, the wooden pavilion steps that may very well have splintered the regal toes of Ranji were at last replaced by wide concrete ones.

During the 1890s and beyond, George Luing's sheep grazed on the outfield between the months of September and March (Mr Luing ran a family butcher's in West Street). As recently as the late 1990s, the same outfield was used extensively during the winter months by Horsham Hockey Club - indeed it was considered to be one of Sussex's premier venues. The last County hockey match took place there in March 1987 and soon afterwards, Horsham HC's 1st and 2nd team matches were transferred to Broadbridge Heath, where the Astroturf pitches necessary to compete at National level were to be found. Despite the obvious inconvenience the Hockey Club still have their matchday headquarters at Cricket Field Road.

The financial wolf again bared its teeth in 1988. An apocalyptic picture was painted of decaying facilities that required an injection of around £300,000. This included urgently needed works to the pavilion, tennis courts and scorebox. In 1986, a controversial proposal to build a sheltered home complex by the river had been howled down by a mix of local politicians and the general public. A less intrusive alternative was also quietly dropped but it was all very sensitive locally. Some indeed were of the view that it was mostly bluff and brinkmanship – that the cricket club was using the threat of a total sell-out and relocation as a negotiating ploy to force the Council's hand. But with new monies clearly needed and development options being whittled away, much effort was invested around this time in persuading the Council to enter into a sale and leaseback scheme.

This acrimonious and long running dispute at its height generated dust-ups with the Horsham Society; features and leader columns in the 'County Times'; furious letters for and against; and heat and light in equal measure, finally reached an amicable conclusion in early 1990. The Horsham Cricket and Sports Club sold the ground, lock, stock and barrel to the District Council for £1. In return the club was granted rent-free use for 250 years, together with an immediate cash infusion of £300,000 for long-overdue repairs.

In 1996, a southerly extension to the pavilion appeared in the shape of a brand new, £210,000 squash court. It received an early baptism from the players, Martin Speight beating Middlesex's Mike Gatting during the dismal Festival weather that year.

Prior to the opening of the 1997 season, a wide-ranging internal review was carried out by Horsham Cricket & Sports Club entitled 'The Future – 2000 and Beyond' which considered a wide range of options for perpetuating/enhancing the wide range of facilities on offer at the ground. These included selling off the groundsman's cottage and bungalow, purchasing a property in Cricket Field Road to facilitate improvements to the hopelessly inadequate access off Worthing Road and creating a brand new Worthing Road access altogether.

Finally, on a dark February night in 2003, the old wooden scoreboard – beloved by many but on its last legs functionally – fell prey to arsonists (yes, even in Horsham!). A new one dutifully arose, Phoenix like from the ashes in a matter of weeks and was opened by Sussex skipper Chris Adams and Dr Dew at lunchtime on the 3rd day of the Championship match v. Notts. It was soon put through its paces for the number of runs scored in that game – 1,339 – was a new ground record.

One thing is certain. Those responsible for cricket at Horsham are keenly aware of the ground's special ambience. They meddle with this at their peril. Time to move on and look at the matches.

Chapter 3
EARLY DAYS 1908-1914

1908: Horsham in the early part of the 21st century is a far cry from the town in Edwardian times. Today, it is a bustling, affluent place with a (by and large) vibrant local economy and strong commuter links to London, Brighton and Gatwick Airport. It has a new town centre and an interesting modern townscape feature in the form of a fountain to commemorate the poet Shelley whose family lived at nearby Broadbridge Heath. The central hub - the Carfax – is now all but completely pedestrianised as are West and Middle Streets but the Causeway, which runs down to the parish church of St Mary and the cricket ground, remains as bosky and charming as it was that early summer a century ago when county cricket first came to town. True, Horsham also features – at No 27 – in the 'Idler's book of Crap Towns of England' (2003), where it is described (among other things) as a 'no fun zone run by old conservatives for old conservatives'. True also that in Victorian times the man responsible for popularising the garden gnome spent his declining years in the town – which for many just about sums it up. Yes, the town centre does tend to go to sleep at 6pm; and yes, there are the usual booze-fuelled problems at weekends involving a minority of vacuous youngsters. But in essence Horsham remains – on the whole – an engaging and attractive place in which to put down roots.

Back in 1908 it was far more compact, the pace of life far slower and its agricultural base much more in evidence. It was almost the quintessential small country town where the way of life for many had remained more or less unchanging down the generations. The big event locally in the Spring of 1908 was a huge fire in the petrol store of Rice Brothers' carriage works in Springfield Road. If you wanted to buy the freehold of a seven bedroom, semi-detached property in London Road with a bow window, large greenhouses and a garden, it was all yours – for the princely sum of £325. And you could lose yourself in the long-running serial in the *County Times* while you did so – 'Five Red Marks' by Mrs CN Williamson, a real gripper.

The local football team had just concluded a highly disappointing season – 2nd from bottom of the West Sussex Senior League, with only three wins and 15 defeats from their 18 matches. Just prior to the county match, Horsham CC tied with Brighton Brunswick, a man memorable as much for the plenitude of his initials as his cricketing prowess – JEBBPQC Dwyer – taking 8/42 for the visitors.

But other things were occupying Arthur Oddie as 1907 turned into 1908. At a Horsham CC committee meeting on 23 December he broke the news that the county had offered to play a match at Horsham against Essex on 15-17 June. 'It was proposed by Mr Chasemore, seconded by Mr Williams, that the Horsham club accept the County Club's offer.' But not all was plain sailing as the record of a Horsham CC planning meeting at the King's Head Hotel in March testifies.

The problem was that some misunderstanding appears to have arisen as to who had the final say in the arrangements. Some misguided local members took the view that they were in charge and made moves to appoint their own committee to manage things. But a letter from Colonel Bruce, the formidable secretary of Sussex CCC, made it plain beyond peradventure that authority was to be vested in its appointees - that is, himself, Oddie and Hunt, together with such local gentlemen as they saw fit to co-opt – the simple logic being that as the risk vested in the county, so too should the control. In fact, Cyril Hunt said he had been in Brighton that very day and confirmed that the county committee was 'very determined on the point'.

Even so there was some lingering discussion among local members, either reluctant to let go or genuinely still unclear, about whether local co-optees should have as much control as county nominees. Horsham CC secretary Alec Chasemore actually thought the county were looking to them to sort it out. Mr MH Vernon was keen to ensure that they should but at this point Oddie – blood pressure no doubt rising - had heard enough. He stepped in and declared firmly but succinctly 'Absolutely not, I assure you.'

With this little contretemps out of the way, Oddie, Hunt and their committee got down to work. Their planning bore all the thoroughness of a military campaign and benefited materially from the administrative infrastructure already in place in connection with the Horsham Carnival. It was largely a question of dusting this off. A network of sub-committees running to around 150 people contacted all cricket clubs in North-West Sussex and tickets for all three days of the match were on sale in local villages. Courtesy of the headmaster Dr Upcott, Christ's Hospital promised Oddie the use of 900 chairs. Sir Merrik Burrell of Knepp Castle lent tents, and wooden forms for other seating were quickly produced by a local builder. The octogenarian Sir Henry Harben up at Warnham Lodge even arranged for his carter, Mr Cook, to have his own sightscreens, roller, chairs and tables towed to the ground by farm horses! No one could accuse the local grandees of not rallying round.

With civic pride at stake the town centre was a mass of colour and 'looked in thorough holiday trim'. Tradesmen and residents alike had responded with a will to appeals to decorate their homes and businesses. Flags and bunting were everywhere and at the West Street Brewery the decorations were exceptionally pretty. Large numbers of flags and streamers spanned many of the thoroughfares. The slogan 'Success to cricket' was picked out in various colours on rosettes, while after dark, outlined in fairy lights, were the initials SCCG (Sussex County Cricket Ground) and HCC (Horsham Cricket Club), with a 'capital sketch of a cricketer at the wicket with upraised bat.'

Pre-season, Horsham CC had, at some considerable expense, spread red Nottingham marl over the square. Courtesy of Mr Williams the scorebox had been moved 'by the unemployed and free of cost to the Cricket Club' so that it now faced the pavilion (this was generally held to be a great improvement). Oddie fired off several letters to the local paper urging locals to turn up and support the match, adding for good measure that 'a county match is bound to render the town a vast amount of good, and a week of county cricket in the town still more so – that future rests in your hands'. The organisational die was cast. All that was needed now was something even Arthur Oddie couldn't command - the weather.

The main talking point prior to the match was the increasingly unreliable behaviour of Sussex's captain, the legendary C B Fry, which fuelled rumours he was about to leave the county and join neighbouring Hampshire. To Sussex's chagrin, Fry did little or nothing to dispel the chatter (in the event he did join Hampshire but not until the following season). As Iain Wilton put it in his 1999 biography of Fry 'In mid-June, with Sussex entertaining Essex at Horsham, he was expected to make his first appearance of the season and, when he failed to arrive on time, the start of play was delayed for his benefit. In due course, however, a phone call revealed that he was not merely running late but had no intention of playing after all'. In the event, the side was captained by another legendary 'Golden Age' figure, the exotic KS Ranjitsinhji.

Sussex came into the match in fine batting trim. The previous week Ranji had made 153 n/o and 78 in a high scoring draw against Middlesex at Lord's. Joe Vine scored 119 in the first innings – though not to Wisden's satisfaction, his knock being described as 'at times tedious to watch'. Horsham's own Tim Killick made 101 n/o in the second innings of the same match.

Opponents Essex were an interesting outfit. Only admitted to the Championship in 1895, they were not perhaps the most glamorous of opposition but among their ranks were two England captains (one past, one future) and two other England internationals - one of them among the quickest bowlers in the country – to say nothing of two serving soldiers and a full-time clergyman.

Meteorologically, Oddie's wishes were granted - at least initially. The weather on the opening morning was gloriously fine with bright summer sunshine being only slightly tempered by a cool breeze. Sadly, despite all his pre-match endeavour, 'a somewhat meagre assembly of spectators' was present to witness the early exchanges. Ranji won the toss but because of the delay wondering whether Fry would turn up or not, play never actually got under way until 12.25pm with Johnny Douglas (at the Church, or Town, end) and Claude Buckenham opening the bowling to Vine and Bob Relf. Relf placed the very first ball of the match confidently to leg for a couple and dominated the early scoring. Lunch was taken on a prosperous 95 for 1, the only wicket to fall being that of Relf, who had hit cleanly through the off side for 54 before falling to McGahey.

During the luncheon interval 'the prettiness of the scene was enhanced by the large numbers of ladies charmingly attired in light summer costumes in the enclosure; while the space from the Pavilion to the screen at the country end was filled with row upon row of yellow-stockinged scholars from Christ's Hospital' (estimated at about 400). Archie MacLaren was present, as was Albert Craig, 'the Surrey Poet'. For long periods of the day the Horsham Silver Recreation Band did its stuff but excellent though their music was the true English sportsman, it was adjudged somewhat censoriously by the *County Times*, 'would enjoy it (*the cricket*) the better for non-accompaniment of any sort.'

Douglas and Buckenham resumed the attack after lunch but the much-awaited highlight of the afternoon session was the appearance of Ranji, 'who came in to the accompaniment of hearty applause all around the ring'. Sadly the silken-shirted maestro was to disappoint his legions of admirers. Having scratched about for 8, he was LBW to the persevering Charles Benham, having looked 'slow between the wickets'. But on his home ground Killick made a most attractive 48, often jumping out to meet the slow bowlers while Vine 'put much more vigour into his batting' in making 53. Tea was taken with the score on 197 for 4. Bert Relf was holding things together skillfully. He took 12 off an over from Buckenham in the final session before adding 20 more from two successive Douglas overs. He was eventually taken at third slip by Perrin for a very fine 69. Vincett at No 10 lifted McGahey over the heads of the crowd to the press box before being run out and after just over 4 hours 30 minutes the innings closed for 298, Benham achieving the best figures of his brief career with 7 for 60 off 29.4 overs. Bert Relf opened the Sussex attack from the town end in tandem with Warnham's George Cox. After one over apiece and the clock showing 6.30pm play closed for the day with Essex on 2-0.

What followed was a cruel anti-climax. On the Tuesday rain fell steadily until 1.30pm. There was then another shower with frequent mists at 3pm. After that conditions improved and a rapidly increasing crowd frequently demonstrated its impatience at the lack of action. Umpires Attewell and West inspected the wicket at 4.25pm and again 25 minutes later, announcing emphatically that it was 'impossible to start yet'. This of course was the cue for the sun to break through and as the weather remained generally fine the crowd waited expectantly for play to get under way. Indeed a section in front of the pavilion started barracking, at which point Messrs Attewell and West emerged again - and drew stumps. This gave rise to more hooting and, with hindsight, stumps might perhaps have been drawn earlier. Ironically, some local sages felt that the pre-season application of Nottingham marl actually militated *against* a quick-drying wicket. Through all the hubbub the Horsham town band played on gallantly.

Rain fell all night, completely ruining the already saturated wicket. At 11.30am, the umpires made a no-doubt perfunctory inspection before reading the last rites over the game. Ranji invited both teams, umpires and scorers across to Lord Leconfield's country house at Shillinglee Park but there are no prizes for guessing what happened next – the sun shone mockingly forth for the rest of the day and a good number of folk actually turned up hoping to see some play.

The circus then rolled out of town – Sussex to Aylestone Road to try conclusions with Leicestershire and Essex the short cross-country hop to the Angel ground, Tonbridge to face Kent.

So, how was 'the experiment of playing a county championship match at Horsham' (as *Wisden* put it), viewed? The London dailies were unanimous in their praise. One of the morning editions waxed particularly lyrical: 'Set in the midst of a rich meadow land studded with trees...and redolent with the odour of new-mown hay, the scene is one of great rural beauty, and the good folk of Horsham came nearly 4,000 strong to look at their county team, had the additional advantage of paying court to Ranji.' Wednesday's *Daily Mail* carried two photos of Craig addressing the Christ's Hospital boys and one of Ranji at the wicket executing a glance. Another wrote 'This opening cricket game at Horsham was an experiment, from which it was hoped that the Sussex County Cricket Club would receive such a return in revenue and added membership as to be induced to provide the Town with an annual match.' *Leather Hunter* agreed: 'Horsham is certain to get another county fixture allocated in the near future' he pronounced authoritatively, having demonstrated so amply that 'enthusiasm for the grand old game in the Horsham division is most refreshing.'

1909: Oddie claimed to have been promised by the powers that be at Hove that if 1908 was successful, Horsham would be awarded a plum fixture against Surrey in 1909. And so it proved. Traditionally, Surrey were big draw-cards yet despite great expectations it was a stodgy old game. An opening day crowd of over 4,000 saw the visitors grind their way to 187 all out, Queenslander Alan Marshal top-scoring with 58 (Marshal was something of a stormy petrel: told once by Surrey skipper 'Shrimp' Leveson Gower that he was overdrawn at the bank, he replied: 'That can't be right: I was looking at my cheque book only this morning and I still have three cheques left!'). Sussex could only struggle up to 146 in reply as Walter Lees and Bill Hitch shared nine of the 10 wickets. Second time round, Surrey made a much better fist of things. With two of their lesser lights to the fore – opener Harry Harrison (81) and William Davis (89). Their 355 all out left the home side 397 to win in 330 minutes. This was never remotely likely and after a few early alarms Bob Relf (100) and Vine (76) piloted their ship gently home to harbour and an 'honours even' draw on 291/5. A ground collection for the two men (arranged by Oddie) realised £15.12.0.

1910: If the match in 1909 was largely uneventful, the one in 1910 was a cracker. Surrey were again the visitors and again batted first. With Hobbs, Harrison, Ducat and skipper Morice Bird all back in the pavilion cheaply, the 'chocolate caps' were indebted to the vastly experienced Tom Hayward. His solid 64 steadied the ship allowing others to play more expansively. William Davis rattled up a quite brilliant 106 in 110 minutes to see his side up to 295. Sussex replied with 331 (Vine 83, RB Heygate 74), as 'Razor' Smith picked up 6-93 with his sharply spun off breaks. *Wisden* was unimpressed, referring to Sussex's seven hour effort as 'strangely lifeless...although they never stood in a position of real anxiety.'

Second time round, Surrey openers Hobbs and Hayward got their side off to a solid start and at close of play on the second day a draw seemed inevitable. However, they collapsed in quite unaccountable fashion on the final morning to Bert Relf (6-53) and Joe Vine (3-28) for 160, leaving the home side unexpectedly requiring 125 to win the game and plenty of time in which to do it. Smith opened the bowling at the town end and without a run on the board had Bob Relf taken at short leg by Hitch. Wickets and runs were evenly exchanged as the tension mounted. With Smith turning the ball ever more sharply, Leach and Cox moved the score along to 110 when Smith dismissed the former and then, with the very next ball, Bertie Chaplin.

Cox and Vincett took the score to 123 when the former, attempting to hit Smith to leg to win the game, was bowled. Last man Harry Butt was an old sweat who had seen it all before but was nevertheless all at sea against Smith. He played and missed at all three balls remaining in the over, the second of which passed over the top of off stump by no more than a whisker. With the clock showing 5.25pm and the tension in the ground palpable, Vincett, to everyone's inexpressible relief, hoisted the third ball of Bird's next over over square leg 'clean over the oak trees into a field, near where the present scorebox stands', a blow that was to be recalled for many a year. Reflecting no doubt on life's vagaries, 'Razor' Smith finished with 6 for 42 to give him match figures of 12-135. This was to stand as the best match return by an opposition bowler until overhauled by George Tribe in 1952.

1911: 'Oh dear!' best sums up 1911. The first date offered by the county – in July against Lancashire – had to be declined because it clashed with the Sussex County Agricultural Show which was being held literally just up the road in meadows off the Worthing Road. Even Arthur Oddie couldn't compete against that – particularly as the date also had the misfortune to clash with Goodwood Week.

Horsham was then offered the Hampshire match in August – only for this too to be deemed unacceptable because it clashed with Warnham Lodge's cricket week and they had no wish to upset 'one of our most generous supporters, Sir Henry Harben'. A match against Warwickshire was then considered but not taken forward because: a) it was still too close for comfort to the Agricultural Show and b) the town of Chichester, which allegedly 'has had the worst luck possible with their County Fixtures, wished for a match just then.' Noble to a fault – or perhaps resigned to his fate - Oddie and his committee gave them preference. The net result of all these 'after you Cecil, after you Claude' machinations was that the fledgling Festival, which had opened in such encouraging fashion, risked shooting itself in the foot.

1912: However, to everyone's relief, 1912 saw the town allocated not one but two fixtures. Richard Streeton, in his 1981 biography of PGH Fender, considered that 'This was a compensatory gesture to local supporters', adding that 'A Horsham and West Sussex Week, as it was designated, was an experiment, therefore, and (was) watched closely by the Sussex authorities.'

Regrettably, Oxford University were to prove no match for the home side though as Wisden pointed out: 'Sussex had all the luck that was going, for they batted on a perfect pitch and then dismissed Oxford twice on ground that was drying after heavy rain.'

The story is quickly told. Against bowling that as the innings wore on one London daily described as being 'so ineffective as to positively invite punishment', the Sussex innings prospered. Nineteen year old Fender smote about him hip and thigh, reaching a quite brilliant 133. With the score on 414-8, compiled in a mere 4 hours 40 minutes, the storm which had been gathering since tea finally broke and drove the players in.

The remainder of the match was badly messed about by the weather. Rain had set in by the following morning and with a gale blowing and the pitch drying quickly, Chaplin promptly declared. The Varsity side started with deceptive ease but from 167-5 they were unceremoniously bundled out on an increasingly treacherous surface for 186, Vine finishing with four wickets.

The second innings was a rout from start to finish. Bert Relf and Harry Simms opened the attack, both men 'making the ball turn a lot and being practically unplayable.' In no time at all Oxford were reduced to 18-6 and at tea were even deeper in the toils at 52-7. The *coup de grace* was applied with the total standing at 81. As *Wisden* observed, once the Dark Blues had failed to save the follow-on their fate was sealed. Relf captured 6-36, living up to his pre-match billing in the programme as keeping 'a fine length with plenty of spin.'

The second match was once again against Surrey and opened in dull weather, which fortunately picked up as the day wore on. Around 3,000 spectators witnessed the opening exchanges of a curiously uneven game in which a brilliant start in all four innings was followed by an equal number of more or less inexplicable collapses. Surrey set the ball rolling, only to squander a flying start given them by the three 'Hs' - Hobbs, Hayward and Hayes – and crumbled unaccountably from 195-1 to 281 all out. Sussex replied with 254 to make it virtually a one innings game. After the early loss of Hayward, Hobbs and Hayes raised the 100 in only 75 minutes but thereafter their side 'fell to pieces in a remarkable way.' Three wickets, including that of Hayes for a faultless 69, tumbled with the score on 175, and the last seven for 25, as the visitors crashed to 178 all out, Fender taking five wickets and Cox four. This left Sussex 206 to win on the final day.

The deciding factor was the pitch which, as *Wisden* acknowledged, 'wore badly on the last morning.' For an hour or so it played pretty well but as time wore on the turf dried on top and became increasingly treacherous. This was all the encouragement Messrs Smith and Rushby needed. They operated virtually unchanged as the home side slumped to 96-6 at lunch. The end arrived part way through the afternoon session with the score on 127. Five men were bowled and four LBW as only Bob Relf put up any sustained resistance. He was third out for 50, Smith's 6-54 giving him match figures of 11-132. He at least wished he could come to Horsham every year...

1913: The weather in the week running up to the 1913 Festival had been wretched with around three inches of rain falling in the town. In consequence the wicket was very soft, but easy paced but the opening day attendance was as gloomy as the weather – a mere 850. Visitors Northants opted to bat first but could only muster 154. Bert Relf operated throughout from the railway end returning 6-68. As it turned out, this rather modest offering was to go a long way towards determining the outcome.

Confronted by a 'queer wicket and deadly bowling', Sussex's reply on the fast drying turf was pitiful – 59 all out in 100 minutes, their lowest score of the season. It was also to stand as their lowest on the ground for 33 years until an unspeakable 35 all out v Glamorgan in 1946. The wickets were shared equally by Northants' left-handed skipper Sydney Smith 'who skilfully varied his pitch and pace and got considerable work upon his deliveries' and the utterly dependable George Thompson, a big, burly man with a drooping moustache known as 'the Northants

Nugget'. These two held an admirable length throughout despite Thompson being hit for three early fours to leg by Bertie Wilson. At one point Thompson took three wickets (Cartwright, Cox and Lang) in four balls.

Northants clearly decided to go for broke second time around and were all out in 110 minutes for 115 (Cox 5/31). This left Sussex 211 to win but it was apparent to all that under the hot sun the wicket was fast becoming very tricky indeed. Bob Relf started boldly, taking 10 off Thompson's opening over, but it was a false dawn. Relentlessly, he and Smith tightened their grip for a second time. Fender played 'a short but merry innings' but it was left to No. 9 Lang – a Cambridge Blue who was lost in action two years later during the Great War – to top score with 31. Bowling unchanged, Smith and Thompson shared the wickets equally for the second time in the match, the only occasion in the entire history of the Festival that two men have bowled unchanged throughout both innings. Concerned no doubt by the weather, the attendance of around 1,500 was again disappointing. With the match over in two days, Oddie persuaded both sets of players to take part in an Over 30s v. Under 30s match on what would have been the final day. He must have wondered why he bothered for the weather continued cold, cheerless and drizzly; the turnout was again poor and to cap it all the game was hopelessly one sided.

After this fiasco it must have been with some relief that they welcomed Lancashire. Mercifully, a large and rapidly increasing crowd (which eventually peaked at 3,000) was greeted by delightful weather. Chaplin won the toss and – unusually - put Lancashire in. For whatever reason it was a turgid day's play. One notable exception was the celebrated veteran JT Tyldesley. His side's 236 all out owed much to Tyldesley's flawless 107, made in a little over 2 hours 30 minutes. Bert Relf took 6-56 including his 100th wicket of the season but Chaplin's handling of his bowling again came in for criticism from the London dailies.

Sussex's reply was wretched. In less than two hours they were bundled out for 81, just failing to save the follow-on. Dean, with his swerving left-arm deliveries and Huddleston took all 10 wickets. Following on, Sussex batted with much greater conviction. Anchored by Lang's watchful 71 and entertained by

Fender's breezy 49, their 332 left Lancashire a modest 178 to win but in *Wisden*'s words, this proved 'altogether too big.' This time Chaplin got his bowlers right for after opening briefly with Norman Holloway he chose Jack Vincett to partner Bert Relf. These two repaid their skipper's faith by claiming five wickets apiece as the Red Rose first wilted then withered away on the vine. From the relative heights of 83-3, Lancashire's 112 all out was an undeniably dismal effort, Relf's 5-52 giving him a match return of 11-108.

Some rare cine-film footage was shot of the cricket and of the Carnival. Lasting for around seven minutes, it clearly depicts (among others) Fender, Cox, Cartwright, Bert Relf, Vincett and umpire Albert Trott emerging from the pavilion. Also captured are scenes in the 'paddock' with men in boaters and ladies in the long full-skirted dresses, puffed sleeves and huge, wide-brimmed hats of the period. There are views too of Denne Hill and large crowds making their way down The Causeway.

1914: Against an increasingly sombre political backdrop, 'disappointment was freely expressed' in the town at the fixtures allocated to Horsham in 1914 – Cambridge University and Hampshire. Admission prices were held at 6d (1/- per match or 2/- for the whole week), and – a sign of the times - 'A large storage room for motor cars and bicycles' was provided at the Worthing Road entrance to the ground.

Hampshire were the first visitors. Opening the bowling for Sussex was a promising 19 year old by the name of Maurice Tate but he and the rest of the Sussex attack were unable to prevent their neighbours running up 396, opener Alec Bowell's faultless 114 being punctuated by many pleasant off drives. Sussex's reply was anaemic. Alec Kennedy, a dapper little man with sleek dark hair and an India-rubber physique, took 6-49 as the home side were hustled out for 146 and forced to follow-on. Once again they were to bat with far greater conviction second time round. In a heartening display two youngsters, Vallance Jupp (69) and Ted Bowley (83), combined to show their more experienced colleagues how it should be done with a judicious mix of defence and attack. The tail wagged enthusiastically and Sussex's 329 all out invited Hampshire to make 80 to win in around 100 minutes. After a careful opening, the match seemed to be moving gently along towards its pre-ordained conclusion. However, with Holloway somewhat unexpectedly to the fore, the visitors suddenly found 29-0 translated into 58-6, to 'a tumult of cheering' from the home supporters. For the first time in what had been a hitherto depressing match Sussex scented victory but the experienced Kennedy was not to be denied. With 15 minutes showing on the clock he shepherded his side nervously home by two wickets in what had been a marvellous game of cricket. Holloway took a splendid 6/39, but despite carrying all before them on the final day, Sussex were left ruing their ineptitude for most of the previous two.

The Week's second visitors were Cambridge University. The visitors batted in far too cavalier a fashion and would have been disappointed with a mid-afternoon 173 all out. Sussex too seemed to enter into the carnival spirit and by stumps were intriguingly placed on 174-7. Continuing the 'entertain at all costs' theme, the final three wickets added a further 92 runs in pretty rapid order, Wilson and Chaplin both completing fine half-centuries. By lunchtime the Light Blues were 25-2 with little hint of what was to follow. As *Wisden* put it, 'As on the previous day, there seemed no good reason why the Cambridge men should not make plenty of runs, but their batting broke down badly against Albert Relf's deceptive spin and accurate length, and their failure was even more pronounced than before.' Two run-outs didn't help – one of them being Davies, who perished 'responding to an unreasonable call.' But however you dress it up, 102 all out was a mediocre effort, Relf capturing 5-32. At 4pm, Bowley and George Street set off in pursuit of the 10 needed for victory. Eight of these came in Morrison's opening over but four successive maidens then followed before Sussex eased home.

Who knows what was in the thoughts of these men as they left the sun-dappled ground on that late June afternoon. World events were closing in and would soon bring to an end a whole, seemingly immutable, way of life. Five of the protagonists would never again smell new-mown grass on an English cricket field in the Springtime. In addition to Sussex's AH Lang, Hampshire's promising Cambridge blue Alban Arnold was killed in 1916, aged 23. *Wisden* was not alone in predicting a bright future for him. Another Hampshire man to die was Arthur Jaques, who had just picked up five wickets with his unthreatening version of leg-theory. He perished on the Western Front in 1915. This obscene 'war to end all wars' also took its toll from among the Cambridge ranks. The same GB Davies who was run out 'responding to an unreasonable call' was also killed in action in 1915. Of him, Wisden remarked unequivocally: 'there can be little doubt that, but for the War, he would have developed into an England player.' Closer to home, Kenneth Woodroffe was an unflagging fast bowler of great promise, who had already made his mark with Sussex: he lost his life near Neuve Chapelle on 9 May 1915, aged 22. Two of his three brothers were also killed in action, all within 13 months of each other. And Frank (Lieut FAJ) Oddie (Middlesex Regiment, attached Royal Berkshires), the apple of his father's eye and only appointed county secretary in 1914, was killed in October 1917. As the casualties continued inexorably to mount, it was enough to make the strongest and most resilient of men wonder how – and when – it would all end...

But perhaps the most poignant death of all did not take place on some foreign field. It was that of Arthur Oddie himself, that rumbustious character who more than any other had brought county cricket to Horsham. In October 1914, he was suddenly cut down at home by a combination of double pneumonia and heart failure. Right to the end he was serving others – in this case Belgian refugees who were coming to the town in numbers. In the words of the *County Times* 'everywhere this week in Horsham has been asked "what shall we do without him"...A devoted Romanist...he in no way allowed his religious views to interfere with his untrammelled human sympathies.' Even in his final days, Oddie was still 'hustling and pushing his way with good tempered bluster' in his endeavours to equip one of his own cottages and other accommodation for the refugees. After a requiem mass at St John's, he was buried at Hills Farm cemetery in the town, with George Street (among others) representing Sussex CCC among the mourners. 'Throngs of people en route and at Hills Cemetery made the funeral a public occasion to a degree seldom seen. The procession was of great length...all who came into contact with him (will) miss and mourn him.'

With Arthur Oddie's passing, it really was the end of an era...

Chapter 4
GOLDEN SUMMERS PART I: 1919-1929

Prelude

The War years had not been kind to Horsham cricket. Indeed things were so parlous that in July 1917 'an appeal for help at a critical juncture' was made by Horsham CC president Charles Lucas with the objective of 'saving the Club from extinction.' A crowded AGM in 1919 heard that 'Very little had been done to (the ground)...and it had got into a very bad state'. Against this troubled backdrop there was no question of the town being in a position to stage county cricket in the strange season of 1919 when, experimentally, matches were played over two long days rather than three. However, with the horrors of the Great War still a raw wound for many, local people needed the reassurance that an early return to familiar peacetime activities such as cricket. What was termed a 'Comrades of the Great War' cricket week was staged in early August, in which sides representing the Chief Constable of West Sussex played two-day matches against a 'Comrades XI' and Sussex Club and Ground. Friendlies they may have been but there were some pretty fair players on parade such as George Cox, Bertie Chaplin, the Relf brothers, Jack Mercer and the former Middlesex and England bowler JT Hearne, now 52.

Perhaps the most extraordinary event to take place on the ground in 1919 didn't even involve cricket. An estimated 2,300 people gathered to watch the world-renowned local athlete Alfred Shrubb compete in a five-mile (or 25 laps of the perimeter of the ground) race against Kitty M, a noted local trotting horse. Born in nearby Slinfold in 1879, Alf Shrubb ('The Little Wonder') was a fascinating character in his own right and one of the great unsung heroes of British track athletics.

1920: The two matches in 1920 were against neighbours Kent (championship runners-up in 1919) and Gloucestershire. Sussex skipper Bertie Wilson, who had lost his previous seven tosses, won one at last and took first knock on a day that was notable for two things: a quite remarkable innings from Vallance Jupp and an even more unaccountable Sussex collapse after tea. Dropped on four and again on 30, 'Juppy' made 151 in four hours. He scored the bulk of his runs on the off side, unfurling a wide range of drives and cuts. However, the rot set in when he was caught shortly after tea. 258-4 all too rapidly became a hugely disappointing 287 all out as Frank Woolley and 'Tich' Freeman ran through the tail like the proverbial dose of salts, taking all 10 wickets between them.

Attractive but steady cricket was the order of the second day as Kent moved methodically to 261 all out, all their batsmen seeming to get in but no-one sticking around to play a really big innings. Maurice Tate was the pick of the home bowlers. In the two hours till stumps Sussex had moved smoothly along to 120-3 with Ted Bowley, unbeaten on 60, holding things together. Just before the close he launched Freeman for an enormous six that pitched in the tea enclosure and travelled to the far end of the large tent. The match was nicely poised...

The final day saw Sussex perform in fits and starts on a wearing wicket but their 215 all out left Kent 242 for victory, a task that was by no means straightforward. Woolley then played an innings that elevated the art of batsmanship to a quite different plane from anything seen hitherto in the match. Coming in with his side in some difficulty at 38-2, he stroked and caressed his way to a quite sublime 139 not out with all the style and grace that made him such a drawcard wherever he went. (Robertson-Glasgow once remarked that Woolley was 'easy to watch, difficult to bowl to and impossible to write about'). By 5.15pm it was all over, the locals not knowing whether to feel privileged at witnessing such brilliance or aggrieved at seeing their side lose. Wilson's captaincy again came in for criticism: he employed seven bowlers, some of them very much 'part-timers' but chose not to use Jack Mercer at all.

In the second game, Gloucestershire's 201 all out was well below par. Only skipper Philip Williams (who played in the 'Comrades Week' matches in 1919, his father being Chief Constable) with an attractive unbeaten 85, showed to advantage. Coming on as 4th change, George Cox produced a startling spell of bowling, rifling through the tail and taking 5-18 as the last four wickets fell for 19 runs. In the two hours left for play Sussex had raced to 188-4, Jupp continuing his excellent run of form with 95.

The tide continued to flow strongly in favour of the home side on day two. The Haywards Heath amateur Kenneth Higgs made a carefree 85. Warnham's George Street weighed in with a chanceless 87, his highest first-class score to date. The rest rather fell away but 351 was a decent enough effort. Percy Mills took six wickets with his mix of medium pace and off breaks. Heavy rain stopped play when, with six wickets in hand, Gloucestershire still required 99 to avoid an innings defeat.

There was to be no miraculous reprieve for them on the final morning – indeed in less than 90 minutes the match was all over, Sussex emerging victorious by an innings and 21 runs. Nobody made more than 25 as Mercer (for once) took centre stage with four wickets.

1921: Horsham's two visitors in 1921 were Hampshire and Leicestershire. In heat that was almost too intense, Hampshire skipper Lionel Tennyson won the toss and took first knock. Although wickets fell at intervals during the afternoon session, the imperturbable Philip Mead – whose three previous scores somewhat ominously had been 87, 45 & 280 n/o - went on his own sweet way and it was something of a surprise when he was ousted by a clever catch by Bowley at short leg. He had batted 3 hours 15 minutes for his 113 and the innings closed for 260 shortly after his dismissal, a total that was somewhat below expectations.

Runs and wickets were traded with almost reckless abandon on the second morning but few could have anticipated what lay in store. While Bert Relf kept him more or less passive company, Tate 'settled down to the best innings of his life, hitting with remarkable vigour' all round the wicket. His 50 came up in 45 minutes, his century in 70. In the first 40 minutes after lunch he scored 92 as the score soared. Alec Kennedy was smashed for five 4s in one over and the 300 was hoisted after less than four hours. Sadly, all good things must come to an end and after 90 dazzling minutes Tate's coruscating innings ended on 142. The innings itself closed with Sussex 99 to the good. So stunned were Hampshire by this unlooked-for reversal in their fortunes, that in less than an hour's play half the side were brushed aside for 65. At this point Mead and Kennedy came together and put on 113 in 75 gloriously entertaining minutes, Kennedy being bowled in the last over of the day.

The final day belonged entirely to Mead, though events might have taken a different turn had he been held in the slips by Cox off Gilligan when on 75. He put together a monumental 224 with 32 fours and one splendid six onto the pavilion roof that broke several tiles. Mead was last out with the score on 411, his innings standing as a ground record until 2004. He remains the only player in the history of the Festival to score a century and a double century in the same match. As a measure of the extent to which he dominated his side's innings, no one else made 50.

Sussex opened their second innings without even the remotest prospect of making the 313 needed for victory and as so often happens in such unreal situations it all went horribly wrong. Four wickets fell quickly to give Hampshire a faint scent of victory but when Bert Relf (88 n/o) got set, this quickly evaporated and both captains happily settled for the draw.

Never very strong even at their best around this time, Leicester won the toss and batted in gorgeous weather. Ewart Astill was caught behind off Gilligan without a run on the board and this seemed to set the tone for the day: 189 all out was woeful and Sussex put it all in context when racing – perhaps a little over adventurously – to 196-5 by stumps with half-centuries for Jupp and Bowley. Jupp's dismissal was curious: an LBW appeal had been answered in his favour when (unbeknown to him) others noticed that the ball had trickled back onto the stumps, dislodging a bail. Leicester's woes were compounded when their veteran opening bowler Bill Benskin injured his ankle and was unable to bowl a ball. Almost 400 runs and 15 wickets constituted a pretty good day's cricket, but it paled into insignificance compared with the fireworks that lay in store.

As the *County Times* put it, 'Exceptionally fast scoring characterised the match on Thursday morning'. They weren't kidding. Bert Relf took three fours off the first over sent down to him and this was just the beginning. Relf, his captain and the 27-year-old, Oxford-educated amateur Hardit Singh Malik – resplendent in a blue turban – scored at a terrific rate. Gilligan and Relf added 100 in an hour; Relf and Malik a further 175 in only 70 hell-for-leather minutes. Batting in a most attractive fashion, particularly through the off side, Relf eventually holed out to long on for 153, made in only two hours 40 minutes. Malik's 106 included one six that landed on a motor car and the innings eventually closed for a gigantic 519 in only 100 overs. Three bowlers conceded over 100 runs with poor old Astill returning a heroic 6-187. This remains the highest number of runs conceded by an opposition bowler in an innings. Sussex's total was to stand as a ground record for over 80 years until eclipsed by their gargantuan 619/7 v. Notts in 2003. Arthur Gilligan recalled Malik as being 'a great favourite with the crowd...a hard hitting bat and a splendid fielder'.

A dispirited Leicester started woefully. Arthur Mounteney was caught off the very first ball from Gilligan and after only 50 minutes play they had slumped to 48-4. The doughty veteran Jack King then got his head down. Astill, coming in at No 6 after his exertions with the ball, hit 63 in 45 minutes, and another left handed veteran, Sam Coe, also made 50 as Leicester displayed increasing resilience. But they were only playing for pride (and the hope that it might rain). At stumps the score had reached 228-6 which meant that the fortunate patrons had witnessed over 550 runs and 11 wickets in the day. Robertson-Glasgow related an amusing anecdote concerning King: 'In his latter years he was a slowish mover between the wickets, and once, being run out...by many yards while facing the ...pavilion, was told by umpire Reeves to "keep on running, John, while your legs are loose." '

With Benskin unable to bat the end duly came the following morning – but full marks to Leicester for gallantry in a hopeless cause. Their last wicket pair of George Rudd and wicket keeper Tom Sidwell blazed merrily away, putting on 69 in only 35 minutes, before Cox wrapped things up.

1922: The two visitors in 1922 were Gloucestershire and Surrey. The West Country side lacked depth and were to finish in 13th place. They won the toss and batted in lovely summery weather. A crowd approaching 2,000 witnessed steady rather than pulse-racing fare. As might be expected from a side led by Arthur Gilligan, the Sussex ground fielding was a feature of the day though their catching left something to be desired. The local papers were not charitable. The 3rd wicket partnership between Alf Dipper and Sheppard was described as 'long and dreary'; and Dipper 'mostly concentrated upon defending his wicket'. The pre-lunch session was 'exceedingly dull'. However, things perked up after the break. Corbett emerged from his shell to hit five fours in quick succession and although Dipper was still hanging on in there, at 157-6 things looked to be going Sussex's way. However, Mills rode his luck and, hitting cleanly, took 15 from one Harold Gilligan over. Dipper's epic eventually ended on 117 (his first century of the season), made in over four hours. To rub salt further into the wound, the Gloucester tail then wagged with venom. Mills made 92, his highest first-class score, as the innings closed for 320. Play had been held up for a short while after lunch to enable running repairs to be carried out to George Street who suffered a cut nose when a return from Wensley struck the wicket and sent a bail flying up into his face.

Sussex's reply was almost too cavalier. In the two hours till lunch, half the side were out with only 134 on the board. Bowley was caught shortly after the resumption for a stylish 65 but Curly Roberts (62) and Arthur Gilligan (39) continued to play freely and the innings eventually realised 273, a deficit of 47. It might have been less but for shoddy Gloucester out-cricket. Colonel 'Jacko' Watson's brief but violent innings thrilled the crowd, 'who were perhaps fed up with the stereotyped cricket'. He helped himself to 19 off one over from Mills, including two huge sixes. Tate bowled Captain Green with the very first ball of the Gloucester second innings but bad light ended play prematurely with the visitors on 103-4.

The third day's play was notable for a second century by 'Old Dip'. Despite a somewhat agricultural appearance his workman-like 103 anchored his side's 245 all out, Roberts being the pick of the home attack with 5/66. Pedestrian though it may have been, it gave Gloucester a total they could work with.

Sussex's reply was bedevilled by showers, but given they had no hope of making the 293 needed to win their batting was 'risky in the extreme'. Downright irresponsible more like – and this after a careful 2nd wicket stand between Street and Edwin Harris seemed to have earned them a draw. Other than an urge to entertain, it is difficult to imagine what – if anything - was going through their collective minds, particularly against such experienced practitioners as Dennett and Parker. Colonel Watson hit a huge six over long off - but was then caught off the very next ball. As *Wisden* put it, Sussex simply 'threw it away by reckless batting'. With only the extra half-hour to negotiate, the score stood at 150-6. Tate and Harris were well set and men of the calibre of Higgs and the captain were still to come. A draw should have been easily achieved, but 'disaster followed disaster' – most of them, it has to be said, self-inflicted. Having taken 20 off one over from Parker, Tate then lashed out once too often and was bowled, having contributed a breezy 31 out of 46 in half an hour at the crease. In 15 crazy minutes the last four wickets fell for an equal number of runs and Gloucester had, somewhat improbably, triumphed by 137 runs. Only Roberts, enjoying the best season of his career, emerged with any real credit taking eight wickets in the match and scoring 66 runs for once out. Apart from four token overs from Bessant, the two slow left-armers Parker and Dennett bowled unchanged second time round. They captured 16 wickets in the match and neither needed any encouragement from such wilful batsmen.

The second visitors were their old friends from Surrey, captained by Percy Fender. On the opening day, 'all records were broken…and the ground was absolutely crowded.' A huge crowd, estimated at around 6,000, saw the visitors take first knock. The old firm of Hobbs and Sandham opened confidently against Roberts and Tate and by lunch the score stood at 101-1. Although not at his very best, Sandham (124) was still in occupation at teatime as five further wickets fell and 159 runs were scored in a thoroughly entertaining session. However, persistent drizzle became heavy rain and any further play was out of the question.

Rough weather on the Sunday afternoon did considerable damage. Two unusually strong gusts of wind snapped one of the main poles supporting the big marquee and tea enclosure. The marquee had to be taken down, but emergency repairs were carried out to rectify damage inflicted on the small marquee nearby. Nothing daunted, Alf Street continued to serve teas on the Monday as though nothing had happened. Not so fortunate was 'the fine old elm tree close by the pay box on the church side of the river' which was also badly knocked about.

The whole of the second day was washed out and even though there was little prospect of a result another large crowd turned out for the third. Sussex quickly polished off the Surrey innings for 294, Arthur Gilligan sending Sandham's 'off stump flying yards out of the ground'. Any hopes that the wicket might prove sticky were quickly dispelled as Bowley and Street put on 80 for the first wicket, setting about the bowling 'in free and delightful style'. Sussex continued to throw the bat in the afternoon - which at least was some consolation for the crowd - and were eventually all out for 248. Surrey shuffled their batting order about and their wholly irrelevant second innings had reached 109-4 when stumps were drawn, Hobbs and Alf Jeacocke putting on 77 in 40 minutes. But it was a shame the weather ruined such a promising match between two enterprising and energetically-led sides.

1923: Horsham had been allocated two very different opponents for 1923, Nottinghamshire and Glamorgan. With the exception of their captain Arthur Carr, Notts were an all professional side who had been runners-up to Yorkshire in 1922 and were destined to finish runners-up again in 1923. They were as tough as old boots. By contrast, Championship newcomers Glamorgan finished second from bottom in both seasons. They were a poor side who were struggling simply to survive and lived a hand to mouth existence.

Carr won the toss and took first knock on a dull, cold day in poor light. Ominously, 'A good pitch had been prepared...but moisture in the air kept the turf from drying and, with the change of pace, the wicket was always difficult'. But no-one could have foreseen quite how difficult. Notts came into the match unbeaten but against quality bowling from Tate and Gilligan – one reputedly the deadliest bowler in the land, the other the fastest - their innings was a shambles. By mid-afternoon they were all out for 94. The enigmatic George Gunn was an exception. He seemed in little trouble and at one point 'caused amusement by walking in to get to the pitch of Gilligan's fastest ball', but when he played-on for 30 the game was up. Bowling unchanged, Tate took 6-22 in 23.2 devastating overs, 'Perfect length, with a slightly varied pace and some break, gave him his command over the batsmen'.

If that was bad, worse was to follow. In 25 disastrous minutes, Sam Staples and burly ex-miner Fred Barratt had reduced Sussex to 11-4. Tea was taken at a desperate 41-6. Coming in at No 9, Gilligan determined to go down fighting. He began by straight driving Staples for six and in 10 minutes had scored 24 in six hits before he 'hit over what was almost a yorker from Barratt and his middle stump went flying'. The end came after a mere 100 minutes with the score on 79, Staples and Barratt taking five wickets apiece. By dint of what the *County Times* construed as 'excessive caution', Notts' experienced opening pair of Gunn and Dodger Whysall had added 35 circumspect runs by stumps to round off a highly eventful day.

Early on the second morning Gilligan and Tate changed ends and Tate, now operating from the town end from which he had wrought such havoc in the first innings, immediately sent back Gunn. Thereafter he and Gilligan again scythed through the visiting ranks, only Whysall (34) seeming able to resist them for any length of time. Gilligan split a stump bowling Lilley and shortly after lunch the innings closed for 121. Of the 186 runs coming off the bat, Gunn and Whysall between them had contributed 98. Tate took 7-46 off 31 overs to complete quite astonishing match figures of 53.2 overs, 13 for 68. It was the first time a home bowler had taken seven wickets in an innings and his match return has only once been bettered as we will see shortly.

Sussex therefore required the highest score of the match – 137 - to win. When Harold Gilligan and Tate (the latter playing-on for the second time in the match) had both been bowled by Barratt with only 13 on the board, it seemed that the visitors would cruise home. But in a match where the unexpected was commonplace, they were in for a rude awakening. Starting slowly at first, Bowley and Higgs gradually gained the ascendancy before an absorbed crowd, 'every good piece of batting or fielding (being) heartily applauded'. Carr rang the changes but Bowley reached his 50 (out of 94) in 90 minutes with shots all round the wicket before being beaten by Matthews with the score on 115. With an off drive for four and a single off John Gunn, Higgs (62) saw his side safely home. Neither man had given a chance and - no doubt a mixture of delight and relief – 'There was a big ovation at the close.'

The Glamorgan match couldn't have provided a greater contrast. With admission costing 1/- (6d for children) proceedings opened in fine weather, the visitors winning the toss and batting. They put up a sorry show and in 2 hours 30 minutes were routed for 86. Again operating from the town end, Tate simply picked up where he left off against Notts. He was far too potent for

Glamorgan's collection of journeymen and took 8-30 in 28.2 irresistible overs. The tone was set at the outset, Tomlinson being bowled by the second ball of the match. The most stubborn resistance was put up by the last wicket pair of Stamford Hacker and Frank Ryan, the latter a colourful character who liked his drink and was once found asleep under the covers overnight because he had forgotten where the team was staying!

Despite the early loss of Harold Gilligan the Sussex batsmen went for their shots. Cook in particular 'indulged in some merry batting'. His first six scoring shots were all boundaries and in a 75-minute final session the score fairly raced along. Bowley, driving powerfully, took three fours in a row off Davies while Jack Holmes hit Tomlinson out of the ground as the home side closed on 202-3.

In fine weather and before a good crowd runs continued to flow on the following morning. Holmes eventually departed for 93, his highest score to date for Sussex but there was no denying Bowley. He was eventually bowled for 120, made in 3 hours 10 minutes, the county's first centurion of the season. But the fun had only just begun as an increasingly ragged Glamorgan attack was put to the sword. Regan conceded 19 in one over while the lusty Colonel Watson, hitting with great vigour, despatched one massive six clean over the large marquee. Tate struck 16 off the first over after lunch and he and Arthur Gilligan took 13 from the next. In 40 frantic minutes together they put on 91, Tate's 76 taking only 45 minutes. The Sussex innings eventually closed for 447, their highest total of the season to date. In less than 2 hours 30 minutes play 245 runs had been scored.

Roberts and Cox took the new ball second time around and it wasn't long before a demoralised and hopelessly outclassed Glamorgan were deep in the toils again. Wickets fell with (for them) depressing regularity and after 53.1 tortured overs they were finally put out of their misery for 91, leaving Sussex victors by the monstrous margin of an innings and 270 runs. Not such welcome news for the financial coffers because for the second time in the Week a match was over in two days. 'Birdie' Mathias completed a pair as, bowling unchanged, Cox picked up 6-46. Neither Tate nor Gilligan deigned to bowl at all. As *Wisden* – accurately but rather cruelly - put it: 'Sussex had a holiday task...(having) everything their own way from start to finish'.

1924: With George Street's tragic death still fresh in the memory Horsham welcomed their first visitors, Leicestershire, a consistently mediocre outfit. Gilligan and Tate were among *Wisden's* five Cricketers of the Year and were both away playing for England. This was balanced to some extent by George Geary being unavailable for the visitors because of a bad neck. The match commenced in glorious sunshine and a large crowd, estimated by mid-afternoon at some 4,000, saw Colonel Watson lead his men into the field on losing the toss. Parts of the outfield were still damp after recent heavy rain and openers Lord and Sidwell were probably quite relieved to be facing 'Tishy' Browne and Wensley rather than Tate and Gilligan. The pitch was dead and progress early on was equally lifeless: two singles only in the first 20 minutes, the total still in single figures after 35. Lunch was taken with the score on 36-1. Even as the day wore on the scoring rate remained funereal – so much so that the crowd were provoked into ironic applause whenever a run was made. 'Painfully unenterprising' the *County Times* called it. Astill plodded wearily along and his fifty 'was mostly composed of singles', though in mitigation, he more than most was all too aware how fragile his side was. Although 168-4 at one point, Leicester's over-cautious approach then began to unravel and they found themselves 186 all out in an astonishing 109.5 overs. Bowley with his leg-breaks was the pick of the home attack taking 5-27 but it must have been desperately dull stuff.

The second day's fare was more enterprising. After a wobbly opening - Harold Gilligan and Bowley were back in the pavilion before the score had reached double figures – Sussex's innings eventually closed for 233, a lead of 47. Nearly all the batsmen got starts but, coming in at No 3, Street's replacement, 'the miniature wicket keeper' 'Tich' Cornford, top scored with 50. There were four wickets apiece for Astill and the bespectacled Alec Skelding. It was no surprise that a ground collection among his home supporters for George Street's dependants realised over £80.

Then, as the *West Sussex Guardian* put it, 'came the sensation of the match'. In a curious bowling change Cox was taken off after only one over and replaced by Jimmy Parks, a 20-year-old colt from Haywards Heath, playing only his third match for the county. Parks specialised in slow-medium away swingers, which over the course of a lengthy career were to prove steady rather than earth-shattering. Today however he proved completely unplayable. By the close Leicester had slumped to a shocking 27-7. Among the witnesses were the Earl of Leconfield and the Bishop of Lewes.

Unsurprisingly, there were very few present on the final morning to witness the doleful procession continue. After 51.1 angst-ridden overs, the *coup de grace* was applied with the total showing 51. This was to stand until 1946 as the lowest innings total witnessed on the ground. What was going through the military mind of Leicester skipper Major Fowke is probably best left to the imagination. Fowke had came in at No 4 and was left high and dry on 15 at the close as young Parks left the field with the scarcely credible analysis of 7-17 from 24 overs. With only five required and scarcely anybody present to bear witness, Sussex's victory took them to the top of the Championship table.

Worcestershire weren't expected to present much of a challenge either for on recent form they were an even worse outfit than Leicestershire. They weren't able to enter a side in the Championship in 1919 and so barren were the 1920s that one of their historians actually 'questioned whether they should have returned to the fray at all'. In four years of the decade they finished rock bottom while in the other six, they never rose above 14th. Things reached their absolute nadir in 1929 when they went through the entire 30-match campaign without winning a game. One member of the side who would have felt at home at Horsham was the Chilean born Maurice Jewell who played in the town's 'Comrades' Cricket Week in 1919, a season in which, curiously, he contrived to play for both counties.

The night before the match a thunderstorm swept violently over the ground but the wicket seemed in no way affected and Worcestershire elected to bat on winning the toss. Pearson was caught at slip off the second ball of the innings but this simply paved the way for a quite remarkable display from their captain Maurice Foster. Maybe he did ride his luck a little but in the highest amateur tradition he went for his shots from the off against an eight-man attack. With support that could best be described as patchy (the next highest score was 29), Foster reached his century after 2 hours 40 minutes. When the final wicket fell deep into the final session he was still there on 157, an innings that had lasted for 250 minutes and contained one six and

14 fours. (He was clearly in good trim, for the previous day had scored 128 against Kent).

As the *West Sussex Guardian* put it: 'In the 45 minutes before the end Sussex, wearied by a long spell of fielding, batted very indifferently'. Indeed they did. At stumps they had tottered to 37/4, all four wickets haven fallen to the vicious late inswing of Fred Root who operated to a field of five close catchers in an arc either side of short leg, a deep third man, mid on, mid off and something akin to a cover. There was some middle-order resistance on the following morning, but Sussex's overall batting display was anaemic. That said, 155 all out actually represented something of a recovery from 58-6. The two bright spots were Arthur Gilligan and Wensley, the latter 'hitting cleanly and with tremendous power on both sides of the wicket' before succumbing to a magnificent running boundary catch. Wensley had the temerity to strike Root for three fours in four balls but for the Championship leaders to be trailing one of its perpetually weaker vessels by 125 on first innings was eyebrow raising stuff.

There was little immediate hint of the fireworks to come but when first innings hero Foster was caught at mid-on attempting to drive Tate, the floodgates opened. Once again Tate swept irresistibly through the breach he had created. There is not much to be said in defence of 57 all out though in his *Cricket Reminiscences* Tate does refer specifically to the wicket for this match – and by inference others at Horsham – as being 'fast (and) inclined to break up'. He returned an astonishing 8-18 and more than 80 years later this remains the best ever individual return by any Sussex bowler against Worcester. Tate and Gilligan bowled unchanged, while poor Edwin Bryant and Harry Rogers rounded off miserable games by completing 'pairs'.

In a complete reversal of the position earlier in the day Sussex now found themselves wanting 183 for victory. Bowley in particular was determined there would be no repeat of the first innings shenanigans: 'by masterly strokes on both sides of the wicket' he reached his 50 in 80 minutes. The score had reached 143 when he was dismissed for a delightful 78. With a Sussex victory now inevitable, Foster sportingly offered them the opportunity to play over time to finish the game off that evening – which they duly did.

We are fortunate to have a lively first-hand account of this match from the pen of Arthur Gilligan. Of the first day he wrote generously that *'The honours...went absolutely to Maurice Foster...He had a little luck, it is true, but he made some glorious off-drives and revelled in doing so particularly off Maurice Tate and me. The back-chat was very marked in this game, but Maurice not only won this easily on the day in question, but played one of the very best innings ever seen on the Horsham ground. His innings was an object-lesson to the schoolboys, who came from the neighbouring schools to watch'.*

1925: The visitors in 1925 were again a mix of 'something old, something new'. Hampshire had been at Cricket Field Road as recently as 1921 but it was uncharted territory for Somerset. These were undistinguished times for Sussex's near-neighbours. Hampshire had finished 12th in 1924 and were only destined to move up three places in 1925.

As the recent dry, warm, settled weather continued, Colonel Watson won the toss and batted. Progress was slow against a steady attack but Bowley played his usual confident game – albeit in more watchful vein - and reached 50 after 110 minutes. Tate added a bit of much needed sparkle to the proceedings, hitting 39 in 30 minutes, while the captain and Tich Cornford added a very useful 66 for the 9th wicket in an hour. Unusually for him the Colonel 'played a cautious game, but (eventually) opened his shoulders to some purpose'. The innings finally closed for 255, Sussex's highest of the season to date. Hampshire's reply started shakily. In the 50 minutes left for play, they had advanced timorously to 36-3.

The weather on the second day was, if anything, even hotter than on the first – blazing sunshine and a temperature of 84 degrees in the shade. A shirt-sleeved crowd saw Sussex sweep all before them as Hampshire never really got to grips with things. By lunchtime they were all out for a modest 124, only Mead and Captain Jameson tarrying long. Yet it might have been worse. 'The Sussex fielding, perhaps due to the heat, was not of such a high standard as usual'. This uneven-ness continued when Sussex went back in. Leading by 131 on first innings, they contrived somewhat carelessly to be bowled out for 179. The author of their demise was Hampshire's man for all seasons, George Brown. He hadn't been required to bowl in the first innings but now answered his side's call, taking 7-60 with his gentle medium pacers in an innings notable only for an immense straight drive by Colonel Watson off slow left-armer Stuart Boyes that has passed into legend. This mighty blow pitched in the tea enclosure by the tennis courts and bounded through the railings into the field by the river, a huge carry.

Sussex's collapse left Hampshire 311 to win on the final day but with Tate continuing to mine his rich vein of form at Horsham – at one point he had taken 5-8 - they never had a prayer. Yet again Tate swept all before him. Before they knew where they were Hampshire's innings was in ruins at 94-8. But the impassive and immovable Phil Mead, who had been watching phlegmatically from the non-striker's end at the chaos all around him, then found an ally in Walter Livsey who sadly seems to be remembered less for his cricketing prowess – he was a wicket-keeper/bat good enough to have played for England – than the fact that he was also Lord Tennyson's butler. These two added 80 for the 9th wicket but were only delaying the inevitable. By early afternoon it was all over. Mead made a faultless and superbly crafted 76 not out, but was overshadowed by Tate's even more admirable 7-44 off 27 overs.

Somerset were an interesting side captained by the Stogumber farmer Jack White, who, in season, would come to matches at Taunton following a spell of haymaking. The 1920s were an undistinguished decade for the West Country outfit and a lowly 15th spot awaited in 1925.

The match again opened in glorious sunshine and a crowd of over 4,000 saw White win the toss and bat. Opening the bowling from the town end Tate broke through with the very first ball of the innings but worse was to follow for the visitors, Wensley taking a wicket with the second ball of *his* opening over. White and Tom Young then steadied the ship until Tate sent back White in the opening over after the resumption. When Young was bowled by Cox for 86 the end was nigh. Somerset's innings realised 199 with Tate picking up a further five wickets. Sussex's reply began equally disastrously, Bowley being bowled by Robertson-Glasgow without a run on the board. This set the tone for the innings and by stumps the home side were perilously placed at 121/6 with Wensley unbeaten on 44. But, ominously for the side batting last, the wicket was already showing signs of wear and tear.

The following morning Sussex decided to play a forcing game. All the middle-order contributed and they actually ended up with a modest lead of 14. Colonel Watson drove White for a huge six and Tate made a breezy 29 in even time as Robertson-Glasgow and White took nine of the 10 wickets. Somerset had cleared the arrears by lunch, Young in particular batting with much greater freedom. He was particularly severe on Cox, smiting the veteran for three fours in one over and shortly afterwards, for a driven six. The big hitting Guy Earle – who once took 22 off an over from Australia's Clarrie Grimmett – hit two sixes and three fours in a brisk knock. By contrast, Haywood's 38 (made in over 2 hours) might euphemistically be described as a model of restraint. Opening bat CCC 'Box' Case came in for particular criticism. He 'was painfully slow and his cricket was poor and consisted mainly of putting the face of the bat at the ball to stop it hitting his stumps. Even for pure defence it was most unattractive'. Yet on an increasingly tricky pitch Somerset's 230 was an excellent effort. Sussex were left with 35 minutes to negotiate and lost three cheap wickets, Bowley (worryingly) being caught off his glove defending his face from one that 'flew'.

The weather on the final morning was again glorious but sadly for Sussex their innings was anything but. In fact they only just made it past lunch on a by-now badly crumbling pitch. The only batsman to tarry long was Holmes who stuck it out for 90 minutes. Earle split his little finger trying to catch one of Colonel Watson's skiers but as luck would have it 'Dr Dew, who was on the ground, and who keeps wicket for the Horsham Club, treated the injury'. Well supported by George Hunt's medium pacers, Robertson-Glasgow, who 'bowled very fast and had all the Sussex batsmen in trouble all the time' completed match figures of 9-111 as his side eased home. *Wisden* had little doubt about the determining factor: 'All through the match the pitch, baked hard by the sun, gave bowlers assistance'. But you can never please all the people all the time. 'Taken as a whole', the *West Sussex Guardian* opined a bit sniffily, 'the second game was not so bright and interesting as the first and there were times when it was rather tedious to watch'.

We are again fortunate to have a first-hand account of the game from one of the protagonists and doubly so in that it comes from the witty and perceptive pen of Robertson-Glasgow. Encapsulating the very essence of the match in a few elegant paragraphs, 'Crusoe' was to write in his autobiography '46 Not Out':

'My only success was...at leafy Horsham, and here the pitch was so fast and uncertain that my natural pace of fast-medium was enough. Our own first innings amounted to 199... In the first over of their innings, I bowled Ted Bowley for 0. Wicketkeeper 'Tich' Cornford, opening the innings as if he'd never heard of places 10 and 11, batted very soundly. Two or three times a ball from me bounced over his head from a length, and the crowd barracked in defence of the little man. 'Tich' was much amused, and said to me "The trouble is, Mr Glasgow, they forget I'm not very far above the ground". I had him lbw for 30 and soon half Sussex had gone for under 100. But we were held up by that admirable all-rounder Bert Wensley, and the cunning George Cox senior, then in his fifty third-year. When these were parted, Maurice Tate whacked around like a genial policeman. So, for a shorter space, did the lusty Colonel AC Watson...Eight of us reached double figures in the second innings. Tom Young added 48 to his 86, and that miracle of vigilance, CCC Case, stuck for 19. Guy Earle shook the trees of Horsham with a brisk 31, and George Hunt, chewing impassively at number ten, made 28 not out. Bowley brought our own little battle all-square by having me lbw for 0. So Sussex needed 217 to win; the ideal match. They lost 4 wickets for less than 30, and though AJ Holmes batted gallantly for 40, and George Cox was unbeaten for 23, they never quite looked like doing it, and we won by 76. There's nothing like a victory to think over as you tootle home on a motor-bicycle through an evening in June.'

1926: The first game of the 1926 Festival has gone down in national cricketing history as George Cox's Match and shortly we shall see why. But against a backdrop of the National Strike, Horsham's visitors were again comprised of one side familiar with the venue (Gloucestershire) and one who was not (Warwickshire). Sussex would no doubt have recalled ruefully their remarkable encounter against the latter at Edgbaston in 1925. They called the shots for the majority of that match, finally setting their heavily outgunned hosts a mammoth 392 to win – which they achieved with 45 minutes to spare for the loss of only one wicket! However, the Warwicks attack, quite frankly, was lightweight and their record for 1926 tells its own story - P28, W2, D17, position in table, 12th.

With Tate and Arthur Gilligan on Test duty at Lord's (the latter in his capacity as a selector), Warwicks skipper Bob Wyatt won the toss from Harold Gilligan and took first knock on a glorious summer day. The Sussex out-cricket was uncharacteristically shoddy with catches being spilled and several misfields. A 3rd wicket stand of 111 between Len Bates and the veteran Willie Quaife helped the score along to 171/2. Bates was to become well-known in the Horsham area. After retiring in 1935 he became coach at Christ's Hospital, a position he held until 1963. He was also father-in-law of the future Horsham and Sussex fast bowler Don Weekes. WG (Willie) Quaife was even better known – indeed was on Sussex's books as a youngster. Many years later George Cox recalled that he and Quaife first played against each other back in 1887 in a village match between Warnham and Ockley! Bates struck two 6s in his 77, but when Quaife fell, the innings went into a rapid decline and concluded for a disappointing 257. The star of the home side's attack was veteran slow left armer Cox. In 38.4 overs he collared 8/56, at one point only conceding four runs in 11 overs. 'There was mild barracking after the tea interval when Kilner and Croom declined to take liberties with (his) puzzling deliveries'.

Initially the tide flowed in Warwicks' direction on day two and at 94/6 Sussex were struggling to avoid the follow-on. However, marshalled by Holmes' splendid 87 and supported heroically by the tail, they actually contrived a first-innings lead of four. Warwicks started their second innings confidently and there was little hint of what lay in store. Wyatt and Jack Parsons put on 72 for the first wicket in a mere 50 minutes. Bates picked up where he left off the previous day and the 100 was raised in a mere 90 minutes. But then Cox went to work again. By the close the visitors had crashed to 126/6, Cox having claimed five of them.

The Warnham man continued to dominate on the third day – but not immediately, for heavy rain and mist delayed the start. In 36.5 overs he returned 9-50 - which was to stand as the best individual analysis on the ground until 1948 - to complete astonishing match figures of 17/106. As though mesmerised Warwickshire had subsided to 177/8 at lunch, Cox – despite being hit for six by Jack Smart – having seven of them. He bowled Mayer with the first ball after the break and Peare in his next over to leave Warwicks 177 all out. (For the record, Bert Wensley was the man who prevented 'the Guv'nor' from picking up all ten).

It was said – and George never denied it – that part of his success was down to delivering the ball out of a background of dark trees at the town end! John Marshall, in his 1959 history of Sussex CCC, leaves us with a nice vignette involving George and his old-sparring partner Quaife. Somewhat embarrassingly, Willie had misjudged one in the first innings and been clean bowled shouldering arms. As he passed his nemesis en route back to the pavilion he muttered wryly out of the corner of his mouth: 'That one turned a bit quickly George'. 'Must have pitched on a dandelion' replied George, equally drily – which for a long while puzzled his impressionable young son who wondered what on earth a dandelion was doing on a county wicket!

All this left Sussex 174 to win but the real question was: would the weather allow them sufficient time in which to do it? One factor in their favour was that their opponents were hardly the most formidable bowling side in creation. They started boldly enough. In between the showers Bowley and Wensley went for their shots but the weather seemed determined to have the last laugh, particularly when both men were out in successive balls to Wyatt - 71 to win in 33 minutes. Now it was the turn of Harold Gilligan and Cook to take up the cudgels. Gilligan was run out with the score on 141 (at one point Cook lent him his bat after Gilligan's own had smashed rather than waste time waiting for a new one to be brought out). The formidable smiter Colonel Watson contributed 19 in 13 minutes before he too was run out. Incoming batsman Holmes was waiting at the pavilion gate and in his anxiety not to waste so much as a second, 'did part of his journey to the wicket at the double'. Eleven runs were needed in 6-7 minutes as Holmes and Cook scampered for just about everything. Eventually, Holmes late-cut the first ball of the final over of the day for the winning run 'amid prolonged cheering...(and) great enthusiasm'.

Again we are fortunate in having an account of proceedings from the pen of Arthur Gilligan: *This game was memorable for the finest bowling performance ever rendered to Sussex by that wonderful 53-year old veteran George Cox, who in the December of his honourable career...showed all his old wiles, and his variation of pace and a fair amount of spin made him absolutely unplayable. He hit the stumps nine times...In July, at Hove, there was a splendid function held in front of the pavilion, when George...was presented with the ball suitably mounted'.*

John Marshall too paints a wonderfully atmospheric picture of this match recalling how old George *'Bowling from the river end...had the batsmen shuffling from unease to helplessness, getting an edge to it – or not even an edge at all – baffled and bewildered. Varying his pace with his old skill – the faster one still had a bit of bite in it too – imparting a disconcerting amount of spin...The ovation that followed was not forgotten by old George Cox and will never be forgotten by George Cox junior, a spellbound spectator, who has the ball, a treasured heirloom, at his Warnham home today...There was an air of melancholy about the Horsham ground when 'the guv'nor' played his last match'.*

Could the Gloucestershire match provide similar excitement? On paper, 'No' because their brilliant young strokeplayer Walter Hammond missed the entire season and in consequence they fell from 6th to 15th. Their skipper, 42-year-old Lt Col Douglas Robinson, played for Essex in the first-ever county match on the ground back in 1908.

Sadly, the match was plagued by rain and it is greatly to the credit of both sides that they contrived to make such a good game of it. Gloucester won the toss and batted. After the early loss of 'old' Charles Barnett, Dipper and Smith took the score up to 107. But then (for them) disaster struck and once again the agent was George Cox. Even by their modest standards 144 all out was a major disappointment, Cox adding six more wickets (for 45) to the 17 he had just taken against Warwicks.

Right on cue it started to rain and no play was possible until after lunchtime on the second day. Once under way Charlie Parker – who was something of a jinx to Bowley – duly dismissed his 'bunny' without a run on the board and the innings proceeded by fits and starts to 163, a lead of 19. Even this wouldn't have been possible but for a fighting unbeaten half-century in an hour from Arthur Gilligan but Gloucester only had themselves to blame -

Gilligan was dropped twice and in all no fewer than five catches went down, all off the luckless Reg Sinfield, who for good measure conceded 110 of the 157 runs scored off the bat. Batting at the railway end, Gilligan struck Sinfield for one six onto the tennis courts and another into the nearby tea enclosure - each one a goodly carry by any yardstick. By the close Gloucester were wobbling at 26/2.

On the final morning Colonel Robinson, the 'giant captain of the visiting side', injured his leg so badly he had to be helped off the field by his opposite number. In untrustworthy weather the visitors' scoring rate was pedestrian and their declaration left Sussex an hour in which to score 128, a somewhat improbable undertaking against Parker on a wicket tailor-made for him. And so it proved. Perhaps because they shuffled their batting order around, perhaps because they weren't sure whether to stick or twist, and perhaps because of some really fine bowling, Sussex at one point were actually in some danger of losing. By the close they had stuttered nervously to 54/7 with only Harold Gilligan, who had opened the innings and was still there on 29, keeping the ship afloat. But spare a thought for poor Bowley. Coming in at No 5, he was bowled by Parker for his second duck of the match. Including the match earlier in the season at Gloucester, this was the 4th time he had fallen to his nemesis in five balls!

Let Gilligan have the final word: *'Rain ruined a sporting return match with Gloucestershire, though we had a game more reminiscent of country house than of county cricket. George Cox took 6 for 45 in their second innings, bringing up his aggregate for three innings to 23 wickets. The strain of so great a performance left its mark on him, and anno domini played its part afterwards. To use George's own words "If I had had another pair of legs, some of them would have to answer for it"'.*

1927: Horsham's first visitors in 1927 were none other than Warwickshire again. For the visitors the 1920s were summed up by club historian Robert Brooke as 'notable only for consistent mediocrity' and 1927 – an abnormally wet summer – witnessed them string together a run of 15 consecutive early season draws, which secured them an 11th place finish in the Championship table.

Harold Gilligan won the toss and batted. A crowd estimated at 3,500 saw Bowley and Tate tuck into the visiting attack with gusto. Tate in particular played with great vigour, surviving two hard chances to hit three legside sixes. He was eventually caught in the deep for 72, made in even time. When Cook joined Bowley runs flowed at an even greater rate. They put on exactly 200 in 115 minutes against an attack that sorely missed fast bowler Harry Howell. Bowley looked particularly assured 'depend(ing) almost entirely on the drive, the pull and the leg glance.' His century came up in 135 minutes and he was eventually 4th out for a quite magnificent 176, scored in 205 minutes. This was to stand until 2007 as the highest individual score on the ground by a Sussex batsman. At tea the score stood at 333-2 and although Warwicks took three quickish wickets in the final session, Harold Gilligan then proceeded to flog a tired and demoralised attack all over the place. He and Jim Parks had plundered 79 in 35 minutes before rain cut short the final session. Even so, Sussex's 480/7 was scored at a storming rate of 100 per hour.

The weather on the second morning was delightful with bright sunshine and a gentle breeze. Re-invigorated, Warwicks – and in particular Wyatt, with a burst of 3/8 in 14 balls - quickly polished off the Sussex innings for a mammoth 515, in which not one of the batsmen was bowled. No doubt with some trepidation, Tiger Smith and Norman Kilner commenced Warwicks' reply. Kilner was run out with only four on the board but his comrades dug in with commendable resilience. If they were going to lose, they weren't going down without a fight... They batted doggedly through the remainder of the day. Much clearly turned on whether they could make the 365 needed to avoid the follow-on and this contest ebbed and flowed throughout a fascinating day. Late on, Bowley strained a tendon in his leg and was treated by Mr A Williams, Horsham Football Club's masseur, who chanced to be on the ground.

Resuming on the final morning with 71 still needed, Warwicks fell well short and duly followed on. However, the weather then decided to intervene. The players were on and off for rain until stumps were finally drawn at 5pm. But give Warwicks credit for by then the combined efforts of Kilner (55), Parsons (56 n/o) and Croom (41 n/o) had pretty much seen them to safety after a bumpy opening. The latter pair had already put on 101 in 85 minutes when the match splish-splashed its way to a soggy and inconclusive finale.

The Week's second visitors, Kent, had a reputation for attractive cricket and even without the talismanic APF Chapman, they were usually worth watching. Arthur Gilligan won the toss and batted but on a lively pitch wickets soon started to clatter. So much so that by mid-afternoon, Sussex were all out for a distinctly ordinary 160. Only a stand of 52 for the 5th wicket between Bert Wensley, who top scored with 45, and Reg Hollingdale prevented it from being even worse as the Kent seamers George Beslee and AC Wright took most of the honours. By the close, Kent had raced ominously to 174/2 thanks in the main to a quite wonderful unbeaten century from Wally Hardinge, a solid and reliable opener who had made his first-class debut at the age of 16 as far back as 1902.

The weather certainly favoured Sussex on the second day. Heavy rain before the start rendered the wicket increasingly tricky to bat on as it dried out. The morning session was clearly going to be crucial to the outcome of the match and it went completely Sussex's way. Hardinge only added one to his overnight score and in around 75 minutes Kent's last eight wickets tumbled for the addition of 73 runs, Jim Parks taking 5/39. By mid-afternoon the balance was still – just – in the visitors favour, but Wensley and Captain Isherwood changed all that. Batting with increasing confidence they cleared the arrears and paved the way for some classic late-order hitting from the Gilligan brothers. The mercurial Harold – who didn't always do himself justice at Horsham (or indeed generally) - struck 10 fours in a brilliant 66. This enabled his side to reach 292, leaving Kent 203 to win. They started badly, losing the valuable wickets of Bill Ashdown and Hardinge for 23 in the 30 minutes to stumps.

Initially there appeared little prospect of play on the final day as rain fell through most of the morning. However, when events did get under way, it was clear that for the second time in the match Kent had to contend with an awkward wicket as well as an attack led in exemplary fashion once again by Tate. It wasn't long before the rot set in, with Gerry Legge the only man able to resist for any length of time. But when he fell to Tate (who else?) for 60, many in the crowd sensed the game was up. And so it proved as Sussex polished off their visitors for 172. Tate ended up with 8/68 off 28.5 overs but who would have dared forecast such an amazing transformation at the close of the first day?

1928: The 1928 Festival saw the return of Surrey and Hampshire. Surrey finished 6th in both 1927 and 1928 but in a batsman's summer their record of P28, W5, D20, L3 tells its own story. Other than skipper Percy Fender and Alan Peach the attack struggled to bowl sides out even in favourable conditions.

The match opened with the visitors looking to protect/extend an unbeaten record. A decent sized crowd of 2,750 saw them take first knock on an excellent wicket and in glorious weather. The early exchanges went very much their way. The forceful Andy Ducat was quickly into his stride but – perhaps ominously soon in the piece – Jim Parks was extracting spin before lunch. Ducat made the most of two chances – on 1 and 48 – and completed an excellent century but against a clever and varied attack he could find no-one to stay with him. He was left high and dry on 101 as Surrey's innings broke down completely in the afternoon session. 226 all out was a major (and unaccountable) disappointment, their last seven wickets tumbling for a mere 68 runs. Bowley and Jim Parks opened Sussex's reply against Peach and a new young fast bowler making his debut for the county, Alf Gover. By the close they were handily placed on 98/2.

Heavy overnight rain affected the scoring rate on day two and Sussex – usually among the more free-scoring sides in the country – were obliged to play steady rather than forcing cricket. An exception was the versatile and under-rated Wensley who cut and drove in splendid fashion. He was within three runs of a richly deserved century when beaten and bowled by a slower ball from Gover. The wicket was so lifeless that even Tate was obliged to play cautiously. The innings eventually came to an end on 387, compiled over a marathon 155.5 overs. Jim Langridge made 77 but everybody chipped in in what was a real team effort. At this point rain fell in torrents.

Surrey had nothing to play for but the draw on the final day but on a treacherous, fast-drying surface they struggled from the outset. Four top wickets were down by lunch as they fought to survive. Fender and Ducat steadied the ship, putting on 72 for the

5th wicket in 90 minutes. At tea they only needed 16 to make Sussex bat again with Fender well-set and five wickets in hand. 'So likely did a draw appear…that a good many spectators left early'. They should have known better for the immediate post-tea session witnessed some sensational cricket. Fender was caught behind off Gilligan from the very first ball and the hitherto 'Bored spectators' looked on in amazement as the last five wickets capitulated in 20 thrilling minutes to the England duo of Tate and Gilligan for the addition of only 11 runs. 'The mild barracking of the afternoon was succeeded by hearty cheers on the part of the big ring of onlookers, numbering well over 1,000'. From a match that was drifting nowhere, Sussex had improbably conjured up an innings victory, Surrey's 156 having taken 108.1 overs. As an aside, umpire Jack King became the first of several men to have played and officiated on the ground.

Hampshire's problems were the same as for several seasons past – and indeed the same as many county sides in the decade immediately following the Great War – weak bowling. That they finished as high as 12th was due largely to a burst of three wins out of five in August.

Harold Gilligan took over as captain but for the 9th time in 13 attempts Sussex lost the toss. On a beautiful summer's day a crowd amounting at its peak to almost 3,700 was treated to a stodgy day's cricket. Hampshire's problem was that while any number of their men got starts, no one could fully capitalise. Hampshire captain Alec Hosie, who opened in rather uncertain fashion against the pace of 'Tishy' Browne, soon got his powerful drive going and top scored with 54 but from the relative heights of 179/5, 199 all out was a grievous disappointment. Browne celebrated his selection by taking 6/50. Sussex's reply couldn't have started in worse fashion, Bowley playing-on to the first ball of the match from Peter Utley. By the close they were 73/3.

On the second morning, Sussex's innings followed a curiously similar pattern with Nos 2-7 all making double figures. Cook (45) and Jim Langridge (38) top-scored but it was only the assistance of Mr Extras (36) that enabled them to take a first innings lead of 33. Pick of the visiting bowlers was Utley, who was later to join the Church. With Browne doing likewise this was one of the few instances in first-class cricket in which both sides opened the bowling with a future 'man of the cloth'. Hampshire started badly second time round. Newman was run out without a run on the board but along came the reassuring figure of Mead. With Brown for company he saw things through to the close without any further alarms.

Rain ruined the final day but not before Mead and Brown had given the crowd a batting masterclass on a capricious wicket. Mead batted for over 2 hours 30 minutes for his 75 but despite having to use a runner his partner was still there on 67 when the declaration came at 214/6. This left Sussex 182 to win but the infernal rain then set in again and prevented them from starting their innings until 4.30pm – far too late for either side to harbour thoughts of victory. They had moved to 55 for the loss of Bowley when stumps were drawn.

1929: Horsham's first visitors in 1929 were Essex, who hadn't been seen in the town since their inaugural visit 21 years and one World War earlier. The 1920s were a long, rather featureless period for Essex cricket. They were never bottom of the pile, yet never particularly near the top of it either.

Harold Gilligan won the toss and took first knock. Sadly, rain wiped out virtually the entire pre-lunch session but afterwards, Bowley in particular seemed in good touch. A smallish crowd watched expectantly as Duleepsinhji took strike but just as he was getting into his stride he leg-glanced a fast delivery from Nichols and was magnificently caught at full stretch by wicketkeeper Eastman. Bowley treated all the bowlers in the same confident manner and was 4th out shortly after tea for exactly 100, made out of 156 in 130 minutes. Bad light then ended play prematurely.

Rain again poked its unwanted nose in on the second day, the start being delayed for 45 minutes. A feature of the truncated pre-lunch session was a swashbuckling innings from the erratic Harold Gilligan, on his day a superb clean hitter. He shepherded the score along to 248 in the face of Essex bowling that was competitive throughout. His 51 only took 20 minutes and included a magnificent off-driven six. In the 20 minutes to lunch, Essex lost both openers. Two of their all-time greats, Jack O'Connor and CAG (Jack) Russell, then added 85 for the 3rd wicket but when they were parted wickets began to tumble again. By tea, the score stood at 125/8. Somewhat improbably the last pair of Raison and Eastman then put on 69 audacious runs in 50 minutes to boost the total to 194. Bowley was dropped at the wicket off the first ball of the home side's second innings but was bowled soon after by a shooter from Nichols. Nevertheless, Sussex were handily placed at stumps being 80 runs to the good with nine wickets in hand.

Rain ruined the final day. The feature of the Sussex innings was some heroic fast bowling from Morris Nichols. Operating at the railway end with the assistance of a strong wind, the Stondon Massey man took 6/34 with his ungainly but highly effective, flail-like action as the home side was routed for 106. Coming in at No 5, Jim Langridge alone stood firm but apart from a flamboyant cameo from Gilligan it was a poor effort. In bowling Grimston, Nichols sent a bail an estimated 50 yards. This flaccid Sussex display meant that Essex were set 161 for victory in 105 minutes and but for yet more rain, who knows what might have happened? By the close Essex had moved watchfully to 53/2.

Glamorgan were the second visitors. They would have little cause to recall their only previous visit to the ground with any affection. On that occasion they played some truly wretched cricket and failed to reach 100 in either innings. 1929 was perhaps the gloomiest season of a gloomy decade for them. They finished bottom of the Championship with 19 defeats and a mere three wins from their 28 matches. Their batting was fragile and their bowling even worse.

Arthur Gilligan was back in charge, won the toss and batted. The crowd settled back expectantly to watch the visiting attack take its ritual caning. Bowley was in a good run of form and was anxious to oblige. Having played himself in quietly, he opened up in quite delightful fashion scoring freely all round the wicket. For the 4th consecutive home match he reached a century – and in doing so became the first man in the country to reach 1,000 runs for the season. He made 130 and put on 143 for the 3rd wicket with Cook (43) but other than 47 from Wensley the support was modest, the last seven wickets falling for 98. Gilligan would doubtless have been looking for more than 306 all out as slow left armer Emrys Davies picked up 5/26. But all things are relative and by stumps Glamorgan were in disarray at 57/5.

The tide continued to flow strongly in Sussex's direction on the following morning as Jim Langridge and Wensley combined to see Glamorgan off for 101. Fortified by a lead of 205 and his bowlers still fresh, Gilligan had little hesitation in enforcing the follow-on. They little dreamt what lay in store. In direct contrast to their spineless initial effort the Welshmen batted with far great resolution throughout the remainder of the second day and into the third. Only three batsmen failed to reach 20 although 'Dropped catches were partly responsible for this, and the Sussex fielding in this particular respect was not any too keen'. John Bell led off with 56 and Fred (Birdie) Mathias followed his 'pair' in 1923 with 48 here. Skipper Trevor Arnott, hitting the ball hard in front of the wicket, added 49 but the highest innings of the day – indeed of his career – came from Guy Morgan, a talented all-rounder who won eight Welsh rugby caps but who, sadly, was crippled by rheumatoid arthritis by his late 30s. Morgan hit an unbeaten 91 as Glamorgan made a defiant 408.

Somewhat unexpectedly Sussex found themselves having to chase 204 for victory. On a wicket that clearly was holding no great terrors this should have been a routine assignment, but courtesy of one of those twists of fate that make cricket such a wonderful game (unless you are on the wrong end of them), they put up an inexplicably supine display against Davies and Mercer. As a stunned final day crowd looked on in disbelief, wickets tumbled like skittles – except for that of Cook. He was still there when the score stood at a scarcely believable 80/9 but then found an ally in No 11 Cornford. These two put what had gone before into perspective with a stand of 67 in 66 minutes before Cornford was lbw to hand Glamorgan a victory that was nothing short of miraculous. Cook was left high and dry on 54 as Davies took 4/34 and Mercer 5/77. As the *County Times* generously put it: 'Glamorgan deserve all the credit they can get for pulling this game around from an apparently heavy defeat'. *Wisden* went further, describing it as: 'One of the most remarkable contests of the season.' Few even in shell-shocked Sussex would argue…

On this somewhat downbeat note, time to enter the portals of a new decade…

Chapter 5

GOLDEN SUMMERS PART II: 1930-1939

1930: The new decade was ushered in by two Midlands sides. Leicestershire had been in town twice before but Derbyshire were debutants. The former were a very average outfit around this time finishing in 12th place despite only winning 4 matches all season, all of them in the first half of the campaign.

The visitors would no doubt have been delighted that Duleepsinhji and Tate were away playing for England against Australia. They won the toss and took first knock 'on a wicket that appeared to be good for plenty of runs.' The weather was glorious and sunny and after a bright opening the innings rather fell away and by lunch five wickets were down. The scoring rate was pedestrian and the innings eventually folded for 254, Jim Langridge picking up some late wickets.

On the second morning Jim Parks struck the first ball of the day to the boundary. Two brief rain breaks gingered the wicket up a little but the century was raised after only 110 minutes. Cook and Parks then departed in rapid succession and tea was taken on 173/2. Rain again intervened in the final session as Sussex closed on 235/6 with (seemingly) only a draw to play for.

The final morning saw consistent batting all the way down the order. With the exception of Jim Langridge everyone made double figures as the side totalled 362, the final three wickets putting on an invaluable 125. Not for the first time at Horsham, Astill wheeled away tirelessly and returned 5/105.

This gave the home side a useful lead of 108 but would there be enough time for them to force a conclusion? Leicester's second innings was as sedate as their first - their 158 took them more than 86 overs.

This left Sussex 25 minutes to make 49. As the *County Times* put it: 'In this short space was crowded more thrills and incident than had characterised practically three whole days play.' Shuffling his batting order about, 'Gilligan and Wensley went in first , obviously determined to go all out for the necessary runs or sacrifice their wickets in the process'. Sadly for them, 'Shipman's first ball spreadeagled Wensley's wicket' - 0-1. With only five on the board Snary removed Harry Parks' middle stump. One run later it was Bowley's turn, his 'off stump falling to a straight one from Shipman'. Williams was then stumped in the 4th over - 13/4. All this had taken place in 13 frantic minutes which left Sussex a further 12 in which to get 36. The umpires then took a hand decreeing that as there was insufficient time for Sussex to win it was time to draw stumps 'thus ending the only really thrilling part of an otherwise uneventful match. The bowling and fielding of both sides were object lessons in themselves and it was due entirely to these that almost every batsman appeared slow…Sussex were not favoured with the best of luck, for stoppages through rain and bad light took some of the time off and when they went out for the necessary runs, they were faced with deadly accurate bowling.'

The second visitors, Derbyshire, were another settled, mid-table side. Their batting was adequate without being anything to shout about, but in the shape of Tommy Mitchell, they had a high class leg-break bowler. When the two sides had met a month earlier, Sussex lost by an innings despite the home side only making 191. Jim Langridge completed a 'pair' in three balls.

Sussex welcomed back Tate and Duleep but in perfect cricket weather it was Derbyshire's Guy Jackson who won the all important toss. He had little hesitation in batting before a crowd that was to build up during the day to nearly 2,000. It was a curate's egg of an innings. Storer and Smith put on 71 relatively untroubled runs for the first wicket but Jim Langridge and Bowley wrought a transformation that saw the score slide alarmingly to 90/5 by lunch, Langridge returning 4/16 in the session. This uneven pattern continued through the afternoon as only Jackson himself and wicket keeper Elliott tarried for any length of time. Derby were eventually dismissed for a modest 203 just before tea, Bowley taking 5/63 and Langridge 4/67. Mindful of his recent exertions at Trent Bridge, Tate only bowled eight overs. Sussex's reply was similarly fitful and by stumps they had lost four wickets making 112. This included Duleep's for a most elegant and wristy 39.

Bat and ball strove for domination in time-honoured fashion on the second morning. At 191/7 things were still fairly evenly poised, but there then followed an extended passage of play that was to determine the match. After spirited knocks from Harold Gilligan and Tate had enabled their side to take the lead, Harry Parks was joined by Wensley with the scoreboard showing 241/8. These two put on exactly 100 in 55 furious minutes despite Mitchell trying every trick in the book 'to lure the batsmen out to tricky slows, but they just stepped back onto the wicket and cut and drove him as they had the other bowlers. In one attempt to dislodge them, Mitchell literally dropped a ball towards Parks, who watched it carefully before smiting it lustily to the fine leg boundary.' Wensley struck two successive fours to bring up his side's 400 and his own century. The former had taken 5 hours 20 minutes, the latter a mere hour with 14 powerful boundaries. The new ball was taken but not until the score had reached 419 did Worthington 'dislodge Parks' middle stump', thus bringing to an end a pulsating 9th wicket stand of 178 made in 105 minutes of sustained brilliance. A weary Wensley eventually capitulated for 120 as the home side's innings closed for 429 but the point must be made that this was compiled in the face of 'very good bowling and brilliant fielding. Indeed apart from the great stand, the Derbyshire fielding was the outstanding feature of an eventful innings. Their picking up and returning over a whole day's play were remarkably consistent.' An absorbing day ended with the visitors on 100/3, still 126 adrift.

The early loss of Jackson on the final morning seemed to dishearten his side. Some of them clearly tried to hang it out but it was as though their collective heart knew the game was up. With Langridge, Tate and Wensley each taking three wickets the end came just before lunch with the score on 192. Cook kept wicket after Cornford had to leave the field following a blow to the face. For Sussex it was pay-back time for the hiding meted out to them earlier in the season and brought to an end a run of five matches without a win. As luck would have it rain started to fall just as play finished.

1931: The two visitors in 1931 were more attractive drawcards than those in 1930. Surrey and Nottinghamshire were both riding high in the Championship – as indeed were Sussex themselves. Percy Fender was certainly looking forward to his visit. In a private letter to Horsham CC, he wrote: 'I always feel that the attitude of your public, coupled with the general atmosphere and surroundings...combine to make a match at Horsham a real pleasure...no matter what the result.' Rain had ruined the earlier game at the Oval but not before Bowley (144) and Duleep (162) had put on 250 for the 3rd wicket in three hours.

The opening day crowd was gigantic and is still believed to be a record for the ground. Some estimates put it as high as 7,000 and 'Certainly it was a fine sight to see the great crowd gathered round the playing area...the general view of people, expansive greensward, white marquees, flags flying, trees in full leaf and the parish church spire in the near distance, was as pleasing as any spectator could wish to behold.' Fender won the toss and decided to bat. Hobbs and Sandham justified the decision with an opening stand of 87 but despite several batsmen getting starts, Surrey would have been disappointed with 195 all out off. As so often in the past Tate led the way with 5/46 which included a burst of 4/7 in 11 overs after lunch. By the close Sussex had lost Bowley and John Langridge with only 44 on the board. This was believed to be the match recalled in later years by Arthur Gilligan in which play was held up for some minutes while a number of chickens crossed in front of the sightscreen. Hobbs was on strike at the time and remarked laconically to Sandham, 'This would never have happened at the Oval.'

Despite batting (on paper) all the way down to No. 11, Sussex were bundled out on the second morning for a woeful 113, Edward Sheffield's medium fast inswingers being the primary agent of execution. Finding themselves with an unexpected first innings lead of 82 Surrey started shakily second time round, Wensley trapping Sandham lbw with only two on the board. But it wasn't long before the visitors were easing themselves firmly into the box seat. Hobbs and Ducat put on 92 for the 2nd wicket as Surrey closed the day on 231/7, an overall lead of 313.

They didn't continue long on the final morning, Fender setting the home side an improbable 337 for victory. Despite Duleep's engaging 59 the game seemed all up at 243/8, everybody but Jim Langridge managing double figures. Yet there was to be one final twist. Tate refused to modify his usual ebullient approach and contributed a cleanly struck 57 in only 40 minutes. At this point he was joined by a man well-known to cricket followers locally, George Pearce, a highly popular and well-known member of Horsham CC. Together these two put on 65 priceless runs for the 9th wicket before being parted with the score on 308. When last man Cornford – by no means a negligible commodity with the bat - came to the crease, only 29 were needed. Sadly there was to be no fairytale ending for in a gripping finale the final wicket fell with only five minutes remaining and Sussex only 12 runs short. How they must have rued their first innings frailties...

The second match was fraught with controversy and the genesis for its ultimate degeneration into near farce might be traced back to the fact that counties only played 28 Championship matches. Yet with 17 teams in the competition, it meant that four fixtures each season were arranged and played as friendlies. For 1931 both Sussex-Notts games fell into this category. By the time of their visit to Cricket Field Road, Arthur Carr's still-powerful side were 2nd in the table and immediately after this match had to hurry back to Trent Bridge to take on Championship-leaders Kent. With nothing riding on the Sussex match, Carr and his men must have viewed their long trip south as irksome and largely irrelevant. And all too soon it was to show...

The game got under way promptly despite heavy overnight and early morning rain. Duleep won the toss and batted. To his side's relief the much-feared Harold Larwood was present at the ground but did not play. The previous month Larwood hit a century against Sussex coming in at No 10 and two Sussex men then had to retire hurt after being struck respectively by Larwood and Bill Voce (some 'friendly'!). Jim Parks and Duleep added 143 for the second wicket in 120 minutes, Duleep's 97 including 10 fours. He drove Sam Staples for three onside 4s in one over but the first two sessions were punctuated by poor field placings, lackadaisical fielding and even worse catching. There was nothing like the effort being put in as there had been in the Surrey match and the *County Times* was not alone in its observation that this 'lack of seriousness was most pronounced in the fielding of Notts, which was anything but keen, many boundaries being given away un-necessarily and more than one comparatively easy catch being dropped.' Parks took full advantage going on to make 109, his only century of the season but from the teatime heights of 243/2 Sussex's innings went into a rapid decline. They lost their last eight wickets for 66 runs, Arthur Staples taking 5/83 with his little medium pacers. The wicket seemed to have a bit more devil about it as Barratt made several deliveries rear nastily. Cook was forced to retire hurt after being hit on the hand, his place in the field being taken by local youngster Charlie Oakes.

The second day saw Walter Keeton and George Gunn struggle early on against Tate and Wensley and it wasn't long before wickets started to tumble. By lunch the visitors had subsided to 149/6. The burly Barratt then enlivened proceedings with some big hitting. Having knocked Pearce out of the attack, he lifted Jim Parks high over the boundary ropes near the tennis courts and in his next over hit Parks clean out of the ground. By contrast Hardstaff fashioned an unbeaten 58 in his usual elegant manner as the visitors were all out for 185, giving Sussex a lead of 124.

There then followed a most astonishing passage of play as the home side rattled up 310/4 by stumps in 160 minutes against an attack that – Voce and Barratt apart - was clearly going through the motions. After a slow start John Langridge and Duleep picked up the tempo by putting on 143 for the 2nd wicket in 75 minutes. Tate and Jim Langridge trumped this by compiling 110 for the 4th wicket in 45 minutes, Duleep hitting the left-arm medium pacer Bland for two identical 6s in an over that was to cost 16 runs. By this time boundaries 'were coming with almost monotonous regularity.' In a frenzy of run-scoring, Duleep reached his century in 90 minutes but was bowled immediately after striking Sam Staples for six. Tate simply picked up where his captain left off, taking 18 from one Staples over. Not overly deterred by four men on the boundary for the drive, he reached his 50 in half an hour. At one point wicketkeeper Wheat had to chase 50 yards after the ball because he was the nearest fielder! Tate then hit another six that unfortunately landed on the head of a child sitting near the ring but was out next ball. Arthur Staples' 12 overs cost him 82 runs, his brother's 17 went for 93, while Bland's 9 overs yielded 63.

An overnight declaration left Notts needing to score 435 but rain then took a hand preventing any play until 2.30pm. Sad to relate the visitors made no effort whatever to save the game and in 90 minutes of knockabout cricket were all out for 126. Wensley (4/58) and Jim Langridge (5/56 in 9.5 overs) shared the wickets in this hollow and meaningless charade. The following day a refreshed Larwood returned to the side and claimed nine wickets as Notts steamrollered Kent to defeat in a real power-play.

Notts can't be held wholly to blame as their priorities clearly lay elsewhere, but the paying public were denied a genuine contest between two of the country's premier sides and it was regrettable that such a showpiece match should have been reduced to end-of-the-pier stuff...

1932: Horsham's two visitors in 1932 were Gloucestershire and Worcestershire. With all due respect neither really set pulses racing. For Gloucester, 1932 was to prove a major disappointment as they tumbled from runners-up spot the previous season to a nondescript 13th.

The match opened 'under anything but cricketing conditions: in fact it was almost an ideal day for football. All day the skies were dull and grey and there was a very chilly wind blowing' while some of the outfield was decidedly squelchy underfoot. Full marks to the locals therefore for a 'gate' of over 3,000 in such inhospitable conditions. Wally Hammond won the toss and decided to bat. There was little hint early on of the fun and games that were to follow as he and the austere veteran Alf Dipper put on 117 for the 2nd wicket in 2 hours. Hammond was in particularly fluent form, driving and glancing at will when, to his demonstrable surprise, he was bowled round his legs by Wensley playing no stroke to a big inswinger. The scoring rate then slowed appreciably. Dipper's 220-minute vigil ended when he was beautifully picked up at slip off Scott for 96. After this the innings went into a steep decline. The bowling plaudits were shared pretty much equally by Tate, Wensley and Scott. In 40 rousing minutes to stumps Jim Parks and John Langridge added 48.

Hostilities resumed in benign weather that during the afternoon session became pleasantly warm. The first session was one of steady consolidation against a tidy attack. Lunch was taken on 143/2 and after 3 hours and 20 minutes Parks completed a richly deserved century (his first of the season) though he should have been stumped off Sinfield when on 99. He was eventually dismissed for 114, he and Duleep having put on 139 for the 3rd wicket in 105 minutes. Duleep's own fluent innings ended on 89 when he was caught looking to step up the pace. This heralded a collapse not dissimilar to Gloucester's the previous day. From 271/3 Sussex fell away disappointingly to 335 all out, a lead nevertheless of 106. In the 30 minutes to stumps Gloucester had reached 32 for the loss of Sinfield.

Following the trend in county cricket at the time a gate of only 1,200 was present on the final morning. The pleasant weather continued as the visitors top pairing of Dipper and Hammond again looked to be in ominously good touch. Mindful perhaps of his first innings dismissal Hammond was particularly severe on Wensley. Just before lunch Dipper was brilliantly caught by Duleep off Bowley's slow leg-breaks to end a stand of 154. Worse was to follow for in the final over before the break Hammond himself, on 95, looked to reach his century in the grand manner by lofting Bowley disdainfully out of the ground, missed and was comfortably stumped. For the third time in the match this heralded a collapse of quite cataclysmic proportions. On a badly crumbling surface they lost seven wickets for 21 runs in a mere 40 minutes. Bowley was the executioner-in-chief as 170/2 all too rapidly became 191 all out. Bowley's 7/28 included a burst of four wickets for two runs with his final nine deliveries.

All this left Sussex 86 to win and plenty of time in which to do it. But the question on everyone's lips was how would they fare on such a treacherous surface against Charlie Parker, one of the greatest slow left-armers of all time? The answer wasn't long in coming. After a token two overs with the new ball Goddard joined Parker in an all-spin attack. With the score still in single figures Bowley, John Langridge and Cook were all back in the pavilion. Bowling unchanged from the railway end Parker may have been in his 50th year but wickets such as this were the stuff of dreams. Duleep was batting on a quite different plane to any of his colleagues but when he was run out the game was thrown wide open again. Wensley and Scott put on an invaluable 19 for the 8th wicket before the former was bowled with the score on 78. 'Now the crowd began to get really anxious. Tate might proceed carefully or he might lash out – and perhaps be bowled. However fears were soon allayed as Tate exercised caution. Scott …made the winning hit with a neat glide to the leg boundary; and so anxiety was over and Sussex had won a memorable game by 2 wickets.' In the slightly unfortunate terminology of the time, 'Parker, who had been making his balls kick a good deal' captured 6/29 off 18 demanding overs.

One feature of this enthralling encounter was the extent to which Duleepsinhji and Jim Parks for Sussex, and Dipper and Hammond for Gloucester, dominated their respective side's batting effort. Sussex scored 400 runs off the bat and Parks and Duleep were responsible for 249 of them. This trait was even more pronounced for their opponents. In total, Gloucester's batsmen mustered 394 runs. Between them Dipper and Hammond contributed no fewer than 303 or 77%. For good measure Sussex completed the double over their opponents in August, courtesy of an even more remarkable match at Cheltenham which was completed part-way through the second day. None of the four completed innings reached 150, no batsman made 50 and Jim Langridge returned eye-watering figures of 11.5 overs, 7 for 8 (13/67 in the match).

Could the visit of Worcestershire live up to this? On the face of it, no, for the visitors were enduring yet another miserable season which was to see them finish rock bottom of the Championship (again) with only one win from their 28 matches.

Sussex took a stranglehold on the game from the outset. There were four wickets apiece for Tate and Bowley as Worcester, having won the toss, slumped a touch too predictably to a miserable 88 all out in only 2 hours 40 minutes. Highest scorer was Maurice Nichol with 24. At his best a stylish bat, Nichol missed most of the 1932 season with pneumonia and tragically was found dead in the team hotel in Chelmsford on the morning of the second day of his side's match with Essex in 1934. By the close Worcester's fate was all but sealed as Sussex closed on 248/5. Highlight of the day was a scintillating display from Duleepsinhji. He eased his way to 116 in 165 minutes (his first century of the season), dominating a stand of 126 in 90 minutes for the 3rd wicket with Cook.

Sussex's first innings eventually closed just before lunch on 343 leaving Worcester the bleak prospect of scoring 255 simply to avoid an innings defeat.

Worcester had a nasty little period before the interval to negotiate which *they* managed safely but not so Cornford, who took a nasty blow on the shoulder in Tate's second over which halted play for a while. By this time the sun was shining brilliantly and Walters and Gibbons determined to make a better fist of things second time round. It was only partially successful as once again the all too obvious frailties in the Worcester side were cruelly exposed. To their credit they clearly tried to dig in. Their 153 was ground out over almost 93 attritional overs and Sussex were forced to employ seven bowlers. Wensley effected the key breakthrough clean bowling Walters for 38, a sterling defensive effort which took 155 minutes 'even if it had not been a particularly interesting one to witness.' Gibbons' two hour vigil ended on 48 and signalled the beginning of the end though Quaife and Perks gave it a bit of a go late on. But with White unable to bat, 149/6 became 153 all out with predictable rapidity. Tate and Wensley again bagged the lion's share of the wickets and Cornford snaffled seven victims behind the stumps. In a melancholy footnote, Worcester played two South Africans, Sid Martin and Frank Ahl, and both made 'pairs'. A crowd of around 2,000 witnessed play on each day. To rub further salt in the wounds the two sides met again at Kidderminster a month later and once again Sussex completed a win inside two days.

1933: George Cox served notice for the future with an early season 212 for Horsham CC, the highest score seen on the town ground since the Great War. Great things too were hoped for from 17 year old Jack Oakes, who was just feeling his way into Horsham's CCs 1st XI. The *County Times* 'doubts whether he will ever be as stylish as his brother, but he should develop into a forcing batsman.' Finally, in something straight out of the Two Ronnies, 'Madam Zelda, the Palmist of London Road issued an apology for not having had time to see all her Clients on her last visit.'

Horsham's two visitors were Hampshire and Essex. Hampshire were to experience a disappointing season. Their position of 14th – down six places from 1932 – was their lowest since the Great War and they only won two games all season, the last of them in mid-June. Informed opinion held that unless Phil Mead got set Sussex would carry too many guns for their near neighbours.

Jessop won the toss for Hampshire and took first knock on a wicket that was considered 'ideal for what one nearly always gets at Horsham in County Week – "good sporting cricket"'. By lunch they had collapsed to 97/6. Mead was a trifle unfortunate in that he was the victim of a quite brilliant one handed catch by Bowley at slip, but the rest seemed intent on playing back when they should have moved forward. Len Creese showed some aggression in the afternoon session 'though for one who is fighting for a place in the team, he showed a surprising hint of recklessness at times.' By mid-afternoon Hampshire were all out for a mediocre 157. Jim Cornford, who had been brought into the side for Cox, operated for a time with five slips and rewarded the selectors by taking 5/54.

Bowley and John Langridge raced to 40 in 25 minutes but this was the brightest spot of the day as Sussex became more and more subdued in their approach. Cook was never confident facing Herman, who 'even bowling up the hill…got a fair amount of pace from the pitch.' He eventually 'played back in a very uncertain manner to a ball that took his middle stump six yards out of the ground.' However, Sussex skipper Robert Scott displayed 'a fine blend of audacity and dourness' as his side's 154/6 at stumps gave them a slight edge.

Thanks in the main to Scott, Sussex gained a useful first innings lead of 120. He and Wensley took their 7th wicket stand to 79 in 70 minutes before 'a real snorter from Herman sent Wensley's off stump flying.' The ninth wicket fell with Scott still some distance from his century but a flurry of strokes saw him home. Full marks to Cornford who, despite not getting off the mark, kept Scott company in a last wicket stand of 44 with the ball flying about a bit. Scott struck Kennedy for two successive fours and then a six which bounced off a car. His 113 took him 2 hours 30 minutes and included one six and 17 fours. It was to be his only century of the season.

Hampshire batted steadily through the afternoon session, openers Arnold and Brown putting on 98 before the former, a 'one cap wonder' at both football and cricket but a fine opening bat at county level, was magnificently caught on the boundary's edge by Cook. 'James Langridge continued to toss up some innocuous looking stuff' as Sussex strove for a breakthrough. Tate thought he had achieved it when he 'bowled' Bailey, only to hear the umpire call no-ball. Tea was taken on 130/3 but in the final session Hampshire squandered all the solid work they had put in earlier. With a shot worthy of his father, Jessop smote a six into the tennis court before being caught at cover. The key moment was the dismissal of Mead, who had progressed unhurriedly to 56 before being cut down by a 'distinctly debatable' lbw decision. The tail soon folded and their 224 all out left Sussex the whole of the final day to make 102.

To Hampshire's undisguised delight, 'Steady and fairly heavy rain' greeted the players on the final morning. There was no play before lunch, but by mid-afternoon it was all over. John Langridge and Jim Parks put on 71 steady runs as Sussex eased home by eight wickets to reclaim 2nd place in the table. Rain was to ruin the return match at Portsmouth a month later.

Essex were expected to be made of sterner stuff - indeed were to prove the most improved side in the Championship, moving up 10 places in 1932 to 4th, their highest-ever placing at that time. Like Sussex they were another powerful batting side.

Scott lost the toss for the second time in the week and - again for the second time - led his men into the field. Tate (from the Church End) and Cornford opened the attack, only for Cutmore and Taylor to put on 111 for the 2nd wicket in only 90 minutes. Morris Nichols held the second half of the innings together and Essex were eventually all out for 259. Cornford again impressed with 6/66 but not so Steyning's Jack Eaton behind the stumps - he conceded no fewer than 29 byes. Sussex lost both openers with only 15 on the board but by stumps had rallied to 73/2. One of the two to fall was John Langridge who, having seen very little of the bowling, was then run out for a duck, his first in first-class cricket.

In the face of some hostile bowling from Nichols, who was making the ball rear nastily, Sussex's batting broke down completely on the 2nd morning. In close, humid conditions their last eight wickets tumbled for 77 runs, Nichols ending up with 5/67 despite the indignity of being struck for 17 in one over by Wensley.

This gave Essex an unexpected lead of 109 which they were quick to consolidate. The sun was shining benignly as Cutmore (again) and Laurie Eastman put on 81 for the 1st wicket. Cutmore and Jack O'Connor then added a further 112 for the 3rd. In the process Cutmore reached his first century of the season and in all was at the crease for 4 hours for an invaluable 117. By instinct he was an aggressive sort of opener and one of the few known cricketers to earn his living as a music hall entertainer. He had a fine tenor voice and appeared in pantomime at such well-known metropolitan venues as the Dominion, Tottenham Court Road. Nichols was never far from the action and a tiring Sussex attack could have done without his breezy assault in the closing stages which included two consecutive sixes off the nigh inviolable Tate as his side closed on 297/6. 'Onlooker' in the *County Times* had some pretty caustic observations to make about Tate after this innings: 'Unfortunately he had a bad match. Frankly, Tate bowled some of the time in surprisingly ordinary style. He may still be able to bowl out the 'rabbits' – that is unquestioned – but it is becoming increasingly risky to put him on to open the attack.'

The declaration left Sussex to make 407 and they were never remotely at the races. On a wicket asking more and more questions of the batsmen's courage and technique, the ubiquitous Nichols took five further scalps to give him match figures of 10/104 (in addition to scoring 103 runs). There were five wickets too for the lesser known Arthur Daer, an amateur fast bowler whose career was blighted by a combination of injury and illness. Daer had match figures of 9-75 as he and Nichols took all 19 wickets (the other being a run-out). Sussex had been thoroughly outplayed and could have few complaints. Only Jim Langridge made it past 25 as Essex cruised home by the massive margin of 294 runs. In doing so they replaced their hosts in 2nd place in the Championship table. In the return match at Chelmsford, Essex rattled up 560/9 declared (Wensley 3/189). Despite following-on Sussex held on for a draw, Harry Parks scoring a century in each innings.

1934: It seems as if the county may have been listening to the town club's continued plea for big-name opposition for Horsham's visitors in 1934 were a repeat of those in 1931 - Nottinghamshire and Surrey. Notts were not quite the force of old - indeed were now a mid-table outfit - but at least the match was a 'proper' one and not a repeat of the farcical events of 1931. Their batting was sound enough but other than the formidable England pairing of Harold Larwood and Bill Voce their attack was expensive.

The match coincided with the Test match against Australia at Trent Bridge. By rights, Larwood and Voce should both have been playing in this but because of continuing fallout from the infamous Bodyline tour it was deemed politic not to pick them. Instead, they were free to unleash their thunderbolts on their own countrymen.

New Sussex skipper Alan Melville got off on the right foot by winning the toss and - with perhaps a little trepidation - sent John Langridge and Jim Parks out to do battle with Larwood and Voce in front of a crowd estimated at 4,500. 'The sun shone down from a cloud flecked sky' as Sussex's experienced opening pair went about their business on what was described – a touch worryingly given the opposition – as 'a good sporting wicket.' Larwood opened up from the Denne Hill end and both he and Voce employed a bodyline field. But Larwood wasn't at his fastest and despite 'opening in an ultra careful mood' runs came at a steady pace. The 50 arrived after 95 minutes but almost two hours had elapsed before the first boundary was scored. There was a curious incident involving Larwood when he was heckled by a member of the crowd near the scorebox, having lost his run-up on three occasions, which led to the offender being given a lecture by umpire Hendren. At lunch the score stood reassuringly at 87 without loss. Larwood and Voce opened up to a predominantly leg-side field on the resumption, but Langridge responded by hooking Voce's first ball resoundingly for four. Parks reached his 50 after 135 minutes and his partner followed suit 15 minutes later. Their stand had reached 155 when Langridge hooked Staples straight to Hardstaff at long leg. Melville opened his account with a beautiful cover drive for four but then suffered a recurrence of back trouble and became much inhibited in his movements. An innings of 'grim determination' was rewarded when, after almost 4 hours 30 minutes, Parks finally reached his century. He eventually fell to Arthur Staples for 104 and by stumps the score had reached 285/4.

The following morning it was an altogether different story. Langridge – who was to score a century in the return match at Trent Bridge in July - was struck on the head early on as a revitalised Larwood 'was putting plenty of fire behind his deliveries'. Wickets soon began to tumble and Sussex's last five men could only muster 17. Within an hour they were all out ('a speedy ending to a slowly begun innings'). Larwood picked up four of them to end with 5/66 and Voce four, both men generating considerable pace and lift. It was noticeable that the 'Notts Express' 'bowled to his slips instead of to short legs.' The national press were quick to spot a bandwagon and as Bradman and his team mates were making hay at Trent Bridge, the call went up for the two Notts men to be reinstated in the national side ('Larwood at his best: pace baffles Sussex' trumpeted one national headline).

Notts' celebrated opening pair of Walter Keeton and Charlie Harris embarked on a long stand in the afternoon session in their sharply contrasting styles. Keeton was forever looking to play shots while Harris 'kept plodding on steadily.' By tea they were still together with the scoreboard showing 164 (Keeton 91, Harris 63). Sadly Keeton was destined not to reach his 'ton'. When on 99 he reached forward to a ball from Jim Langridge and nicked it onto his pad from whence it deflected on to his middle stump. 'He had batted superbly and scored all round the wicket.' His sparkling stand with Harris had been worth 187 in three hours. Profiting from two dropped catches Harris moved into the 90s, then 'jumped in to J Parks and hit him to long on for six, the first of the match.' He square cut Tate shortly afterwards to reach his century as Notts closed the day on 253/4. This was all very fine but with only one day left, where was the match going?

The visitors' middle order all chipped in on the final morning as Notts established a first innings lead of 19 but their 331 all out had extended over a monumental 151.1 overs and took play into the afternoon session. It all meant that Sussex clearly couldn't win but Notts just might…Much depended on the early exchanges. 'Larwood and Voce bowled really fast…for several overs' but, critically, Parks and John Langridge stood firm. They had reached 80 at tea and pretty much taken the match away from the Midlands side. Skipper Ben Lilley clearly thought so for after their opening burst, neither of his star men were seen in action again. The second string attack saw out the somewhat meaningless final session. Langridge and Cook reached their 50s as Keeton, the eighth bowler used, picked up two unexpected scalps; and Vaulkhard his first ever First-Class wicket. John Langridge recalled this critical passage of arms 14 years later, writing in the 1948 Festival programme how 'Poor Jim Parks (was) hit all over his body and had the medals to show for a very long time. I was more fortunate, as being much taller, I was hit more on the top part of the legs.'

Surrey were making their seventh appearance at the Horsham Festival and were always welcome visitors. They remained one of the most attractive sides in the country but were destined to finish 11th in the Championship, their lowest placing since the Great War. The reason, as ever, was not hard to find. Their batting was solid but only Alf Gover took his wickets at under 25 apiece.

The visitors won the toss and batted. The weather was gorgeous and the first-day crowd built up to nearly 4,000. Early on the 'Scoring was extremely slow and neither player was aggressive nor particularly energetic.' Even Hobbs was not above criticism as 'the way he deals with some of the half volleys was half-hearted.' The most remarkable feature was that the first four wickets to fall were all caught at slip by Wensley. Holmes and the bespectacled Squires pulled things round with a 5th wicket stand of 133 in 165 minutes before both fell to Cornford. He ended the day with 6/54 as Surrey were all out for a decent 280. A feature of the day was Sussex's excellent fielding with Scott and Cox to the fore. In taking his 5th catch of the innings Wensley equalled his own county record.

On the second morning John Langridge and Jim Parks embarked on what was to prove a record opening stand for the county against Surrey. More to the point the runs were made at a spanking pace. Future England captain Freddie Brown was hit out of the attack in pretty rapid order – his first five overs cost 35 – as 100 came up after 79 minutes. Poor Fender slipped and cut a leg and when he returned with a plaster over the wound, Langridge added insult to injury by on-driving his first delivery to the boundary. At lunch the score stood at 158, though just before the break Langridge was badly missed by Watts at 4th slip (!) off Gover. 'Boundaries came fast and furious on the resumption, Fender and Gover being treated unmercifully.' After three hours the score had reached 200 – at which point, to Surrey's immense frustration, Parks was caught by Gover off a no-ball from Holmes. After 175 minutes of rich entertainment the stand came to an end when Parks was caught by Fender at slip off the bowling of Brown for 122, the score at this point having reached 258. Langridge's marathon ended moments before tea when he 'allowed Holmes

TWOPENCE. Horsham Cricket Week.
OFFICIAL SCORE, 1926.

Saturday, Monday and Tuesday, June 5th, 7th & 8th.
SUSSEX V. WARWICKSHIRE.

WARWICKSHIRE.

	First Innings.		Second Innings.	
1 Parsons	b Bowley	20	b Cox	50
2 R. E. Wyatt	c Watson, b Cox	33	c Cornford, b Cox	35
3 Bates	b Cox	77	c Wensley, b Cox	30
4 Quaife	b Cox	43	c Bowley, b Cox	1
5 Santall	c Cook, b Langridge	5	st Cornford, b Cox	7
6 N. E. Partridge	b Cox	12	b Wensley	3
7 Croom	c Bowley, b Cox	15	not out	23
8 Kilner	st Cornford, b Cox	28	b Cox	0
9 Smart	st Cornford, b Cox	15	b Cox	23
10 Peare	b Cox	0	b Cox	0
11 Mayer	not out	2	b Cox	1
	Extras	7	Extras	4
Cox—8 wickets for 56.	Total	257	Cox—9 for 50. Total	177

1-48 2-60 3-171 4-176 5-192 6-199 7-220 8-240 9-240 10-257
1-72 2-91 3-99 4-104 5-121 6-123 7-136 8-175 9-177 10-177

SUSSEX.

	First Innings.		Second Innings.	
1 Bowley	b Mayer	8	b Wyatt	53
2 Parks (J.)	c Bates, b Quaife	48	c Partridge, b Quaife	22
3 Wensley	b Santall	5	c Mayer, b Wyatt	40
4 Cook	c Wyatt, b Quaife	20	not out	9
5 Langridge	b Partridge	5		
6 A. J. Holmes	b Partridge	87	not out	8
7 Cox	c Bates, b Quaife	0		
8 A. H. Gilligan	c Partridge, b Parsons	20	run out	15
9 Col. A. C. Watson	b Partridge	11	run out	19
10 Parks (H.)	b Mayer	14		
11 Cornford	not out	12		
Quaife—3 wickets for 34.	Extras	31	Extras	8
Mayer—2 wickets for 15.	Total	261	Total	174

1-23 2-29 3-75 4-94 5-94 6-94 7-123 8-147 9-205 10-261
1-46 2-122 3-122 4-141 5-164 6- 7- 8- 9- 10-

Umpires: Young and Street.   Scorers: Austin and Isaacs.

Luncheon, 1.30 to 2.15.   Tea, 4.15.   P.T.O.

1. George Cox's swan-song. Eighty years on his match return of 17-106 is still the only occasion a Sussex player has taken 17 wickets in a match.

2. Educated at Collyer's Grammar School when it was situated at the bottom of The Causeway, the bespectacled Tim Killick (4 matches) made his debut for Horsham CC in 1892. In 1894 he took six wickets and scored an unbeaten century against Brighton Teachers. A talented amateur musician, he was much in demand at local concerts.

3. George Pearce (4 matches). Very much a local boy, George's family ran a butcher's shop in East Street. His mother helped run the whist drives during the Carnival.

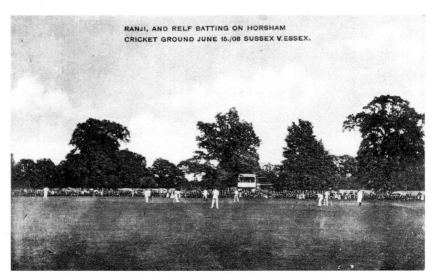

4. The legendary Ranji's only appearance at Horsham was a disappointment – he was described as being 'slow between the wickets'.

HORSHAM COUNTY CRICKET FESTIVAL.

GREAT Fancy Dress CARNIVAL

THURSDAY, JUNE 9th, 1932,

Assemble in Horsham Football Ground at 5.30 p.m.

Competition Judging at 6 p.m.   **Procession starts about 7 p.m.**

COMPETITION LIST.

Class No.	Description	Entrance Fee	1st	2nd	3rd	4th
1.	Fancy Dress, best home-made and best advertisement (boys under 8)	3d.	5/-	3/-	2/-	1/-
1A.	Ditto, most attractive (boys under 8)	3d.	5/-	3/-	2/-	1/-
2.	„ best home-made & best advertisement (girls under 8)	3d.	5/-	3/-	2/-	1/-
2A.	„ most attractive (girls under 8)	3d.	5/-	3/-	2/-	1/-
3.	„ best home-made & best advertisement (boys under 15)	3d.	5/-	3/-	2/-	1/-
3A.	„ most attractive (boys under 15)	3d.	5/-	3/-	2/-	1/-
4.	„ best home-made & best advertisement (girls under 15)	3d.	5/-	3/-	2/-	1/-
4A.	„ most attractive (girls under 15)	3d.	5/-	3/-	2/-	1/-
5.	„ best home-made & best advertisement (adults, men)	6d.	10/-	5/-	2/6	
5A.	„ most attractive (adults, men)	6d.	10/-	5/-	2/6	
6.	„ best home-made & best advertisement (adults, women)	6d.	10/-	5/-	2/6	
6A.	„ most attractive (adults, women)	6d.	10/-	5/-	2/6	
7.	Pedal Cycles, best decorated	6d.	10/-	5/-	2/6	
8.	Horse-drawn Vehicle, best maintained	1/-	20/-	15/-	10/-	
9.	Equestrians, best conditioned	1/-	20/-	15/-	10/-	
	All Competitors in Class 9 have a free entry into any ONE of the Fancy Dress Classes (1 to 6A)					
10.	Motor Vehicles (trade), best maintained	2/-	20/-	15/-	10/-	
11.	Motor Vehicles (private), best decorated	2/-	20/-	10/-		
12.	Unclassified		20/-			
	Most Humorous in Classes 1 to 4A; 5 to 6A; 7, 8, 9, 10, 11		10/- each.			

☞ DO NOT FORGET TO FILL IN YOUR ENTRY FORM
ALL ENTRIES CLOSE ON MONDAY, JUNE 6th.

Entry Forms can be obtained from Mr. HUNTLEY, 61, West Street; Mr. WYNCHESTER, 24, East Street; Mr. H. R. BRIDGER, Carnival Secretary, 16, Bostock Avenue.

Prizes will be presented in the Dance Ring by Mrs. J. Ireland Eager, supported by Mr. J. Ireland Eager, President Chamber of Trade.

Admission to Football Ground:
Competitors Free; Spectators, Adults 2d., Children 1d.

[P.T.O.

---

5. The 1932 Carnival was a great success. On a deliciously warm evening, huge crowds thronged the streets and festivities culminated in a flying display in which a car was flour-bombed. This reportedly had 'the greatest effect on the emotions of the spectators.'

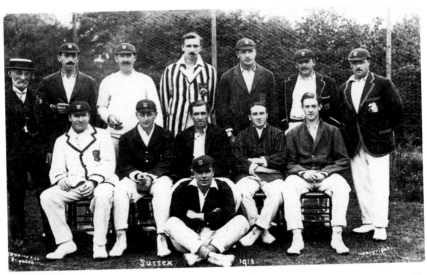

6. Sussex at Horsham, 1913. *Left to right: Back row:* WH Edwards (scorer), RR Relf, AE Relf, PGH Fender, JH Vincett, GR Cox, J Vine. *Middle Row:* P Cartwright, HL Wilson, HP Chaplin (capt), NJ Holloway, AH Lang. On grass: VWC Jupp.

7. Yet more Festival rain in 1946 as Field Marshal Montgomery inspects the Sussex and Glamorgan troops on the first day of peacetime cricket in Horsham. To 'Monty's' right are Sussex players Jack Nye, Jim Cornford, Harry Parks, John Langridge, Jack Oakes and Billy Griffith, while behind Griffith are Hugh Bartlett and Jim Langridge. On his immediate left is Glamorgan skipper John Clay. When play did get under way, Sussex were bowled out twice in under four hours. Their first innings total of 35 is the lowest first-class score ever made on the ground.

Cricket

Horsham Week

SATURDAY, MONDAY and TUESDAY

June 13, 15, 16

Sussex v Surrey

1931

WEDNESDAY, THURSDAY and FRIDAY

June 17, 18, 19

Sussex v Notts

Play commences 11.30 each day.   Stumps drawn at 6.30 the first two days,
and 6 o'clock on the third day of each match.   Lunch from 1.30 to 2.15.

Admission 1s., after 4 p.m., 6d.   Boys 6d.   Enclosure 1s.
Pavilion 2s.   Motors 5s.   All prices include Tax.

For Terms of Membership, apply Secretary, County Cricket Ground, Hove, Brighton.

8. The opening day attendance for the Surrey game in 1931 is believed to be a ground record.
Despite a century from Duleepsinhji the Notts match was to end controversially.

9. A view taken in the 1960s showing Joker Oakes' cottage at its best.

10. A bleak opening day view of the 1935 Festival. Inspecting the rain-sodden pitch are *(left to right):* Maurice Tate, G.B. Cuthbertson and A.W. Snowden of Northants, Arthur Gilligan, Alan Melville and Sussex CCC secretary Lance Knowles. Rain completely ruined both matches.

11. With 12 appearances Surrey have visited Horsham more often than any other county. In 1912 Razor Smith's match figures of 11-132 ensured that the spoils went to the visitors. Sussex wicket-keeper AH Lang (pictured) was among those killed in the Great War.

12. A view from Denne Hill during the match against Cambridge University in 1971. This game was awarded to Horsham as part of the town club's bi-centennial celebrations.

13. John Barclay (4 matches) scored a century against Sri Lanka at Horsham in 1979. In July 1971 the 'local squash club player' was assisting Horsham CC in a league match against Hastings. Barclay's great-uncle played on the ground in 1889.

14. Tony Pigott (8 matches) enjoyed a love-hate relationship with Horsham. A playing member of Horsham CC, three of Sussex's five most expensive bowling analyses in one-day cricket have his name alongside them.

15. By contrast, another of Horsham's favourite sons, Old Collyerian Paul Parker (6 matches) has a remarkable one-day record at Cricket Field Road averaging over 70. Another 'Dewdrop', Parker is one of only two Sussex players to have made a first-class and one-day century on the ground. With Allan Green he holds the Sussex record 2nd wicket stand in first-class matches at Horsham.

through to his wicket' for 160 with the score on 307. If a weary Surrey felt they could now relax, they were mistaken, for at 349/5, Harry Parks was joined by Cox and these two pasted a tired attack all round the ground, putting on 103 in 75 minutes. Parks reached his 50 with a six as the day ended with Sussex in complete control on 452/5.

With Sussex declaring at their overnight total, Surrey's task was straightforward enough. 172 adrift on first innings, they simply had to bat out most of the final day to secure a draw. Drawing on all his long experience Hobbs carefully set out his stall for the maestro too was inching his way towards one last personal cricketing milestone - a career target of 200 centuries. In the event he was run out for a meticulously crafted 79 but couldn't find anyone to stay with him. It wasn't easy for Surrey fought tenaciously but Tate, Cornford and Jim Parks worked their way steadily through the card. The final wicket never fell until well into the final session, Surrey's 224 having taken 109.5 overs. There were two more slip catches for Wensley giving him seven in the match, a county record that still holds today. Sussex were left to make 53 in an hour for victory and despite the early loss of first innings hero Langridge, there was never any real doubt about the outcome. Surrey were to take full revenge in the return match at the Oval in August.

There was a poignant edge to Hobbs' innings. All too aware that time was running out, he came into the match on 197 centuries. In his 1960 biography of the great man, Ronald Mason tells the story thus: 'He showed himself perfectly capable of playing Tate still, and his second innings nearly brought him one (century) nearer…So near he was to the hundred and yet through his own error it eluded him, for he ran himself out for the second time that season. Was his frustration at last beginning to disturb the coolness of his native judgment?' Others went further for Hobbs played very little cricket after this match. Some felt that as a direct consequence of his experience at Horsham, he finally accepted that there just wasn't enough gas left in the tank to make three more tons. And having concluded that if he couldn't do it at 51, he was hardly more likely to do it a year later, Jack Hobbs retired with all the grace and dignity he had displayed throughout a long, glittering career.

1935: The visitors in 1935 were Northamptonshire, who hadn't been seen in the town since 1913; and Hampshire. They were hardly the biggest draw-cards in the Championship – Hampshire were to finish 16th in the table, while – for the second successive year - Northants were to finish rock-bottom. True, they had just won their first match of the season but any hope this may have engendered was soon extinguished – it was to be their sole success in a disastrous campaign that saw them suffer 16 defeats out of 24 matches, including a dismal run of 13 on the trot.

Skipper Alex Snowden had luck on his side with the toss, winning 10 on the trot - all the more pity that he didn't have a stronger side to take advantage of it. His luck held again at Horsham but it must have been with some trepidation that he decided to take first knock. Rain fell from around 8am and continued spasmodically for several hours. Play finally got under way at 4.45pm though only around 200 hardy souls were on the ground to witness it. By stumps Northants had struggled fitfully to 72/4. The highlight of the day for many locals – including of course his proud parents – was a county debut for Charlie Oakes on the ground where he was almost literally born.

Resuming before a desultory crowd of only 300 or so, Northants continued to struggle on the following morning, the end of their feeble innings arriving in something of a rush with the score on 124. 'Being early closing day, the crowd was considerably increased in the afternoon' and they were treated to a spectacular spell of bowling by Melville, who in nine deliveries took 3 wickets for one run.

Sussex's reply began brightly enough but then disaster overwhelmed them. John Langridge was given out off the third successive lbw appeal from Nobby Clark whose very next ball to Melville 'lifted his off stump clean out of the ground.' It was said of the enigmatic Clark that you could tell what sort of mood he was in when he paced out his run. If he paused to pick mud off his spikes, the slips retreated a pace or two because they knew he meant business. And Clark at full throttle on a less than perfect track would test the courage and technique of the best batsmen in the world for he was a genuinely quick left-armer who, in the words of *Wisden*, 'Possessed every qualification of a great bowler except temperament' – or as Robertson-Glasgow so beautifully put it: 'the wind of his temperament veered like a cardboard weathercock.' He was a moody, stroppy individual who moaned about everything – footholds, lack of support from his fielders – even the birds in the air weren't safe from his blaspheming. Sussex had a real fight on their hands. At 109/9 Tate joined Jim Langridge who had been soldiering stoically on while all around him perished. These two had brought the scores level when Tate, of all things, was stumped. In the 30 minutes remaining, Northants had slumped to 10/2.

The melancholy batting procession continued on the final morning. The only bright spot was the batting of AL Cox. Coming in at No 5, his robust 40 included two 6s off Melville and was the highest score of the entire match. Encouraged by his first innings success, Melville gave himself an extended bowl second time round and was rewarded with 5/37 as Northants sank beneath the waves for 109.

This left Sussex 110 to win in three hours. How they would have fared will never be known because right on cue the rain returned. At 4.30pm the umpires called it a day, thus bringing to an end what the *County Times* was doubtless not alone in referring to as 'A sorry affair.' But as far as Melville was concerned, failing to see off such a poor side as Northants was not in the script. The portents were clearly unpropitious for the first match between the two sides a month earlier at Northampton had been even more comprehensively ruined by rain.

Melville clearly hoped for better luck – on the field and above it – against Hampshire. Still headed by the seemingly indestructible Phil Mead (now 48), their batting wasn't too bad but on paper this was another highly winnable encounter. Sussex won the toss and elected to bat – but not immediately for yet again rain held things up. They were an hour late in getting under way but it wasn't long before John Langridge and Jim Parks were giving the innings a solid foundation. The partnership had reached 93 before Parks was out. Langridge fell just before tea for a steady and well crafted 84, at which point Cook took centre stage. In contrast with some of his colleagues he scored freely all round the wicket pretty much from the off. He and Jim Langridge put on 122 for the 4th wicket in 100 minutes, but perished for 76 in the final hour as Sussex closed the day on a healthy 315/6.

The tail wagged with some vigour on the second morning, the final four wickets realising 68 runs in just over an hour. Wensley was bowled by Lofty Herman 'just as a local hooter was sounding noon.' Cornford hit merrily and in a typically breezy effort, Tate at No 11 struck Lowndes for a six into the tennis courts before being bowled by Hill 'who lifted the off stump clean out of the ground.'

The veteran Mead lumbered dutifully to the crease with the scoreboard showing 31/2. He had an impressive record at Horsham (and indeed at most other venues) and 'received a wonderful reception' from a crowd who sensed that he probably held the key to the outcome of the match. He was visibly shaken when hit on the leg by a wayward return from the outfield and fell to Jim Langridge shortly afterwards. This sent the Hampshire innings into a sharp decline. Only Lowndes and Hosie tarried long and by late afternoon they were all out for 144, Jim Langridge taking 5/22.

Adrift by 239 runs on first innings, Hampshire were invited to follow on. They quickly made their intentions clear. Arnold and stop-gap opener McCorkell 'stonewalled Tate and Wensley to such an extent that there was some barracking.' After 45 minutes, with the score on 20 (off 22 overs!), an appeal against steadily worsening light was upheld and yet another frustrating day's play ended prematurely.

Worse was to follow for there was no play whatever on the third day as yet more prolonged and torrential rain swept across the ground. This was a disaster both on and off the field for through no fault of their own Sussex had failed to beat the two weakest sides in the table on their own soil. With rain interfering in three of the six days, the public was understandably reluctant to hand over their hard-earned cash at the turnstiles. The attendance figures tell their own story: in 1934, a lovely hot summer, there were 7,148 paying customers for the first game alone. In 1935 there were only 5,989 for the entire six days. Some of the outgoings make interesting reading 70 plus years on – police, £12-12-0; players' lunches, £44-7-7; gatekeepers, £35-8-6; scoreboard attendants, £3-5-0.

1936: 'Groundsman Oakes has been putting in a considerable amount of extra work on the ground, which looks in fine trim' - a fact appreciated no doubt by his son Jack. Playing for Horsham CC against Christ's Hospital in May, he ruined an otherwise unexceptional game by scoring 157 with 5 sixes and 20 fours (including 25 in one over), and followed this up by taking 5/33.

Warwickshire were in town again. For them, 1936 was to prove a depressing campaign. Their batting was extremely brittle and in consequence they failed to win a single home game all season and dropped to 13th in the table. They only won four matches in all and to add to poor results on the field there were serious problems off it. Unusually for those times it was an all-professional eleven that took the field.

Jack Holmes won the toss and elected to bat – but not before an all-too-familiar spectre put in an unwelcome appearance. Rain tumbled from a leaden sky but mercifully relented in time to allow play to get under way in mid-afternoon. At 44/3 – all three falling to lbw decisions – things were looking rocky for the home side but Cook and Cox set about a repair job. Their stand had yielded 135 in 105 minutes when Cox became yet another lbw victim for a spirited 66. The truncated day ended with Sussex on 199/4.

The second morning was nothing short of catastrophic, the last six wickets falling for a paltry 34. In mitigation there were several brief rain breaks in this period – indeed a shower fell just as Cook's three-hour vigil ended. He was caught at slip for a fine 95 and the fielders ran off with him. The rain had clearly freshened up the pitch and in no time at all Warwicks found themselves 6 for 3. Despite a defiant 45 from Santall they never really recovered and were all out for an equally miserable 104, all five Sussex bowlers returning flattering analyses.

Now it was Sussex's turn to face the music again though at least they had the comfort of a healthy first innings lead. Yet again the dolorous batting procession continued and they ended the second day on a perilous 73/6. Twenty-two wickets had fallen in all and it was a great shame that there were only 921 spectators present to witness it.

The rout continued on the final morning. Sussex lost their last four wickets in fairly rapid order and perhaps the best thing that could be said for their meagre 109 all out was that it left Warwicks 239 to win, the highest total of the match. Destroyer in chief was

Danny Mayer who, bowling unchanged, took 7/51 in the innings, 10/114 in the match.

Warwickshire were soon deep in the toils at 24/3 and it seemed a question of when Sussex would polish them off - or whether they could hang it out for a draw. However, there then followed just about the most unexpected passage of play in the entire match. Dollery came out to join Santall with the scoreboard showing 54/4 and together these two put on 159 runs in 120 minutes. There was little indication initially of this total turn-around but the pitch must surely have eased markedly. Crucially, Santall was dropped by John Langridge when he had made 53 but it was perhaps fitting that it was he who scored the winning single off Jim Parks to earn his side a victory that few in the painfully thin crowd of 262 would have dreamt possible at the start of play. This brought his own score to 104, his only century of the season. Ironically, the return match at Edgbaston a month later was totally ruined by the weather.

This was a facer for Sussex. Could they pick themselves up in time for the visit of Surrey? Their neighbours were to finish 6th in the table and as usual were an attractive side to watch. Their batting was especially powerful with six men making 1,000 runs or more.

The match opened in – wait for it – 'excellent weather.' Holmes (ERT) won the toss from Holmes (AJ) and despite the loss of two early wickets, Surrey made hay in the sunshine. A feature of the morning's play was the enthusiastic fielding of George Cox: 'The crowd was delighted with their local favourite's work and he received round after round of applause. His was the one bright spot in what otherwise was dull cricket...Would that Sussex would try more lively players like him' opined the *County Times* tartly. Barling in particular started to play more fluently in the afternoon session but his was the first wicket to fall, his 110 being made in 180 minutes with one six and 10 fours. The screw continued to tighten when Fishlock came to the crease. Sussex had good cause to remember him for less than a month previously he had made a century in each innings in the first fixture between the sides at the Oval. He and Gregory put on 138 in 90 minutes and although Sussex picked up a few late wickets as their visitors closed the day on a daunting 386/7. By this time Fishlock was unbeaten on 79 but

Gregory had finally fallen to John Langridge for a monumental 166.

Then that old nemesis returned – rain. Owing to a heavy storm, no play was possible at all before lunch on the second day when it was announced that Surrey had declared at their overnight total. 'It was on a sodden pitch and in sultry weather' that play finally got under way and there was an air of foreboding about the place – 'Sussex were doomed to disappoint their supporters' as the *County Times* so apocalyptically put it. With Gover in particular a real threat from the Town end, wickets soon started to tumble. Sussex's biggest debt was owed to Jim Langridge who remained unbeaten on 68 as the home side closed the day on 174/7. But without doubt they had had rough luck with the conditions.

And that was it. All the old horrors of 1935 were revived as rain fell incessantly on the final day when not a ball was bowled. Sussex still needed 63 to avoid the follow-on, so in that sense it was probably just as well.

No-one was to know it at the time but this marked the final Festival appearance of the great Maurice Tate ('big feet, a big heart and pace off the pitch'), arguably the finest Sussex bowler of all time (and as we have seen, a lovely clean hitter on his day too). Maurice actually retired at the end of the 1937 season but wasn't selected for either of the Horsham fixtures despite being on the ground and available. His record of 150 Festival wickets is surely safe for all time.

1937: Horsham was allocated two 'plum' fixtures for 1937. The first of these was Gloucestershire, who had finished 4th in 1936 and were to finish 4th again in 1937. Spearheaded by Walter Hammond, their batting was always reliable and sometimes brilliant though their bowling lacked depth.

To everyone's inexpressible relief, the sun shone. History was made too in that for the first time there were live BBC broadcast commentaries twice a day from the ground by Howard Marshall. It was hoped that in addition to the actual play, Mr Marshall 'will probably bring Horsham to the fore with his descriptive remarks.' Holmes won the toss and Sussex took first strike. Runs came at a brisk rate as all the frontline batsmen took it in turns to make hay on one of Alfred Oakes' more benign tracks. John Langridge top scored with 93, but was closely followed by Cox (89). Highlight of the day was their stand of 135 in 89 minutes either side of lunch. By tea the Sussex score had advanced smoothly to 315/4. After the interval Holmes hit the first six of the day and home fans were delighted to see Charlie Oakes move to 25 by stumps when the score stood at 436/8.

The second day dawned even hotter than the first. To the disappointment of a large crowd Oakes, batting at the town end, 'let Barnett clean through to his middle stump with that bowler's first ball.' The innings closed for 443, made in 138.3 overs. Gloucester's reply started with a bang. Barnett sent the first ball of the match from Cornford whistling to the boundary. The second went for four byes, the third was driven to the off boundary for four more and a cut for two saw the score on 14 at the over's end. Although several men got in, nobody seemed able to fashion a match-defining innings and Gloucester's last wicket fell 'as the clock of the parish church tolled out 4pm'. They would have been disappointed with 230 all out on a blameless wicket. Jim Hammond picked up 6/78 and Jim Parks 4/51 as Holmes sent the visitors back in. Yet again they went for their shots but at 139/4 were still 74 adrift when play ended for the day. Their main hope for the morrow was clearly Hammond (52 n/o), who was looking at his fluent best.

There was a sparse attendance on the final morning as a heavy overnight storm threatened to disrupt proceedings. After a crisp stand of 67 between Hammond and Crapp, the predictable collapse set in as the hot sun began to do its insidious work on the drying turf. Hammond's innings had to be seen to be believed: like that of Frank Woolley back in 1920 it was on a different plane to anything seen hitherto in the game. When Tom Goddard at No. 11 made his way out to join him the Gloucester score stood at 216/9, a lead of precisely three. Hammond at this point was on 98. These two added 71 in 35 dazzling minutes of which Goddard's share was eight. When Hammond jumped out once too often to Jim Parks and was bowled he had struck 24 fours in a quite stupendous 160 made out of 256 scored while he was at the crease. Curiously enough, despite scoring 50,000 career runs, Hammond had a comparatively modest record against Sussex with only four centuries in 42 innings.

All this left Sussex 75 to win and oodles of time in which to do it. Gloucester wasted no time fiddling about with token overs from medium pacers: the ball was turning sharply and spinners Goddard and Sinfield opened the attack. Despite the loss of two early wickets Sussex opted for a cavalier approach. Nine came off the opening over as they galloped to 50 in only 45 minutes. Cox struck a rapid 30 before falling to Goddard and despite the loss of several more wickets their knockabout 75/5 made them realise how lucky they were not to have been chasing 175. This victory took them to the top of the Championship table. Could they sustain it against their next visitors?

Derbyshire may have been surprise winners of the Championship in 1936 but it was no fluke. Indeed but for injuries sustained by key bowlers Copson and Mitchell they could very well have retained their title. As it was they finished 3rd in 1937, their strength lying very definitely in their attack where Copson, Mitchell, the Pope brothers, Stan Worthington and – latterly - Dusty Rhodes proved a formidable unit.

Derbyshire won the toss and batted. Runs came steadily and then freely. The beefy Worthington wasn't slow in tucking into Charlie Oakes but was eventually caught and bowled by Hammond for 90, leaving Alf Pope to hold the second half of the innings together. At tea the score stood at 300/6 but Pope's aggressive 100 minute 86 (his highest score to date in first-class cricket) contained shots all round the wicket and enabled his side to reach 342, a pretty fair effort. Sussex had then to negotiate an awkward 50 minutes against one of the strongest pace attacks in the land and Jim Parks and John Langridge did well to close the day on 43/0.

There were heavy rainstorms locally on Sunday and Sussex must have feared the worst when play resumed on the second morning under a warm sun. Copson picked up two early wickets but Langridge found a stout ally in Cook. Together, they put on 120 for the 3rd wicket and by lunch the score was a prosperous 160/2. After 3 hours, 40 minutes, Langridge duly reached his century and was given a wonderful ovation by an appreciative crowd who clearly recognised how hard he had been made to work. Holmes spanked an aggressive 32 and at 232/6, Sussex were slightly ahead of their visitors at the same point in their innings but it was all downhill from there. The last five wickets evaporated for 18 and before they knew what had hit them Sussex were all out by mid-afternoon as Copson and Mitchell scythed through the tail.

Openers Smith and Alderman were swiftly into their stride for the second time in the match but the stand that decided the outcome came when Worthington joined Alderman. Together they put on a spanking 166 for the 2nd wicket in two hours as Derbyshire closed the day in full control on 244/2. The neat and unassuming Alderman had added 103 to his first innings 50 before being picked up at square leg off Wood. Worthington was unbeaten on 97 and as stumps were drawn for the day, Sussex must have feared what the morrow might bring...

And with good cause. Derbyshire's declaration set Sussex the little matter of 411 in five hours. Worthington was left on 133 not out and Sussex must have been sick of the sight of him. At Derby earlier in the season, he was forced to retire with cramp and his scores against Sussex in 1937 were 238 n/o, 30 n/o, 90 and 133 n/o.

Sussex lost John Langridge in the second over, which set the tone for the innings. So much so that it became 'little more than a procession from wicket to pavilion.' Lunch was taken at 103/8 with only Cook putting up anything of a show. Charlie Oakes was defending gamely when he was struck a fierce blow on the left hand by Copson and forced to retire with a fractured finger. When Copson hit Wood's middle stump 30 minutes into the afternoon session,the match was all over, with Derbyshire triumphant by 281 runs. It was Sussex's first defeat of the campaign and there was no gainsaying the margin of victory. For the record, Derby went on to complete the double over Sussex courtesy of another crushing victory which saw Copson take eight first-innings wickets.

For completeness, it should be mentioned that this wasn't the only county cricket played in Horsham in June. On the 10th the High School for Girls staged a ladies match between Sussex and Hampshire, which ended in a draw. Despite it being held on a weekend the *County Times* regretted 'that there was such a small attendance...as the standard of cricket was well worth seeing.'

1938: The two visitors in 1938 – Surrey and Hampshire – could hardly be termed strangers to the town. One major advance was that spectators would have been able to travel for the first time by electric train.

Surrey remained a popular and attractive side and were to finish 3rd in the Championship. Their batting remained consistent – runs were rarely a problem – and for once their bowling had a bit more of a cutting edge. The match opened in ideal summer weather before 1,443 spectators. Although at the ground, Sussex captain Jack Holmes was unfit to play so the side was led by Robert Stainton who won the toss and elected to bat. John Langridge was an early casualty but Jim Parks and Cox took the score up to 115. Then, alas, it all started to unravel. So much so that when Hammond joined Charlie Oakes the scoreboard was showing a troubled 175/6. Charlie clearly relished the Surrey attack for he had registered his maiden century against them the previous season at Hove. Showing little regard for what had passed previously, these two went for their shots and put on 167 in two hours either side of tea. Having spent 70 minutes compiling his first 50, Oakes, by dint of his 'remarkable strength in driving' fairly raced to his second in a further 35 minutes, completing his century just before tea. Sadly he fell to Gover shortly after the resumption for the dreaded 111, an innings which included one six and 12 fours. Unsurprisingly, 'having rescued Sussex in such gallant style, he was given a wonderful ovation by the crowd.' Hammond was last out for 60 as the Sussex innings reached 362.

Sussex's opening attack of Douglas Smith and Alf Tuppin was the least experienced ever seen at a Horsham Festival and it was no great surprise that the second day belonged entirely to Surrey. Although none of their batsmen made it to three figures, they all – with the exception of the captain – contributed solidly to the cause. Barling top scored with 82 but there were half-centuries from Fishlock , Gregory and Parker. Sussex toiled away manfully but their moderate attack was simply too blunt to seriously trouble their visitors. Barling and Parker put on 142 for the 5th wicket in two hours and the end never came until well into the final session with the score on 438, a useful first innings lead of 76.

This left a no-doubt leg-weary Sussex with an awkward period to negotiate before the close. Their failure to do so was to have serious repercussions. A crowd of over 2,100 looked on apprehensively as Jim Parks was caught behind off Gover without a run on the board. Tich Cornford was sent in as night watchman and although he did his job, others didn't and by the close the innings was in some disarray at 20/3.

Lowering skies on the final morning matched the sombre mood of the home contingent among a small crowd but Sussex prayers were answered in the form of an old adversary – rain. There was no play at all until late afternoon and with Cornford and Stainton digging in, a draw seemed inevitable. However, in a season when they were as powerful a batting side as any in the land, Sussex's penchant for producing the unexpected resurfaced in frightening fashion. After tea they lost their last five wickets for 19 runs in 45 crazy minutes. Charging in with his arms pumping like pistons, Gover was destroyer in chief with a burst of 3/11 as Sussex's batting broke down quite inexplicably. Even allowing for the rain, 80 all out was as shocking as it was unexpected. What the stoical Jim Langridge made of it all is probably best left to the imagination. He came in at No 6 and was 17 not out at the close.

This collapse left Surrey five to win. Probably because as wicketkeeper he still had his pads on, Brooks opened the batting. Charlie Oakes bowled two balls, Brooks hit them both for four and that was it.

This was a facer. What would they make of Hampshire? On paper they were an easier proposition although with 12 wins and 16 losses (the latter equalling their worst-ever in the Championship) there were few shades of grey about their play. Had they not lost seven of their last nine games a fate better than 14th in the table would have awaited them. Unlike a number of counties during the inter-war period Hampshire's problems in 1938 lay largely with their batting, which was spectacularly inconsistent.

Favourable weather returned as Stainton again won the toss and again elected to bat. All seemed well at the outset as John Langridge, Jim Parks and the captain prospered. But then, just as in the Surrey match, it all began to unravel – and this time Charlie Oakes couldn't dig them out of trouble. Although there were cameos from Harry Parks and Oakes the end came on a hugely disappointing 227. Langridge was caught six runs short of his century as the hard-working Herman, generating above-average bounce with his high, easy action, took 5/74. At stumps with Hampshire on 86/2, the visitors had more cause for satisfaction than their hosts. A Saturday crowd of 2,745, some standing five and six deep, witnessed proceedings.

The second morning witnessed an even contest between bat and ball. A number of Hampshire batsmen got starts but none seemed able to push on. The end came part-way through the afternoon session and Hampshire captain Cecil Paris would have been as disappointed as Stainton was earlier with his side's 209 all out. Their downfall was wrought almost single handedly by Jim Wood's left arm medium pacers, his 7/52 being a Championship-best. A great trier, Wood always regarded Horsham as his favourite ground ('A pitch I would have liked to carry around with me').

Thanks to his efforts Sussex held a slight lead on first innings – which they promptly set about squandering. As in the second innings of the Surrey match, only Jim Langridge seemed able to resist the Hampshire pace attack for any length of time. Coming to the crease with his side already tottering on 32/3, the fact that they reached even the modest heights of 165 was due largely to his unswerving patience. He remained unbeaten on 68 as Herman (4/58 in the innings, 9/132 in the match) and Heath (5/50) swept all before them. Herman was a man for all seasons with the ball, being able to bowl virtually anything from fast inswingers to slow off breaks.

This meant that Hampshire had the entire final day to make 183. With the pitch now showing distinct signs of wear it wouldn't be easy if the Sussex attack put the ball in the right place often enough. The evening before at the theatre Holmes informed the audience that 'you should witness a fine finish to the game with Hampshire. They are a great sporting side and if they 'pip' us, then they do 'pip' us.' And so it proved – a classic ebb-and-flow contest with the advantage tilting first one way and then the other. At 104/6 the odds were slightly on Sussex. At 173/7 the match was Hampshire's to lose. At 179/9 it was anybody's guess. Walker top scored at No 3 with 37 having been joint-top scorer in the first innings with 42. Budd at No 8 weighed in with a fighting 35 but it was all-rounder Boyes who secured the points for his side with a boundary off Smith, who nevertheless was the pick of the home attack with 5/25 in a brief county career that only had four more matches to run. Sussex were to take their revenge in the return match at Portsmouth in August, Jim Langridge winning the game with a six into a refreshment tent.

1939: Storm clouds may have been gathering over the nation as the fateful summer of 1939 unfolded but 'business as usual' appears to have been the watchword for those responsible for cricket in Horsham. The visitors were Warwickshire and Surrey, the latter paying their 4th visit in six seasons. The weather coming into cricket week was among the hottest on record. In early June, Horsham sizzled as temperatures soared into the 90s and on two consecutive days an exposed thermometer on the lawn of an amateur meteorologist in Roffey showed 105 degrees. A cyclist found unconscious by the roadside at Billingshurst was diagnosed as suffering from sunstroke.

All three sides were to finish in mid-table and for broadly the same reasons. Warwickshire ended up in 11th spot, thanks in large part to a dismal run-in which saw them win but one of their last eight matches. Their batting was solid enough but their bowling a little too dependent on 'old faithfuls' Hollies and Mayer. On paper there seemed nothing much between all three sides and so it was to prove.

The opening match got under way in tropical heat. To the inexpressible relief of his team, Peter Cranmer won the toss from Hugh Bartlett and consigned the home side to a spell toiling in the field. Local interest would doubtless have been heightened by the inclusion of Charlie Oakes' younger brother Jack.

The Warwickshire innings was a curious affair. All but three of their batsmen made it into double figures but only Hill went on to convert his start into a half-century. Poor Bob Wyatt was in the wars. Coming in at No 4 he was struck over the heart by a rising ball from left-arm seamer Jack Nye and knocked semi-conscious. Revived by a brandy and water, he appeared fit to resume but clearly wasn't and eventually had to leave the field. A later examination revealed a clot of blood had formed inside a large bruise. The turning point was the introduction into the attack of Jim Langridge. From 179/4 the visitors collapsed spectacularly during the afternoon session to 217 all out. Having missed the four previous matches with lumbago Langridge eased himself gingerly back into action, yet in a spell of 18 balls broke the back of the Warwickshire innings, picking up four wickets for four runs.

This unexpected collapse meant that the old firm of John Langridge and Jim Parks was open for business far earlier than they might have expected. But not for long. At the close of Danny Mayer's opening over the scoreboard showed 1 for 2. Left to reflect, no doubt, on life's little ironies Langridge and Harry Parks, fresh from a stand of 307 the previous day against Kent, were dismissed in successive balls for 0. The slump continued and at 27/4 Bartlett, captaining the county for the first time at Horsham, must have wondered what he'd let himself in for. Thankfully he and Charlie Oakes steadied the ship, putting on 99 for the 5th wicket, though the loss of the latter for 47 just before the close was a sore blow. Sussex closed an eventful day on 126/5 with Bartlett still there on 64.

The second day brought no respite for the home side, their last five wickets capitulating for 53. Mayer, who had troubled Sussex before at Horsham, captured 6/70 as his side gained a useful first innings lead. The injury to Wyatt meant Warwicks had to reshuffle their batting order and this seemed to unsettle them. As in the first innings, several of their upper order got starts but were unable to capitalise. A stricken Wyatt came in at No 9 and almost immediately had his thumb burst open by Nye. He was again obliged to leave the field, leading the *County Times* to speculate with no obvious irony: 'It is probable that he will rest a while from cricket.' Dollery top scored with 41 as his side were dismissed for 167.

All this left Sussex with 205 to win. With the pitch clearly acting capriciously the match was within the grasp of either side. Early honours again went to Warwickshire as Sussex declined to 45/4. This time it was Jim Langridge who stood firm and he found a doughty ally in Charlie Oakes. These two steadily turned the game round, putting on 110 for the 5th wicket as Sussex closed the second day in much greater heart on 154/4. Both men had half-centuries against their name as a mere 51 remained to be made on the morrow. Oakes fell without addition to his overnight score but thankfully Langridge, with 87 not out, piloted his ship safely to harbour thus enabling Sussex to end a run of three consecutive Festival defeats. Coming in at No 7, Jack Oakes was struck painfully on the hip and no doubt had a word or two to say to his dad about it in the evening. A spirited performance but could they keep up the good work against Surrey?

Surrey would finish 8th in the table, two places above their hosts. They started the season well with seven wins in the first 10 matches and concluded with four straight victories but the period in between was largely barren. As with Sussex and Warwickshire the batting was strong but their bowling a bit too reliant on Gover and his brother-in-law, Eddie Watts.

For those who believe in such things, Surrey came into the match with a distinct psychological advantage. The two sides had met at the Oval not much more than a week previously when Surrey routed their neighbours for 63 to win by the bruising margin of 388 runs. With Sussex no doubt anxious to turn the tables Bartlett won the all-important toss and with temperatures again climbing into the 90s took first knock. Once again the home side flattered to deceive. Seven men reached double figures but no-one played the really big innings that would enable them to control the match. John Langridge batted steadily at the top of the innings for 54 and his brother Jim at No 5 was unbeaten at the close on 59 which included a fine legside six just before tea off Squires. Gover dismissed Nye and Jim Cornford with successive deliveries early in the final session to finish with 5/75 as Sussex were dismissed for a below-par 265.

Surrey started briskly in reply. Fishlock took three fours off Cornford's opening over and the 50 was hoisted in only 35 minutes. After an hour 84 was on the board, at which point Fishlock unaccountably played no stroke to Jim Parks and was bowled. This clearly unsettled the visitors for despite Squires – who had made 107 and 97 n/o in the earlier match - also reaching his 50, five wickets were down for 141 when stumps were drawn. The game was nicely poised.

Led from the front by Garland-Wells, Surrey decided to force the pace on the second morning. He and Brooks put on 105 for the 6th wicket in 75 minutes but worse was to come for the home side as Watts, coming in at No 9, drove the ball furiously to all corners.

His rapid 66 included 11 boundaries and changed the entire complexion of the innings. From somewhere near parity Surrey ended up with a lead of 89. In reply the Parks brothers then featured in one of the brightest partnerships of the match, hitting freely all around the wicket. They added 112 in 90 minutes with Harry at one point taking 17 off an over from Gover. Their dismissals let George Cox in, and it wasn't long before he too was into his stride. Jim Langridge had to retire hurt for a while after being struck on the elbow but at the close Sussex were in complete control at 282/5 with Cox on 73. With two men well set; a lead of nearly 200; runs coming at a furious pace (five an over); and the wicket still 'plumb', it was difficult to see where a result was coming from.

Gover was scheduled to bowl the opening over of the final morning but was obliged to leave the field for a few moments. Watts therefore stepped into his shoes - and in that over turned the match completely on its head, taking no fewer than three wickets (Cox, Griffith and Jack Oakes). Shaken rigid by this the end came all-too-submissively for the home side, their last five wickets falling for a paltry 25 runs as Watts ended with 5/88.

This unexpected turn of events left Surrey requiring 221 to win in 200 minutes. In rollicking good heart they set about their task with a will and galloped across the finishing line with nine wickets and a full half-hour to spare. The left-handed Fishlock seemed to enjoy playing against Sussex. He was 107 not out at the close and was partnered most of the way by Barling who had reached 88 when the end came. These two had added 178 in 115 minutes against an increasingly dispirited attack which saw seven bowlers – most of whom taking heavy punishment - turn their arm over.

Press coverage was muted. Attendances were substantially down on previous years – partly because of the intense heat but partly too because in its own small-town way martial preparations were already under way in Horsham. Few departing the ground on that deliciously warm, sun-dappled Tuesday evening could have guessed that for the second time in a generation, a terrible darkness would soon descend upon the land...

Chapter 6
DECLINE, DISILLUSIONMENT AND DEPRIVATION: 1940-1956

Prelude: The Wartime Years

Despite the hostilities – and unlike the Great War - there was a considerable volume of club and services cricket played at Cricket Field Road. In May 1940 when it might be imagined that people had rather more important things on their minds, Horsham CC decided to introduce Sunday matches despite having canvassed five 'clergyman and ministers in the town asking if they were opposed to Sunday cricket' and receiving responses from three to the effect that they were. There was even talk of a 'county match on 22 August between Arthur Gilligan's XI and a Horsham XI' but no record appears to have survived of the outcome if in fact it did take place.

Three local cricketers were selected to play for Sussex in 1941, thus adding to the 'ever increasing list...which Horsham has supplied to the County team.' On 24 June 1943 the great Australian all-rounder Keith Miller actually played at Horsham - for Sussex against an RAF XI. A flight sergeant in the RAAF, Miller made 11 runs opening the innings and took 3-41 in a match won by the RAF by five wickets.

Highlight of the 1944 season came on Saturday 19 August when the ground hosted the first county cricket match to be held south of the Thames since the outbreak of hostilities. It was a one-day affair against Northants. By 3.30pm the visitors had progressed to 207/8 when proceedings came to an 'untimely end'. For unspecified reasons and with a good finish in prospect the match was abandoned. The Sussex side was an interesting mix. Captained by AK Wilson it included pre-war regulars such as John and Jim Langridge, Harry Parks and Jack Nye and some local 'horses for courses' – George Pearce, Percy Godsmark and John Dew.

There was virtually a full programme of matches in 1945, for the most part against civilian club sides. The season opened in late April 'under conditions more in keeping with football than cricket.' Historically, perhaps the most interesting match took place on 16 September when the wartime London Counties side – a number of whom would turn out after working all night at munitions factories - played its final fixture against George Pearce's XI. For the record they won in a canter, making 118 (Somerset's Frank Lee 38) against their opponents 45 all out (Middlesex's Jack Young 5-8, LA Smith 5-25).

1946: In the eyes of many locally Horsham was in no fit state to stage county cricket in 1946. It is to the town's considerable credit that, despite the many privations, they managed to do so. On 31 May, Sussex and Glamorgan had concluded a rain-affected draw at Newport. The following day the same two sides tried conclusions again at Horsham. Glamorgan were destined to finish 6th, their best placing since entering the Championship in 1921. Their success was founded on a battery of penetrative bowlers.

All who had worked so steadfastly to bring county cricket back to Cricket Field Road were to be cruelly rewarded by the 'clerk of the weather'. Spectators for the eagerly awaited first day of peacetime cricket were greeted by low, black clouds scudding ominously across a slate-grey sky. 'The cricket field was deserted and sodden marquees hanging limply on guy ropes completed the dismal picture.' While poor old Alf Oakes and his helpers were striving valiantly to dry out the soggy sward, Field Marshal Viscount Montgomery of Alamein was introduced to both teams in front of the pavilion during the (extended) luncheon interval. Later on he distributed the prizes at Collyers Grammar School.

By mid-afternoon the rain had ceased. Glamorgan's John Clay won the toss and – doubtless with some fingers crossed – decided to bat. In the circumstances an attendance of 1,213 wasn't too bad. Dyson and Emrys Davies took strike against Nye and Horsham-born Paul Carey who had played a lot of Army cricket in India during the war. After the fall of two early wickets, Dyson and Willie Jones (55) came together in a stand of 70. Newport policeman Arthur Porter's dogged 69 held the remainder of the innings together though no fewer than eight men made it into double-figures. Given the conditions Clay would probably have been content with 265 all out. It may have been ground out over 119.4 overs but the priority was to put runs on the board. It would be a long while before those present would forget what happened next.

Glamorgan's innings extended well into the afternoon session of the second day. At 3.02pm Harry Parks opened Sussex's reply with John Langridge. By 4.20pm, after a mere 22.1 overs, it was all over. The entire side had been dismissed for 35, only two fewer than their all time Championship low of 33 in 1939 against Yorkshire as the war clouds gathered. It was an utter shambles from start to finish as Austin Matthews (6/13) and Peter Judge (4/18), well supported by a cordon of close catchers, did pretty much as they liked. Just over 800 stunned spectators watched as Parks and Langridge made their way to the crease for a second time a mere 90 minutes later. Indeed according to local legend, some late-comers thought initially that they were witnessing an extended first wicket stand in the first innings!

It almost beggars belief but as the pitch continued its capricious drying-out process, Sussex wickets went down like skittles second time round also. Ten minutes before the scheduled close of play they had been dismissed a second time – this time for a slightly less awful 127 – to lose a remarkable match by an innings and 103 runs. Only Griffith and the two local boys – Charlie Oakes and George Cox – made it past 20 as the wickets were shared round between Matthews and the two spinners, Emrys Davies and Clay himself. Sussex had been hustled out twice in under four ignominious hours.

Somerset were making their first visit to Horsham since 1925 and, like Glamorgan, were to enjoy their best-ever Championship placing. After a slow start they really came alive from late June, embarking on a 16-match unbeaten run that included 12 victories. They were also an attractive side to watch – a good blend of amateurs and professionals and by all accounts a happy outfit who invariably played with smiles on their faces.

Yet again wretched weather intervened. Rain fell almost continuously until mid-afternoon so an early decision was made to call play off for the day. An hour later the clouds broke and the sun came out...

Billy Griffith lost the toss for the second time in the week and for the second time led his men into the field. Mindful perhaps of the horrors of the Glamorgan game both sides must have viewed batting with some apprehension and it wasn't long before the tumbrels came a-calling for the men from the cider county. Lee and Lawrence put on 40 for the 2nd wicket and Luckes and the comfortably built Hazell 38 for the last, but a mediocre 150 all out was as many as they could muster. But the imp of the perverse was still in the pitch for as *Wisden* put it, 'the Sussex reply was a tale of almost unbroken disaster.' For the third time in as many days their batting broke down completely. This time it was 95 all out with only Griffith making it past 20. By stumps Somerset had lurched to 28/3. A decent sized crowd (1,083) had witnessed 273 runs scored and 23 wickets fall on a day that must have seen Joker Oakes double his usual intake of snuff.

Any hopes that Somerset might fall apart on the final day were quickly banished by Johnny Lawrence, described by Somerset historian David Foot as 'A Yorkshireman not much higher than the stumps.' For the second time in the match this gritty little player top scored for his side. His 66 was a fine innings and he was given good support by Bertie Buse, a solicitor's clerk from Bath whose idiosyncratic stance prompted John Arlott to liken him to a butler bringing out the tea. Buse would have recalled the ground from a match he played there in July 1944 for a scratch side cobbled together from the RAF camp at Faygate when he scored 44 and took 4/45. These two worthies added 90 for the 4th wicket and enabled skipper Bunty Longrigg to declare just before lunch at 146/5, thereby challenging Sussex to make 202 for victory in a little over two hours. (The match was scheduled to finish at 4pm to allow Somerset time to return to Taunton).

It wasn't long before the terrible, haunted procession began again and at 33/4 Sussex looked doomed. At this point, enter that most popular of saviours – George Cox. With dependable old Jim Langridge for company they added 82 to make the game safe. Cox's was the innings of the week. Driving briskly and refreshingly he hit a six and nine fours in his 71 not out as Sussex limped uncertainly to safety at 145/7. A crowd of 771 paid to see the final day and would doubtless have smiled ironically as the match ended in bright sunshine.

1947: For 1947 Horsham had been allocated games against Worcestershire and Derbyshire. Cox and Charlie Oakes wasted no time getting an early look at the pitch and were among the Horsham CC eleven that took the field in an early season match against Cranleigh. George's look (he made 79) was rather more extended than Charlie's (1).

Worcestershire were a solid, middle-of-the-table side around this time and in 1947 were to finish 7th. Their batting was sound rather than spectacular and their spin bowling quite potent. Their main weakness was the absence of an incisive new-ball partner for veteran ex-England seamer, Reg Perks.

The match opened in perfect cricketing weather. Well over 4,000 spectators saw Hugh Bartlett win the toss and bat first 'on a wicket that looked perfect.' It may have looked perfect but in the very first over it was noticeable that Perks made the ball lift sharply on several occasions. Despite Sussex reaching 301 part-way through the final session it was a curiously uneven innings with Harry Parks hitting a quite magnificent 170 in 4 hours 15 minutes to save his side's bacon. His innings included three sixes and 16 fours and was virtually without blemish. However, apart from a furious 60 from Jack Oakes, nobody else reached 25. In another ominous sign, Charlie Oakes had been bowled first ball by one 'which turned sharply off the pitch.' Perks and the fair-haired Peter Jackson operated unchanged throughout the opening session but when spinner Roly Jenkins was introduced into the attack, Parks promptly hit him for a six and a four. Jack Oakes responded by smashing Howorth over the sightscreen at the railway end for another six as 60 runs came in 17 minutes. Oakes was unstoppable. He straight drove Howorth for a four and a six to reach his 50 before pulling off the biggest hit of the day, striking Jenkins high into the tennis courts, a prodigious carry. But all good things must come to an end and he perished as he had lived, caught on the boundary edge attempting yet another six. 46 of his 60 runs came in boundaries as he and Harry Parks added 152 for the 5th wicket in 85 scintillating minutes. Sussex's final collapse was quite dispiriting, their last three wickets falling with the score on 301. Despite conceding almost five runs an over leg spinner Jenkins did most damage picking up 6/77.

Carey scattered Fred Cooper's wicket 'all over the pitch with one of his express deliveries', but at the end of an eventful and well-balanced day the visitors were comfortably placed on 52/1.

The second day dawned under dull skies and a chilly north-east wind. Eddie Cooper (77) and rising star Don Kenyon added 68 for the 2nd wicket and Cooper and Ronnie Bird 89 for the 3rd as a brilliant sun emerged. Despite a flurry of wickets these two stands slowly drew the sting from the home attack. Jenkins and Bird took their 6th wicket stand to 105, paving the way for Jenkins (63), Young and Yarnold to play increasingly breezy knocks down the order. It was a classic exercise in wearing an attack down with one man (Bird) acting as the constant and others playing cameos round him. Bird was eventually caught off the persevering Carey for an invaluable 105 as his side took a first innings lead of 105. Everybody in the Sussex side except captain and wicketkeeper tried their hand with the ball as a marathon 163 overs were sent down. But with two-thirds of the time gone, the wicket still in reasonably good shape and only one innings each completed, it was difficult to see where the game was headed.

Worcester entrusted the bulk of their attack on the final day to Perks and Jenkins. Taking advantage of being dropped twice, Bartlett drove spectacularly for 54. Charlie Oakes made 49 not out and others supported stoically as the Sussex innings ground on well beyond tea. They cleared the arrears with only three wickets down but Perks and Jenkins stuck to their task and took four wickets apiece as the innings eventually concluded for 228.

This left Worcester 65 minutes to score 124, a stiff ask. Would they go for it? The answer appeared to be yes, for they completely remodelled their batting order with skipper Allan White coming in at No 3. His stand of 77 with Kenyon effectively sealed Sussex's fate. They 'hit out at everything and succeeded in getting the runs with four minutes to spare.' Kenyon 'hit lustily at anything short of a length, flashing the ball to the boundary off the back foot on several occasions.' As wickets fell, incoming batsmen literally ran to the crease. But in a thrilling finish it was White who made the difference. His unbeaten 53 was 'a mixture of powerful drives and highly unorthodox swipes, which included a six skied high over the wicket keeper's head to the fine leg boundary and a haymaking sweep for six which rattled half way up the scoring box.' Full marks to Worcester, of course, but what was Bartlett thinking about with his bowling? Cornford was economical enough – and picked up four wickets – but Carey's 9.5 overs cost 77 runs. If only to slow things down a little, why on earth didn't he give one (or more) of the others a go?

Derbyshire were the second visitors and arrived at Cricket Field Road hard on the heels of a quite remarkable victory over Somerset at Chesterfield on 11 June where they won by an innings *in one day*. On a lively wicket George Pope took 6/34 and 7/16 against a procession of 'irresolute batsmen.' They were destined to finish 5th in the Championship and in a vintage year for batsmen (1947 was the famous golden summer of Compton and Edrich) their success was founded on a formidable pace trio of Pope, Gladwin and Copson. Well supported by AE (Dusty) Rhodes, Derbyshire's was arguably the strongest attack in the land.

After the nightmare of 1946 rain again intervened malevolently, washing out the entire first day. This was doubly cruel as Saturday was the traditional highlight of the week and 1947 was otherwise such a spectacularly glorious summer.

Play got under way promptly on day two with Bartlett winning the toss and (unusually) electing to field. This was a bold move and the first time any captain had inserted the opposition since Bertie Chaplin against Lancashire back in 1913. In the short-term his gamble was well-founded as the damp, drying pitch provided every encouragement for his seam bowlers. Carey removed Townsend with the fourth delivery of the day 'a ball that kept low and came through very fast.' George Pope (61) drove vigorously and with Dennis Smith for company, put on 81 for the 5th wicket - yet only a last-wicket stand of 30 enabled them to reach a modest 217 all out, with three wickets apiece for Carey, Cornford and Wood.

The Sussex innings opened spectacularly. With only four on the board Griffith was bowled by Pope playing no stroke. Harry Parks fell almost immediately to the same bowler, lbw trying to hook. Bartlett and John Langridge mended a few fences and the Oakes brothers must have put a smile on their dad's face with a fighting stand of 77 for the 5th wicket. However, Jack Oakes fell for 40 just before the close leaving Sussex on 158/6.

George Pope (5/63) and Gladwin (3/36) in particular were not to be denied on the final morning. In only 35 minutes the Sussex tail was swept unceremoniously aside, leaving their visitors with a modest first innings lead. Derby's second innings was a curious affair. In a tactical repetition of the Worcester innings earlier in the week, Albert Alderman (68) dropped anchor while others hit briskly round him. (Alderman, it may be recalled, scored a century on the ground back in 1937). Elliott made 32, Smith 40 and Worthington 36 not out as the visitors, intent on making a game of it if they could, raced to 193/4 before declaring. This time Bartlett used no fewer than nine bowlers in 60 overs.

All this activity left Sussex exactly two hours to get 213 against a renowned bowling side on a rain-affected, final-day wicket. Would they pick up the gauntlet? It appeared so initially but after losing four top wickets for only 79, they started to play out time. But against the Derby attack this was easier said than done as Pope and Rhodes started to pick off the middle order with worrying ease. Peter Doggart at No 8 then found an unexpected ally in No 11 Cornford and these two blocked it out until an agonising two balls from home when the former was clean bowled by – who else? – Pope. Again full marks to both sides for fashioning such a decent game in only two days with so little artificiality but in the final analysis Sussex only had to hold on for 37 overs for a draw, yet failed to do so. It was the introduction of Rhodes for Gladwin that changed the course of the match. Alternating fast-medium outswingers off a very long run with leg-breaks, it was his burst of four wickets for two runs in six overs that consigned Sussex to defeat, despite Harry Parks' fighting 39.

1948: Horsham's first visitors in 1948 (Northants) were last seen in the town in 1935 but supporters would have to go all the way back to 1913 to uncover the only previous visit of their second (Lancashire). Northants brought with them an unenviable record. They replaced Sussex at the foot of the Championship table in 1947 and were destined to retain that unwanted 'honour' in 1948. Wretched though their recent record was, at least they managed three victories in 1948 which was three more than they achieved in the entire period between May 1935 and May 1939.

Sussex came into the match without a win to their name and their chances of breaking their duck were not enhanced when Bartlett lost the toss and took first knock on what appeared to be an easy paced pitch. It was a day of fluctuating fortunes. After the fall of an early wicket Oldfield and Brookes put on 125 before the former was run out for 54 (he would surely have remembered the ground, having played against Horsham CC in 1946 for Chorltoncum-Hardy). This was the first of three wickets to fall with the score on 143 but an on-drive for four off Charlie Oakes brought Brookes his century after 4 hours 30 minutes at the crease, his third successive 'ton' against Sussex on Sussex soil. Apart from a fairly easy chance to Cox at cover when he had made 18, it was a faultless innings. Brookes seldom seemed in any bother and seldom hit the ball other than along the deck. Bartlett continued, restlessly, to switch his bowlers around and the crowd played its part by subjecting the batsmen – particularly Garlick who stone-walled for almost an hour for 10 - to some 'mild barracking'. Assisted by the tail, 'Brooky' ploughed relentlessly on and to his mortification, Cox – usually such a sound fielder - dropped him again on 123. By dint of steady, unspectacular accumulation the visitors had reached 317/8 by the close with Brookes still in possession.

Only a handful of spectators were present initially on the second morning to witness Northants' marathon innings finally grind to a halt after 147 overs, Brookes being last out for a superb 179 characterised by meticulous defence and strong off-driving. This was the highest individual score seen on the ground since 1921.

Ominously for Sussex a thunderstorm early on had saturated the pitch and the home batsmen must have been fearful how it would play as it started to dry out. There were no immediate worries as John Langridge and Harry Parks put on 55 for the first wicket but the fun really began when spinners Garlick and Broderick replaced the opening attack of Nutter and Bob Clarke. As the wicket dried almost visibly, Lancashire-born Vince Broderick proved virtually unplayable despite team-mate Frank Tyson commenting mischievously that his left-arm spinners 'evinced only negligible turn'. He bowled 25.4 overs and took an astonishing nine for 35 as Sussex were shot out for 123. Only four men made it into double figures. Arthur Childs-Clarke could scarcely wait to enforce the follow-on, a rarity for his side. Once again Langridge (56) and Parks got Sussex off to a solid start – 86 this time - but once again the middle order made a complete hash of it. At 164/6 they were still 55 adrift and with only the tail to come, seemed doomed...

Then on the third day came one of those astonishing transformations that make cricket such a compelling game (unless you are on the wrong end of them), although 'it was ironic that the smallest crowd of the Festival should be present...to see the home county transform a seemingly hopeless position.' In fact, fewer than 400 spectators were at the ground to witness Sussex's three amateur bats – Bartlett, Blake and Griffith – fairly lace into the Northants attack. Bartlett (55) and Blake put on precisely 100 for the 7th wicket and for once, the captain's innings was carefully compiled with only hints of aggression. 21-year-old Blake started shakily but gained visibly in confidence as his innings progressed. He unfurled a number of flowing cover drives before being caught on the boundary for 77. But coming in at No 8, Griffith topped the lot. After a steady start, he suddenly started jumping down the track and with Cornford (1 n/o) providing almost totally passive support added 57 furious runs for the last wicket in 20 minutes. In fact so passive was Cornford during in this passage of play that he only faced three deliveries! Griffith raced to a flamboyant maiden century (106 n/o) in 110 minutes, an innings that included no fewer than five 6s and seven 4s. This time round Broderick returned to the pavilion with 1/119 against his name! All this amazing energy enabled Bartlett to declare at 418/9 and out of nowhere challenge Northants to make 200 in 90 minutes. Hopes were raised as Blake continued a memorable day by picking up two brilliant catches at short leg but despite the loss of a third wicket, both captains – doubtless with mixed emotions - shook hands on a draw with the visitors' score standing at 43/3.

This was quite a start to the Festival: could the second game match it for thrills and spills? Lancashire were quite a different kettle of fish, being traditionally among the more powerful outfits in the land. Even with Washbrook away on Test duty they could still boast seven internationals (eight, if you include the Victory caps won by the tragic Bill Roberts). They were destined to finish 5th in the table largely because of the lack of a regular new-ball partner for Dick Pollard. Invariably full of runs, they were to draw 15 matches in 1948.

The opening day attendance was gigantic – over 6,000, the largest for a single day since 1931. Lancashire won the toss and Sussex dutifully took the field. 'Drawn by fine weather...crowds poured into the ground...By mid-afternoon every vantage point was filled, with spectators in holiday mood sitting on the roofs of cars and perched in trees.' The *County Times* was fairly hard to please around this time. They had castigated Northants for 'only' scoring 317 on the opening day of the first match and now Lancashire came in for some criticism for making a 'dour' 354/7. If the crowd 'expected to see bright cricket, they were sadly disappointed' was the somewhat sour comment. 'Instead, they saw Lancashire's batsmen piling up runs at a pace that made a moderate Sussex attack look positively hostile.' Accusatory fingers were pointed at a number of the visiting batsmen. Place 'progressed sedately to a century in three hours and 20 minutes.' Ikin (61) 'was neither so swift nor so sure. The crowd sat and toiled patiently while he plodded his way to an uncertain 50 that took him 110 minutes.' To rub further salt in the wound, when on 11, he was given out lbw by umpire Hendren and was part-way back to the pavilion when the official decided on further reflection that the ball had struck his bat first and recalled him! Wharton (69) 'progressed even more slowly', while 'Only big Dick Pollard showed any signs of the Festival spirit with a cheery innings.' Against such accusations it is easy to lose sight of the fact that over 350 runs were scored. Place's 111 contained 12 fours and was his second century in successive days.

Lancashire declared at their overnight total and it wasn't long before Sussex were in the toils. Their first innings was punctuated with starts – seven men made it into double figures - yet the highest individual score was 29 by Don Smith. Just before lunch another decent crowd – over 2,500 - got their first sighting of Lancashire's 19-year-old '*Wunderkid*', Malcolm Hilton. The slow-left armer reeled off an extraordinary 10 consecutive maidens and ending with 3/10 off 16.1 overs as Sussex were dismissed for a mediocre 158. Following on, the same doleful pattern repeated itself in the second innings ('Sussex formed a sorry procession to and from the pavilion'), stumps being drawn on a dismal 72/5.

It was no great surprise that 'a mere sprinkling of spectators' were present to witness the last rites - 85 minutes was all it took as Sussex's last five wickets garnered a further 60 runs. Smith (again) with 37 and Griffith 'made gallant efforts to stem the tide of disaster' but to no avail. Lancashire captain Ken Cranston led from the front, picking up 6/58, but the *County Times* was in no doubt as to its hero - Dick Pollard 'who, red faced and perspiring, had toiled for two long spells throughout the two innings'.

1949: Cricket officials in the town were stunned when they learnt of their allocation for 1949 – Cambridge University. Not even Cambridge University and a county. At a stroke Horsham had effectively lost their cricket Week. This was a bitter pill to swallow in a season when Sussex played more county matches than in 1948.

Unlike the Oxbridge sides of today those of yesteryear were more than capable of holding their own with all but the very strongest county elevens. The Cambridge side that saw service at Cricket Field Road included four players – John Dewes, Hubert Doggart, Doug Insole and John Warr – who not only enjoyed full county careers but also went on to play for England. Cambridge's strength lay very much in its batting.

Entry to the ground was free as Griffith, captaining the Sussex side in the absence of Bartlett, won the toss and batted. Making his county debut was 17-year-old Jim Parks, son of Jim (senior), who 'gave very definite signs that the name of Parks would once again be a feature of the Sussex side.' In what appears to have been a fairly pedestrian effort, Sussex batted until well into the final session for their 275 all out. Everybody but John Langridge and Griffith made it into double figures but local supporters would have noted with quiet satisfaction that the two major contributions were made by Horsham men – Charlie Oakes hit a six and 11 fours in his 67 and George Cox's 74 contained 12 boundaries.

Cambridge slumped to 167/9 in reply until finding partial redemption in a last wicket stand of 62 between Hall, whose 49 was his highest first-class score, and fast bowler Warr (32 n/o). Despite being slogged about a bit at the death, Cornford returned 6/87.

Fortified by a useful lead of 46, Sussex set about consolidation. John Langridge made 67, his brother 51 and Charlie Oakes 52. With Cox adding 65, Griffith was able to declare late in the morning session on 265/7, thus challenging the University to make 312 in 4 hours 30 minutes. John Langridge and

Charlie Oakes put on 108 for the 2nd wicket; his brother and Cox 106 for the 4th.

It was a stiff target, but with their strong batting lineup and a fleetness of foot between the wickets that quite frankly put Sussex to shame, it was anticipated that the University would go for it – and they did. Dewes (74) and Morris led off with a stand of 114. Doggart weighed in with 59 and Burnett 40. The key moment came when Cornford bowled Insole with 10 minutes left on the clock. With their last major player gone and over 40 still needed the Light Blues concluded they had done their bit and the match drifted to a gentle conclusion on 275/8. Cornford took a further five wickets to give him match figures of 11/155, the best yield for a home bowler at Horsham for 22 years. 20-year-old David Sheppard – whose family lived in the nearby village of Slinfold – made a quiet Horsham debut.

But however interesting there was no dressing up the fact that it was a poor substitute for a Festival week. To add to the prevailing gloom the Sussex Ladies were also in action in Horsham, entertaining their counterparts from Surrey at Collyer's School – but not for long. In reply to 146/6, Sussex were all out for nine in an innings that contained no fewer than nine ducks. To twist the knife still further much of the damage was inflicted by Doreen Polly, a former Horsham High School pupil, who used to play for Sussex. She took six wickets for two runs.

The *County Times* spoke for all in hoping that 'the absence of Cricket Week will be only temporary and that next year the bunting, the two county visiting teams and all the pre-war trimmings will return in force.' But would they?

1950: In a word – Yes. Whatever the ins and outs that led to them losing their Festival in 1949, Horsham was awarded two county games for 1950 – Essex and Nottinghamshire. It was some while since either side had visited Cricket Field Road – 1929 and 1934 respectively.

For Essex, the 1950 season was to prove a rude awakening. They had finished 9th in 1949 and considered themselves upwardly mobile. To finish with the wooden spoon was therefore as unexpected as it was unwelcome. Plagued all year by inconsistent and unreliable batting and bowling they were to bounce back strongly in 1951 suggesting that there was nothing fundamentally wrong: it was just one of those seasons.

For the entire week leading up to the game the town had been basking in temperatures up in the 80s and the open-air swimming pool in the park had been doing brisk business. Essex captain Doug Insole won the toss and batted. His experienced opening pair of Dodds and Avery put on 61 but Sussex fought back strongly and by mid-afternoon had reduced the visitors to 132/7. At this point Ray Smith (58) and Dick Horsfall (89) put on 102 in 80 minutes with Horsfall digging in and Smith – a ferocious striker of the ball – going for his shots. The upshot of all this was that Essex managed 274, Cornford (in his benefit season) bowling 'accurately and with verve' to return 5/90. John Langridge and Charlie Oakes fell cheaply in the evening session but by stumps Smith and Cox were firmly in control.

They continued to make hay on the second morning and had taken their stand to 161 when Cox was bowled by Vigar for a spirited 83. A crowd that eventually built up to 1,700 saw Smith continue to pull and drive with assurance. He completed a thoroughly well merited century during the afternoon session, his 106 including 13 boundaries. Jim Langridge picked up the tempo with a spirited 60 that included a six and seven 4s but from 317/4, 363 all out came as something of a disappointment, Vigar's leg-breaks bringing him 5/57. Nevertheless with a lead of 89 Sussex had a spring in their step and it wasn't long before they were among the Essex wickets second time round. Insole was unable to rally his troops this time, falling first ball to Cornford, and his side closed the day on a perilous 155/8, a lead of only 66.

Essex's final two wickets could only add 11 runs as the unlikely figure of Jack Oakes ended with 5/33 on his home 'manor'. This left Sussex requiring 78 for victory. First innings hero Smith departed pretty much immediately but John Langridge (48) and Charlie Oakes (25 n/o) took the score up to 76 as the home side strolled to victory just before lunch in front of a crowd of around 200. Four byes saw Sussex anti-climactically to victory but it was a thoroughly professional job... Wicketkeeper Rupert Webb, making his first appearance at Horsham, caught three and stumped three.

Nottinghamshire were destined to fare little better than Essex. They had to settle for 15th spot and only two late wins enabled them to avoid the ignominy of the wooden spoon. Indeed they only registered three victories all season, none of them at Trent Bridge.

Notts' problems started long before the first ball was bowled. They travelled down by coach and never arrived in the town until 1.30am. Seven of the party of 16 had reserved accommodation at the *Station Hotel* and no doubt tumbled wearily into their beds. The other nine journeyed the short distance down to the *Crown* in the Carfax – only to find they weren't expected and there was no room for them! In desperation they returned to the *Station Hotel* where they were found emergency beds. Some of the team had to sleep in the lounge though the poor old coach driver had to find what rest he could in his vehicle!

Against this troubled backdrop they may not have been too distressed when rain thoroughly ruined the first day. Jim Langridge won the toss from England's Reg Simpson and in the two hours play possible saw his side reduced to 63/3.

Fortunately Langridge himself was still there. He and Smith put on 77 in very difficult conditions before Smith was magnificently caught at short extra cover for 59. Langridge and the teenager Parks then eked out 57 invaluable runs for the 5th wicket, all three men taking advantage of some loose stuff from the leg-break bowler Stinchcombe. The skipper eventually fell to Jepson after 3 hours and 30 vigilant minutes for 66, having helped pilot his side to a respectable 226.

Sussex must have feared the worst as Simpson (59) put on 75 for the first wicket with the enigmatic Charlie Harris. With the elegant Joe Hardstaff also batting securely at No 4, Notts looked set for a healthy lead but when these two were parted Sussex scythed through the remainder and actually secured a modest first innings advantage.

With play well into the final day a draw seemed inevitable though Notts may have harboured outside thoughts of pulling off a shock win when Harold Butler, maintaining a fine pace, single-handedly reduced Sussex to 25/4. John Langridge and Cox stopped the immediate rot but then followed a most extraordinary passage of play, with Jack Oakes at the centre of it. In the remaining 67 minutes of the game he flogged the visiting attack all over – and occasionally clean out of – his father's ground. Never having previously made a first-class century he was mortified to be caught on the boundary's edge for a quite astonishing 95, which included two 6s and fourteen 4s. Cox (66 n/o) could only watch in admiration at these pyrotechnics. Full marks to Simpson for leaving on the erratic Stinchcombe – whose 7.3 overs yielded 57 runs – but in truth it was the first-day rain that ruined this as a contest.

1951: In 1951 the town played host to Nottinghamshire (again) and Somerset. Somerset were about to enter one of the bleakest periods in their history. As a prelude to this, 1951 saw them suffer 15 defeats and tumble seven places in the Championship table to 14th.

Sussex went into the match with some optimism, having completed the double over their opponents in 1950. Jim Langridge won the toss and sent his brother and a promising newcomer named Ken Suttle into battle on a roasting hot day. It wasn't long before the pitch started baring its teeth and were it not for the captain the innings would have broken down utterly. As it was Sussex were dismissed by mid-afternoon for a mediocre 163. Coming in at No 4, Jim Langridge was responsible for 68 of these hitting nine boundaries, mainly through the on side. Ominously, the destroyer-in-chief was pocket-sized Johnny Lawrence with his teasing leg breaks - he picked up 7/63.

Harold Gimblett and the neat, sharp-eyed Les Angell led off with 72 but by the close the visitors had slipped to 132/5. If the spectators thought that was pretty good value for money it was as nothing compared with events on the Monday...Buse strove in vain to hold the second half of the Somerset innings together but Cornford and Wood were not to be denied. They quickly ran through the tail as Somerset were dismissed for 178, a lead of 15. Then it was Sussex's turn again – and once again they were hustled out by the Somerset spinners splendidly supported by their close catchers. Jack Oakes top-scored with 28 but it is difficult to know how to defend 123 all out. Lawrence this time took 3/17 and there were four wickets for Ellis Robinson as the entire innings lasted fewer than 47 overs.

This left Somerset to get 109 with one whole day and one session in which to do it. 'The spectators settled down somewhat despondently to watch the visitors make it, as many thought, with ease.' In the event they didn't make it at all - indeed didn't even make it through the one remaining session. Things started off circumspectly enough with Gimblett and Angell putting on 37 for the first wicket. But unlike Somerset, Jim Langridge opted to stay for the most part with his pace attack. On a wicket of disturbingly variable bounce, Cornford and Wood reduced their visitors to 49/6 and worked their way through the entire side in less than 38 overs. Wood ended with 6/51 and Cornford 3/25 as Somerset tumbled catastrophically to 89 all out with five minutes left on the clock. This rounded off an extraordinary day's play in which 258 runs were scored and 25 wickets fell. Well might 'the big and appreciative crowd roar their approval after being held spellbound and rapt during a grand afternoon's cricket.'

Notts were a pale shadow of the side spearheaded by Larwood and Voce and were destined to finish bottom of the Championship for the first time in their history. Simpson and Hardstaff apart, their batting was poor and their attack – for want of a better word – positively threadbare. The omens weren't good...

Hardstaff won the toss and batted. Yet again batsmen of every kidney struggled. Only Cyril Poole (42) and Harris (32) made any sort of a fist of things against Wood (5/50) and Ted James (4/68). There were no stands of any note and part way through the afternoon session the innings was all over for 149. But what goes round comes round and at 73/5 even securing first-innings points must have seemed a long way off. Makeshift opener Peter Doggart stuck it out gamely and paved the way for Jack Oakes who smote two 6s and five 4s in a typically muscular 47. At stumps on yet another eventful day Sussex had struggled to 165/7.

The home side's last three wickets fell on the following morning for 20 runs but a lead of 36 was not to be sneezed at on this track. One shudders to think what Larwood and Voce would have made of it. So in went Notts again – and it wasn't long before the wickets started to tumble. Against the pace attack of Wood, James and Cornford half the side were out for 77 before the sturdy little left-hander Fred Stocks gritted it out for three hours for 66.

He was last to go as James' 5/64 gave him match figures of 9/132. In something of a re-run of the Somerset match this left the side batting last – in this case Sussex – with a modest target and a day and more than one session in which to get them.

They only had to make 118 but having seen what had gone before, it was a brave man who was prepared to forecast the result. In a flash they subsided to 13/2. Then came a stand of 58 between the dependable Langridge brothers. The crowd relaxed – only 49 required and seven wickets still in hand. They should have known better – in another trice they were 72/5 with only Jim Langridge, Oakman and the tail to come. But in yet another twist these two added an unbeaten 48 for the 6th wicket to see their side home. A Festival win-double! Without question an excited and appreciative home crowd had received full value for money with almost 300 runs scored and 18 wickets falling in the day. What the accountants made of both matches finishing inside two days is another matter, although attendances were healthy enough. However you dress it up, questions must surely have been asked about two wickets that clearly were not up to county standard.

1952: Whatever misgivings the county may have harboured about 1951 they maintained faith with Horsham in 1952 and allocated them fixtures against Northamptonshire and Hampshire. These games marked a first appearance in the town as umpire for the redoubtable Syd Buller.

Pre-war whipping boys Northants were now a cosmopolitan, mid-table side who numbered among their ranks the recent England captain (Freddie Brown) and one of the most potent weapons in county cricket (highly-rated Australian leg break and googly bowler George Tribe). Tribe had opened his county career the previous week, taking a wicket with his first ball in the course of a match return of 11-119. He was clearly going to need careful watching.

The match opened under a cloudless blue sky with admission prices pegged at 2/- for adults and 1/- for children under 16. Brown and his men were staying at the *Kings Head* and after a trouble-free night he won the toss and batted. In a re-run of 1951, wickets started to tumble pretty much from the outset. On a slightly green surface the veteran Jim Cornford in his final season before taking up a coaching post in Southern Rhodesia, ably assisted by Wood, maintained a disciplined length and let the pitch do the rest. At 36/5 after less than an hour's play Northants must have wondered what would happen next but displaying characteristic grit, Brown found an ally in Tribe. Mixing stubborn defence and lofted drives these two put on 81 for the 6th wicket but once they were parted normal service was resumed again until Bob Clarke, coming in at No 10, slogged an enterprising 28 n/o. Even so Northants would have been sorely disappointed with 166 all out as Cornford picked up 5/52 and Wood 3/40.

Sussex started circumspectly but all too soon the stocky Tribe was weaving his web. By the close their innings was in ruins at 108/7, the score at one point having stood at 94/3. Brown was observed 'patting Tribe on the back as he came in. Well did the subtle spinner deserve it.' With the ball already turning prodigiously and lifting sharply, batting was again a hazardous undertaking.

To make matters worse Charlie Oakes pulled a leg muscle early on the second morning. Griffith's 'leg stump was sent cart-wheeling' by Nutter but Tribe was not to be denied. The end came with the score on 135, Tribe's figures 7/53. But lo and behold, just when a third consecutive two-day match seemed in prospect, Northants went on a run-spree. Dennis Brookes (62) and the hugely gifted Australian Jock Livingston then came together in a free-wheeling partnership of 143 which completely took the game away from the home side. Livingston was scoring freely all round the wicket and with the score on 182 reached his century with a square cut for three off Thomson before being bowled shortly afterwards by the latter for 105. In the final session Fred Jakeman – who had to retire hurt with an Achilles tendon injury when on 52 – left-hander Des Barrick (43) and Tribe again (40 n/o) all scored with gay abandon against a leg-weary home attack. By the close the score had mounted to 334/7 and Sussex must have feared the worst.

Brown declared at his overnight score and invited Sussex to make 366, knowing that they hadn't a dog's chance of doing so. Not that they didn't try. Cox and Oakman put on a fighting 119 for the 6th wicket with Cox, still grievously handicapped by a leg strain sustained in the first innings, having to bat with a runner throughout. At tea, they were still only five wickets down and although never in a position to win, entertained outside hopes of escaping with a draw. It was not to be. Oakman fell for 65 and Cox's gallant knock ended when he was caught off the seemingly ubiquitous Tribe for 82. After tea the last five wickets capitulated for 12 runs in 34 minutes to Tribe and his captain: 'For the second time in the match, Sussex revealed an alarmingly long and ineffectual tail.' Tribe ended with 5/80, giving him match figures of 12/133 and fully justifying his pre-match epithet 'Terrible Tribe.'

Hampshire were another side in transition and were destined to finish 12th in the Championship table, down three places on 1951.

The match opened in hot, sultry weather. Visiting captain Desmond Eagar must have spotted something amiss for he won the toss and – unusually at Horsham – elected to field. It wasn't long before the home side were in all sorts of bother against Vic Cannings and Derek Shackleton, one of the most incisive opening attacks in the land. Shortly after lunch the Sussex score stood at a catastrophic 88/6, Cannings in particular proving a handful with his late movement. Of the top order only Parks with 31 looked equal to the challenge. Thomson and James partially retrieved the position with a stand of 53 for the 7th wicket and Webb made several attractive straight drives late on. But Cannings and Shackleton then took the new ball and that was that – 178 all out, the former ending with 5/59, the latter 3/48. Hampshire's batsmen too were soon scratching about, particularly against Wood, though Rogers and Walker contrived to put on 52 for the first wicket. By stumps they had crept to 67/3 but it was in all conscience a turgid day's cricket.

Sadly 'with the laborious Rogers as their mainstay' the second day was no better. It was a classic case of the end justifying the means. Hampshire worked on the age-old premise that if you occupy the crease long enough runs will come. Very possibly so, but don't expect the crowd to appreciate – let alone enjoy – it. Rogers and his supporting cast ground on and on at a funereal pace, indifferent to the fact that 'That Horsham rarity, barracking, reared its head mildly in protest.' His long vigil ended after 4 hours

20 minutes for 119, an invaluable knock for his side that included 13 boundaries. Just to twist the knife the visitors' last wicket pair of Dare and Cannings added a surprisingly sprightly 59 in 50 minutes. Their 300 all out constituted a very handy first innings lead.

Sussex made another undistinguished start but then Parks proceeded to hammer the bowling all round the ring. Two successive overs from Shackleton and Walker went for 32 and 60 had been added in a mere 28 minutes of dazzling strokeplay. Sadly, he succumbed to Shackleton just before the close as Sussex's score stood at a perilous 101/4, still 21 runs adrift. Thomson and Webb again raised hopes with a fruitful stand of 53 for the 8th wicket but from 209/7, Sussex declined to 214 all out, Shackleton finishing with 5/70.

All this meant that Hampshire only required 93 for victory. After the loss of two early wickets, Walker (54 n/o) and Gray (28 n/o) put on an unbeaten 80 for the 3rd to see their side home with time and wickets to spare. However, the key to their success was undoubtedly the stranglehold exerted by Cannings and Shackleton, who took 15 of the 20 wickets to fall. Later that same week 'Vic n' Shack' travelled back to Southampton and bowled unchanged through both innings as Kent were dismissed twice in one day on a rain-ruined pitch.

Wisden's verdict was caustic: 'Few county matches graced by brilliant sunshine can have provided such featureless batting. In nearly eighteen hours of cricket only 788 runs were scored at an average crawl of 43 runs an hour. Some people pleaded the excuse that the heavy atmosphere encouraged the seam bowlers...but...only...Parks showed any ability to get to the pitch of the ball. The rest were leaden-footed and unenterprising.'

1953: Horsham was awarded two games for 1953, against Warwickshire and Glamorgan, and offered up a silent prayer for better fortune after the double disappointment in 1952. It was to prove a frustrating season for Warwickshire. A side in transition, they were to finish in 9th spot and a record of W6, D15, L7 tells its own story. Largely because of an attack that lacked any consistent penetration they were unable to convert a number of promising situations into victories.

New Sussex skipper David Sheppard won the all-important toss and elected to bat. Euphemistically the pitch was described as 'lively' but by dint of steady application his side managed (just) to top 300. Highlight of the day couldn't have been more apposite – a debut century on his home ground by 41 year old George Cox. Coming in at No 3 he was hampered by a pulled leg muscle and his innings of 127 (18 fours) was workmanlike rather than spectacular. The only stand of any substance was one of 109 in 90 minutes for the 5th wicket with Suttle (43). Otherwise it was a solid team performance with Cox's the 9th wicket to fall. A welcome and unexpected bonus arrived courtesy of a last wicket stand of 42 between Wood and Webb. Nine of the wickets were shared between the two opening bowlers. Charlie Grove picked up 5/66 and Queenslander Keith Dollery - no relation to his better-known captain Tom – 4/111. At stumps Sussex were very much in the box seat, Warwicks having subsided to 48/3.

Rain severely impeded progress on the second day, washing out the entire pre-lunch session. When proceedings did eventually get under way the home side continued its domination. Almost inevitably, Dollery (Tom) led from the front for the visitors. His 68 contained a wide range of shots but only the graceful Alan Townsend (46) could stay with him for any length of time. Warwicks were eventually dismissed for 181, the main architect of their downfall being Wood whose left arm seamers in the damp conditions earned him 6/43.

Sussex had little option but to throw their bats if they wanted to give themselves enough time to bowl their opponents out a second time. By stumps they were perched a little uncomfortably on 82/5 but in the context of the game, this constituted a lead of 207, so they probably weren't too displeased.

The weather on the final day was cloudy throughout although the rain, which often threatened, never materialised. With the bulk of the attack entrusted once again to Grove and Dollery (K), Sussex were indebted to a breezy stand of 63 between Suttle (53 n/o) and Oakman. Sheppard's declaration shortly before lunch challenged Warwicks to make 232 in 180 minutes.

To their credit they went for it. Townsend – for the second time in the match – and the under-rated Fred Gardner took the score to 101 in pretty rapid order, helped by several dropped catches. After Townsend (53) was held at deep square leg Warwicks' innings went into a sharp decline. At 135/6 David Heath, who had dropped down the order in the run chase, came in to partner Gardner. When play entered the final 30 minutes, 52 were required with four wickets in hand. Throughout his career Gardner's trademark was his solid defensive play but ironically his innings ended on 76 with an uncharacteristic leg-side heave. Charlie Oakes then ran Heath out with only one stump to aim at after the batsman had slipped going for a quick single. Keith Dollery was 'bowled all over the place' by James but Eric Hollies – one of the select band of men to have taken more wickets in his career than he scored runs – hung in there with Ray Weeks until 10 minutes from time when to general jubilation he touched one to Webb off Oakman with his side still 43 runs adrift. It was a splendid game of cricket that reflected great credit on both sides. With 6/91 to his name the lanky Oakman's off-breaks did the trick for his side.

For Glamorgan 1953 was to prove a season of two halves. By early July they were top of the table but only one win in their final 15 games saw them cascade to 10th. A combination of injuries – especially to their colourful and charismatic skipper Wilf Wooller – and loss of form saw them end the season a pale shadow of the side that earlier on had dominated it.

The coin fell sunny side up for the visitors. The kindest way to describe the play was dour. Emrys Davies, dropped by the woody combination of Oakman off Oakes when on 38, occupied the crease for almost four stultifying hours for his 68 and this set the tone for the day. By lunch the score had crawled to 52/1 with one run coming in the 35 minutes leading up to the interval. Phil Clift spent 40 tortured minutes getting off the mark and his 33 took over two hours. By tea it had further advanced - if that is the right word – to 124/4 and only when the light began to deteriorate in the final session did anything of any real interest take place. As wickets tumbled around him the obdurate Wooller, Horatio-like, held firm. His 15 n/o took 90 minutes and he seemed cussedly impervious to an outbreak of slow-handclapping. The only ray of sunshine in an otherwise turgid display came from Jim Pleass who rattled up 30 in pretty rapid order. The Glamorgan innings was littered with men getting starts and then getting out but fortunately for Sussex their four man attack of Wood, Thomson, Oakman and James maintained a consistently high standard and were backed up throughout by top class ground fielding and catching. After almost 123 overs the crowd were no doubt relieved to see the back of their visitors for 239.

The early passages of play on the second morning went Glamorgan's way and at 89/5 the home innings was in some disarray against Don Shepherd and Allan Watkins. But then the captain stepped up to the plate in the most astonishing fashion. Having opened the innings and watched his side toil, Sheppard gave a one-man batting masterclass. Assisted in half-century stands by Suttle, Oakman and Thomson he single-handedly wrested the initiative away from Glamorgan with a stunning, unbeaten innings of 174 which was spread over a six hour 30 minutes canvas and included 27 boundaries. It was the highest score by a Sussex player on the ground since Ted Bowley's 176 against Warwickshire back in 1927 and was a classic example of innings-building which commenced with him happy simply to survive and ended with absolute domination over an 'attack now rendered almost powerless.' Proceedings were enlivened by several personal exchanges with the confrontational Wooller. Sheppard's marathon effort not only enabled him to declare at 305/7 but also to have a brief, unsuccessful dart at the opposition in the gathering gloom before stumps.

We will never know whether two such disparate spirits could have contrived a finish for the entire final day was lost to the infernal rain.

1954: Despite attendances being poor in 1953, Horsham was awarded two games for 1954. But whereas one of them was a county fixture – Derbyshire – the other was against Cambridge University.

For the fixture against the Light Blues, Sussex took the opportunity to blood four young professionals from their nursery. Skipper Hubert Doggart won the toss and took first knock on a wicket that looked full of runs. Smith and John Langridge put on 82 for the first wicket and this set the tone for the day. However the stand of the innings was between Langridge and Suttle, who added 131 for the 3rd wicket. Suttle's was by far the more attractive innings, his 92 taking less than three hours. Having been becalmed for more than 30 minutes on 99, Langridge duly reached what was to be his only 'ton' of the summer – but the 74th of a long and distinguished career - before being caught and bowled by Pretlove for 126. It took him 4 hours 30 minutes and although he never gave any chances his strokeplay was at times uncertain and it was by no stretch of the imagination a fluent innings. However, his adhesiveness did enable Doggart to declare at 322/5 and get Cambridge in for half an hour on the first evening. This brief passage of play was to prove disastrous for the visitors. The first wicket fell without a run on the board and at stumps their score stood at a sorry 10/3.

Heavy overnight rain did nothing to ease Light Blue concerns and the rout continued on the following morning. The only resistance of note came from Smith and the Singhalese all-rounder Goonesena. From an unpromising 49/6 these two added 53 courageous runs for the 7th wicket but it was only staving off the inevitable. Just before 4pm Cambridge were all out for a beggarly 126, Wood and Don Bates each picking up four wickets. Doggart invited the University to follow on. By tea they had reached 20/0 but rain – which had never been far away – prevented any further play.

The final day's play - witnessed among others by the veteran horror actor Boris Karloff – was a revelation. Pretlove, who was later to play for Kent, came in at No 6 and proceeded to bat throughout the remainder of the day (3 hours 30 minutes) for a dogged and unbeaten 115. Despite starting uncertainly he survived to bat with increasing assurance, striking 18 boundaries. He found stout allies down the order in the shape of first innings heroes Smith and Goonesena (52 n/o) who assisted in stands of 89 and 124 (unbroken) respectively. Such stoutness of heart enabled their side to save the game with unexpected ease as Sussex unavailingly tried eight bowlers.

By 1954 Derbyshire had emerged as one of the most dangerous sides in the Championship. Their batting may have been little better than okay but as with the great Derby sides of the 1930s, their success was founded on a formidable pace attack.

Under leaden skies Guy Willatt won the toss for the visitors and elected to bat. The early part of the Derby innings was dominated by their rugged opener Arnold Hamer who made a sparkling 81 out of 110. He received limited support from all-rounder Derek Morgan and wicketkeeper George Dawkes who put on 54 for the 6th wicket, but Sussex's keen and resourceful attack was not to be denied: 213 was as many as the Midlanders could muster as Thomson (4/57) and James (4/80) shared the spoils.

Rain considerably shortened proceedings on the second day but not before Derbyshire's much-vaunted seam attack took full advantage of a damp, green wicket that might have been produced with them in mind. Cliff Gladwin and Les Jackson were among the most feared opening attacks in the land and it wasn't long before they were knifing their way through a fragile Sussex line-up. John Langridge resisted in his stoical way for 40 but although six others made it into double figures none of them progressed past 20. In the circumstances, 148 was probably about par for the course as Gladwin, Jackson and Alwyne Eato (the latter described by Donald Carr as being 'on his day one of the quickest and most hostile bowlers I have seen') shared the spoils. But what goes round comes round. Although armed with a crucial first innings lead of 65, it wasn't long before Derbyshire were deep in the toils second time round. Hamer top scored (again) with 25 but Wood (4/23) took out the top order on the second evening and James (5/31) ran through the tail on the final morning to leave Derbyshire a dismal 85 all out.

Sussex thus required 151 for victory and had all the time in the world in which to do it. To the surprise of most among a painfully thin final day crowd Sussex saw off the new ball threat of Gladwin and Jackson but when these two were replaced by Eato and Morgan three wickets fell in rapid succession. The rout continued as 34/0 became 44/6 when Jackson and Gladwin took up the attack after the resumption. It was perhaps fitting that with the scoreboard showing a dolorous 74/9, Wood swung hard at his first ball from Gladwin and skied it high to third man where it was caught – perhaps fittingly – by Jackson. With a full two hours still on the clock it was all over. As the *County Times* somewhat lugubriously put it, 'All in all it was a terrible anti-climax and as if to really turn the knife in the Sussex wound, the sun came out and shone at its best for the first time during the week.'

It had been a miserable six days. Held to a frustrating draw in a meaningless game by an inexperienced and non-vintage University eleven and roundly thumped in a match that once again turned increasingly into a batsman's nightmare. The weather was poor and attendances, if anything, even worse. The writing really was on the wall.

1955: The New Year had opened ominously. A Horsham CC committee meeting in January heard that, 'There was a feeling among a number of the county cricket club to withdraw county cricket from Horsham and play the additional games at Hove.' In the event the axe didn't fall. Instead, Horsham was awarded another mixed week – a match against Northamptonshire being followed by a second successive visit from Cambridge University. Better still, Horsham CC spokesman Freddy Kensett was able to report that following a meeting he had had with the county secretary Colonel Grimston, 'it had been agreed that Horsham Week should continue until 1958.' As we shall see, this news was to have profound repercussions later on but for the present it was greeted with great delight.

With so much going on off the pitch it was a relief to be able to concentrate on events on it. Northants were destined to finish in 7th spot but on the back of the sensational Frank Tyson were to experience better things in the not-too-distant future. Indeed the main topic of conversation running up to the game locally was whether recent Ashes hero Tyson would play or not. ('Typhoon Tyson May Not Come' ran one headline with a mix of hope and disappointment). In the event he didn't, for the simple reason that he was blitzing South Africa to defeat in the first Test match with a 2nd innings 6/28.

Despite early rain an encouragingly large crowd of around 2,000 was on hand to witness Sussex take strike. Fortunately the wicket, although visibly drying, did not misbehave. The lanky Oakman took full advantage. Scoring freely right from the outset he had advanced to 89 by tea but hopes of a maiden century at Horsham were to be dashed. He became becalmed after the break and with only one run added attempted to sweep Tribe and was bowled. With support that could best be described as variable,

Suttle attempted to hold the second half of the innings together until Tribe clean bowled him for an invaluable 80. Yet again the master magician had woven his insidious web round the Sussex batsmen. Not content with his haul of 12-113 in 1952 his figures here were 7-69 in Sussex's 251 all out.

The second day was pretty dour stuff. Northants struggled throughout and the only batsman to play with any freedom was – who else – Tribe. Coming to the wicket with the scoreboard reading 53-4 he stuck to his post for a typically fighting 64 as team-mates came and went. He had difficulty with Marlar's off-breaks but when the end arrived the Northants score had reached 206. Mr Extras with 29 – 19 of them byes – was the next highest contributor as Marlar and Thomson picked up four wickets apiece. Fortified by their first innings lead of 48, Sussex had advanced cautiously to 23/0 second time round at the close of a dull, attritional sort of day.

Their progress on the final morning continued in 'steady as she goes' vein. Smith made 56, everybody else chipped in and Marlar's declaration on 179-5 invited the visitors to make 228 for victory. In the event it was the skipper himself who saw to it that they didn't do so. You sensed that he was itching to put himself on as Bates and James were given token spells only with the new ball. His instincts were correct. With Oakman playing second fiddle, Marlar's off-breaks were really beginning to bite and fizz. He worked his way through the Northants line-up pretty much as Tribe had done to Sussex on the first day. Only Barrick posed much of a threat. He made a dogged 64 to try to earn his side a draw but to no avail. With the score on 154 Marlar caught and bowled Keith Andrew to earn his side a gratifying victory, his own contribution being 7-53. One particularly nice touch was that Tribe and Northants' masseur Jack Jennings took time out to visit the Horsham Boys Club. They spent nearly two hours chatting to the lads and dads.

Sussex rang the changes against the Light Blues again giving opportunities to several younger players. Batting first their innings was all about Jim Parks. Coming in with the score on 35-2, he proceeded to flog what was in truth a pretty undemanding attack (Gamini Goonesena apart) all round the ground. Marlar eventually called a halt after 99 overs with his side's score standing at 361/7. A weary Parks remained unbeaten on 175 (one six and 23 fours), the second highest score ever made by a Sussex batsman on the ground at the time. But for the declaration there is no knowing how many he might have made. Yet as Parks recalled in his 1961 book *Runs In The Sun* he was in such poor form running up to the match that he 'decided the only way I could recover my touch was to hit myself out of trouble and make my shots without worrying about them. In brief, I went out to have a crack at the Cambridge bowlers'. Others played satellite-like innings around him and there were century stands with Foreman and Cox. Cambridge were wobbling at 35/2 by stumps on what had been a thoroughly entertaining day's cricket.

Marlar and his men didn't have things all their own way on the second day. The Light Blues dug in even if it did make for fairly turgid viewing. Parsons made 46, the hard-hitting Jamaican Vic Lumsden 47 and Swaranjit Singh 39 as their 232 all out spanned a mind-boggling 126.5 overs. Marlar took 5/89 against his *alma mater* and there were three wickets too for Parks who before picking up the wicket keeping gauntlets in earnest was a promising leg-spinner.

By stumps Sussex had progressed to 107-4, an overall lead of 236. It was obvious that the final day would bring a second declaration followed by either a chase or protracted rearguard action.

Marlar's declaration early on the final morning left Cambridge a victory target of 265 in roughly four hours, a pretty stiff ask. Barely 200 spectators were present to witness a fascinating day's play unfold. Cambridge shuffled their batting order around but the defining partnership was that for the 3rd wicket when the lanky Lumsden, in company with 'his dusky friend Goonesena', put on 94 in 75 minutes to completely transform a game that seemed to be heading nowhere. When Goonesena finally skied Bates to Marlar for a spirited 61 it brought to the crease 'another coloured man, S Singh, the bearded Indian who batted in a turban...who swiped at everything that came his way'. Lumsden finally perished for 90, a fine innings that included 13 boundaries. All this activity left them 30 minutes to get 32. To great rejoicing - in their ranks at least – they did so with four wickets and eight minutes to spare when Parsons lofted Marlar to the mid wicket boundary to round off a wonderful game of cricket.

1955 also marked the final appearance on the ground for umpire Frank Chester who first 'stood' at Horsham way back in 1925. Chester still holds the record for the number of appearances by an official (9).

1956: The New Year had opened quietly in the town. Presumably having decided that a change of image was needed, the Horsham Poultry and Rabbit Club changed its name to the Fur and Feather Society. But elsewhere locally the fur had already started to fly... Horsham CC actually knew as early as December 1955 that they were to lose their Cricket Week after the forthcoming season. The principal reason given in a letter from Keith Wilson at Sussex CCC to Dr Dew was a lack of support and consequential poor financial return. Also 'the fact that many Hove and Brighton members...had threatened to resign unless there were more fixtures on the Hove ground on which considerable sums of money had been spent in recent years'. Stan Parsons confirmed that all the meetings he had attended as Horsham area rep had left him in no doubt that 'there was a very large majority...definitely opposed to county cricket in Horsham.' Mr Parsons concluded gloomily that in his opinion, 'Horsham Week could be regarded as permanently lost.'

Reaction in the town (and beyond) was predictable – a rancorous and combustible mix of anger, incredulity, sadness and betrayal. Feelings ran high and many bitter words were written and spoken.

Some considered that in view of the clear breach of the 'four year deal' agreed with the county in 1955, the town should make no effort to support the 1956 Festival. Others took a contrary view – pull out all the stops and let Hove see what a ghastly and ill-judged mistake they had made.

In such a febrile atmosphere it was almost a relief to welcome the cricketers. Northamptonshire were paying their third visit to Cricket Field Road in five seasons while it wasn't that long since Warwickshire had been in town either. For the first time in their history Northants had a team that was capable of winning the Championship and were it not for the fact that also at their peak around this time was the awesome Surrey juggernaut under Surridge and May they might very well have done so. They were to finish 4th in 1956 (their best showing since 1913) and runners-up in 1957.

The crowd was disappointed to learn that on medical advice Frank Tyson would not after all be testing the fitness of his injured leg on Horsham's green-top. One assumes their disappointment was not wholly shared by the Sussex batsmen. The story is told how once in a match against Gloucestershire, fast-bowler George Lambert was sent out as night-watchman against Tyson in none too appetising light. He returned unbeaten, but shaking visibly at what he had just been through. A sympathetic team-mate lined up his pint of beer and added 'here's a whisky to go with it. The bugger will be fresher in the morning!' Tyson did eventually make it to Horsham – but not to play. He presented a well-attended cricket film show at the Black Horse Hotel in March 1960.

Sad to relate, even the weather had it in for poor old Horsham in 1956. On what was traditionally the best day of the week financially it rained with a cruel intensity. More in hope than expectation the players took an early lunch but to no avail. Play was abandoned for the day in mid-afternoon.

In what was now a two-day match, Northants won the all-important toss and had little hesitation in inviting Sussex to take first look at a green, rapidly-drying wicket. It was clear that the batsmen were in for a difficult time of it. Opening bowlers Kelleher and Clarke were given a desultory two overs each before first Jack Manning and then Sussex's old nemesis George Tribe were introduced into the attack. It wasn't long either before wickets started to tumble. The only stand of any substance was that for the 3rd wicket between Smith and Parks. With firm shots in front of the wicket these two put on 55 in 50 minutes though neither really got on top of the bowling. With the exception of Marlar who, coming in at No 10, mowed his way in true rustic fashion at Manning's expense for 26, the remainder was a procession – 'a case of experienced bowlers using a hostile pitch to trundle out inexperienced batsmen.' It's difficult to really argue with this for 125 was as many as Sussex could muster, Manning picking up 6/73 and Tribe 3/28.

When Northants took up the challenge part way through the afternoon session they found it equally tough going against Marlar, Oakman and Smith. But these three didn't pose quite the same threat as Manning and Tribe; and Northants' batting had a bit more about it than Sussex's. That said there was little in it until the final hour when Manning whacked three sixes out of nowhere in a breezy but invaluable 36 that helped steer his side to 186/7 at stumps. Earlier in the innings it was a case of steady, dogged progress, with the other two Australians to the fore. Livingston top scored with 37 while Tribe – so often a thorn in Sussex's side with bat as well as ball – struck 33 as 90 runs came in the final hour's play.

Despite only having a 61-run lead Northants skipper Dennis Brookes decided there was no point in hanging about. Recalling the vulnerability of Sussex's soft underbelly he declared at his overnight total and put his hosts back in. The Sussex second innings was a rout from start to finish. Only Oakman (29) hung around for any length of time. He used his enormous reach to smother the spin for 90 dogged minutes but was the only man to make double figures as the two Australian left-arm spinners again exploited Sussex's collective lack of technique under what were clearly very trying circumstances. With Webb absent through injury, a pitiable 63 all out in 30.4 overs was as many as they could muster, Manning leading the way with 4/20. This wretched showing left Northants only needing three runs to win. Kelleher and Andrew – Nos 9 & 10 in the first innings – were sent in against the bowling of Suttle - who promptly added to the irony by trapping the former lbw. What Horsham had desperately needed was three run-filled days of joyous, sun-kissed cricket: what it got was a damp, bowler-dominated mismatch that was all over in four sessions. Jack Manning was faster and more accurate than his compatriot Tribe – indeed was referred to as the foil to Tribe's rapier.

And so to the Via Doloroso – the final, sorrowful act in Horsham's 48-year, 70-match county odyssey. The visitors were Warwickshire who were to experience a similar season to their hosts. They never really recovered from six defeats in their first nine matches and were to slip from 9th spot in 1955 to 14th this term. In a rain-ruined summer their batting simply wasn't up to it. Their opening attack of Jack Bannister and Roly Thompson was decent enough but - veteran spinner Eric Hollies apart - the support was variable.

Robin Marlar won the toss and – no doubt with some of his fingers crossed - elected to bat. Against both an attack and a pitch that demanded close attention Sussex employed a watchful approach. Foreman seemed better able than most at picking the ball to hit and just after he had reached a hard-won 50 celebrated by straight-driving Hollies for three lofted boundaries. His 3 hour 30 minute vigil ended on 65 when he tried to hit Hollies over the top once too often. Thereafter only Suttle looked at all confident. His bright 45 enabled his side to top 200 – just – as Thompson (5/26) gained some cheap late wickets by way of reward for his skill and industry earlier in the day. He polished things off in pretty rapid order, his last four wickets only costing two runs.

Thanks largely to a 3rd wicket partnership of 79 between Bert Wolton and the clean-hitting Alan Townsend, Warwicks' score at one point on the second morning stood at 109/2 but Marlar worked his way steadily through the remainder. Although the veteran wicket keeper Dick Spooner resisted for an hour for 42 Sussex just managed to claim first innings points as their visitors were shown the door for 194 (in 110 overs!), Marlar returning 5/35. It was now essentially a one innings game.

Enter Roly Thompson. He had wrapped up the Sussex first innings by dismissing Manville and James with successive deliveries and duly completed his hat-trick by having Smith caught off his first ball second time round. Nor was this the end. For good measure he saw off Foreman and Parks – both lbw – in his second over as the home side crashed to 5/3 and had thus taken five wickets in 15 balls spread over two innings'. There was no way back. A beggarly 81 all out was as many as Sussex could put together as Thompson and Bannister took their collective match haul to 14-115.

It was all over before lunch on the final day - yet Warwickshire's efforts to chase down 89 were by no means straightforward. Indeed at 19/4 (one of the four being New Zealander Ray Hitchcock who thus completed a 'pair') the match was in the balance and without a sterling unbeaten 53 from Wolton, Sussex might even have pulled off a shock win. *Wisden* called his a 'masterly' innings 'on a pitch from which the ball came at varying heights.' The varied bounce didn't seem too insuperable a problem for umpires Fred Price and Paddy Corrall – ex-wicket keepers both – who dished out 11 lbws more or less even-handedly.

In his 1990 county history, paceman Jack Bannister penned an amusing account of the match: *Thompson also did the hat-trick...in a rare Warwickshire victory which was notable for two incidents in the second innings. In a much-shuffled batting order following the early-season traumas, Horner was asked to bat lower down, but so badly affected was the opener by having to wait, that captain Hollies decided to quieten the nerves with a large brandy. It made little difference when, with only 89 needed to win, the super-charged Horner went in with his side in trouble and apparently ran out Wolton, who looked to be the last hope. Wolton was called for an impossible single, and was well out of his ground when the Sussex wicket-keeper triumphantly claimed the run-out, which was promptly given by umpire Fred Price. Only then was it noticed that the home keeper had missed the stumps with his gloves, and a relieved Wolton was recalled to score an unbeaten 53...to steer his side home...As Hollies said in the nail-biting last few overs: "I reckon I shall need the brandy soon.*

The Horsham week died bravely. Over 1,000 spectators paid at the gate on each of the three full days play – not brilliant perhaps but an improvement on 1955, particularly as they had to 'put up at times with appallingly slow cricket.' The lunch and beer tents did brisk business and the ground 'had a comfortably filled look that belied the fact that after 48 years the Horsham week was at its last (Hove-decreed) gasp.' If it didn't exactly end with a bang, 'at least it (did) not end with a whimper' either. The largest attendance – 1,419 – came on the opening day of the Warwickshire match; the smallest (240) - perhaps predictably - on the last, when hostilities were all over by lunchtime. Overall attendance was a symmetrical 4,444.

And with this the light of county cricket was snuffed out in Horsham for a generation and darkness descended upon the land. It was to be 16 long years before a full Sussex side appeared at Cricket Field Road again and 27 years before the next Championship match was staged there. The locals hungered and thirsted but the world knew them not...

Chapter 7
INTERMEZZO: 1971-1982

Prelude

Most wounds heal with time. The rapprochement between town and county was complete by 1970 yet although there was a fixture against Cambridge University in 1971 it is difficult to discern any logical pattern to Sussex's dealings with Horsham during this period. An inaugural John Player Sunday League match in 1971 was a runaway success and should have paved the way for another in 1972 - to be followed perhaps by early restitution of Championship cricket. Instead the town was inexplicably ignored in 1972 and 1973, given another – relatively meaningless in commercial terms - University match in 1974, and then nothing at all until 1978, when there was another John Player match.

In three-day terms there was a five-year gap between the Oxford University match in 1974 and another, one-off fixture in 1979 against the emerging Sri Lankans. More silent years followed until the town was finally awarded a Championship match in 1983. Thankfully, this proved to be a permanent arrangement that has continued – more or less – through to the present day. In fairness to the county their initial reticence may have been attributable in part to Horsham CC itself not being in a position to stage a three-day match. By common consent, the wicket was good enough, but the changing facilities etc were not. A key factor in the decision to return was the completion in the mid-1970s of the changing room block and re-siting of the bar area. These works were part-financed by a grant from Sport England and part from the sale of a building plot in Cricket Field Road.

Time to look quickly at this trio of one-off, three-day matches.

1971: The Light Blues in 1971 had some pretty decent players. Their captain Majid Khan was among the most beautiful and gifted strokeplayers ever to come out of Pakistan – referred to by one noted commentator as 'Dignified, intelligent and amiably sleepy'. Nevertheless, he averaged almost 40 from his 63 Tests and enjoyed a highly successful county career with Glamorgan, against whom he once hit five 6s in an over. Dudley Owen-Thomas was a punchy middle order bat who played for Surrey between 1970 and 1975, while Philippe Edmonds and Mike Selvey were both to enjoy lengthy county careers with Middlesex. Both went on to play for England. Opening the bowling with Selvey was John Spencer, a medium-pacer who had already embarked on a lengthy career with Sussex.

Bill Ford had gone out of his way to ensure 'that the ground and pitch are looking as well as they have ever been'. The match saw a memorable performance from Sussex's 42-year-old left-hander Kenny Suttle, now in his 22nd and final season of county cricket but who was being treated most shabbily by the county. In what was only his second match of the season he completed a century in each innings, the first – and to date only - man ever to do so on the ground.

Sussex batted and declared at 299/9. Suttle's first century came in 4 hours 30 minutes and was a study in concentration, technique and effort. He reached 112 before being bowled by Majid and was assisted in a stand of 157 for the 3rd wicket by another nuggety left-hander Peter Graves who helped himself to 76. John Denman hit a spirited 42 down the order as Spencer impressed with 4/49.

Nothing daunted, Cambridge led off with a stand of 140 with the graceful Majid caressing his way to 92 before falling – of all people – to Suttle. His opening partner Michael Barford was less certain but stuck it out gamely. He was within five of his century before being dismissed by Horsham CC's slow left-armer Mark (Rocky) Upton, his only first-class wicket. Owen-Thomas at No 3 weighed in with a belligerent half-century as Majid declared 27 behind on 272/4. He was clearly throwing down a final-day declaration gauntlet to Sussex skipper Mike Griffith.

Sussex made 231/5 second time round. Suttle registered 120 this time before again falling to Majid's under-utilised flat, curling off-spinners. He and Jerry Morley put on 149 for the 2nd wicket, Morley making an even 50 in what was his maiden first-class appearance. The busy Suttle cut, drove and swept in his very best style to record his 48th First-Class century.

Griffith's declaration challenged the Light Blues to make 259 in just over three hours. This was a tall order but took into account that he was without his main strike bowler John Snow who injured his back after bowling just six overs in the first innings. In the event the declaration couldn't have been better timed. Danger man Majid fell early on but this allowed Barford (84) and the enterprising Owen-Thomas (89) to come together in a 2nd wicket stand of 145 that tilted the match Cambridge's way. Wickets then started to topple but Edmonds and Spencer held their nerve to guide their side to victory off the third ball of the final over. Although Sussex had rested a number of key players including Parks, Greig, Joshi and Buss it had been a great game of cricket and just the boost Cambridge were looking for on the eve of the University match. To cap it all the wicket was described variously as 'a triumph'; and attracted 'much favourable comment'.

1974: Sussex returned to three-day action at Cricket Field Road three years later against Oxford University who were 'billeted' for the duration at Christ's Hospital. Oxford had not been seen in the town since 1912. The Dark Blues side of 1974 was not an especially distinguished crop. Medium-pacer Tim Lamb was to enjoy moderate success on the field with Middlesex, Northants and Durham but as chief executive of the Test & County Cricket Board between 1996 and 2004 was to become a major player off it. Unlike their Cambridge compatriots three years previously there were no other top-flight cricketers aboard with the exception of their captain, who was a host in himself. Imran Khan was to enjoy a lengthy career with Sussex but was already a player touched by greatness – indeed many would argue his case for being the most talented cricketer ever produced by Pakistan. At his peak he was among the quickest and most hostile bowlers in the world, a dashing middle-order bat, charismatic leader and so good-looking it made you sick. He has since overcome this latter handicap to become a politician of some standing in his home country.

Against a below-strength home side captained by Tony Buss the Dark Blues batted first and could hardly have got off to a worse start, with both openers back in the pavilion and not a run on the board. No 5 Peter Thackeray stuck around as the descent into chaos continued. At 20/7 he found an ally in David Fursdon who top scored with 23 in an 8th wicket stand of 31. Thackeray was last out for a dogged 17 as his side were put out of their misery in the 45th over for 71 (five wickets for dibbly-dobbly medium-pacer Paul Phillipson). Trying to be charitable it may be that part of the blame could be laid at the door of an abnormally high wind which enabled the Sussex pace attack to swing the ball around at will.

Sussex's reply hardly pulled up any trees either. Opener Geoff Greenidge anchored proceedings with 51 while coming in at No 7 Nicky Wisdom (son of comedian Norman) contributed a useful unbeaten 31 on his first senior outing. In fairness their innings was thrown out of gear by an injury to opener Mike Buss which meant he was unable to bat at all. In the context of the game 181 all out was a reasonable effort.

Oxford made a slightly better fist of things second time round but as with Sussex, their batting was uneven. Opener Trevor Glover made 38 while Thackeray again showed to advantage with a solid, defensive half-century. However, 169 was as many as they could muster and it took them an excruciating 122.5 overs in which to do it. Such mind-bogglingly turgid fare must have numbed the sensibilities of even the most stoical among the sprinkling of spectators who at least had the consolation of not having had to pay to watch such dreadful stuff. The damage was done by Sussex's two slow bowlers: left-armer Chris Waller picked up 5/69 from a marathon 50.5 overs while Barclay's off breaks secured 3/41 from 31.

This monument to tedium left Sussex requiring a mere 60 to win and although three wickets were lost getting there the result was never in question. It would have done little for the Dark Blues' confidence on the eve of the Varsity match and with 481 runs scored in over 280 overs, even less for the cause of brighter cricket. Eminently forgettable...

1979: Sussex's next outing at Horsham was against the Sri Lankan tourists. Back in 1979 Sri Lanka had not been accorded full Test status – that was to follow in 1982 – and were in England primarily for the inaugural ICC Trophy, a 60-over competition involving 15 of the best non-Test playing nations from all over the world. In the event Sri Lanka were to lift the trophy, defeating Canada in a high-scoring final at Worcester. They were a fluent, attractive side whose batting and spin bowling were generally held to be up to Test standard but who were a little light in the pace bowling department. Given their clear aspiration to achieve full ICC membership it was disappointing that the tour – which included several county games - was given so little advance publicity.

There was no charge for admission and a fair sized crowd – estimated at over 1,000 for each of the three days - came along, clearly intrigued at the prospect of seeing a bright, emerging, national side in action. To their credit Sussex (with the exception of Imran) turned out a full strength side. Play got under way late on the first morning because of an overnight storm with Sri Lankan captain Annura Tennekoon winning the toss and inviting Sussex to bat. As predicted it wasn't long before the two spinners, DS and GRA de Silva, were in action. The only stand worth talking about was one of 72 for the 5th wicket between Paul Parker and Peter Graves as the two de Silvas bowled their hosts out for a modest 180.

Sri Lanka's reply was something of a curate's egg. The talented Roy Dias top scored with 51 and was given excellent support by Dilip Mendis in a 3rd wicket stand of 83. In one particularly thrilling passage of play, Dias thrashed an increasingly exasperated Geoff Arnold for four 4s in one over. The middle order then collapsed against Barclay's gentle off-spin (6-61) but the tail wagged vigorously and they eventually led their hosts on first-innings by 68. There was no respite for Barclay for within minutes he and the South African left-hander Kepler Wessels were out in the middle again. The two de Silvas were again wheeled into action after a token few overs with the new ball. Over the years, Wessels has acquired the reputation of being a dour, rugged sort of player, but on the second evening here he celebrated his recent wedding by caning the Sri Lankan attack all round the ground, making 66 out of an opening stand of 91. At stumps, Sussex were 106/2, an overall lead of 38. Much would depend on events in the first session the next day.

Initially, things went very much Sri Lanka's way as Sussex lost two early wickets, but they had reckoned without the obdurate Barclay. He and Parker stopped the rot as the two de Silvas – who were to bowl 86 of the 99 overs sent down by their side – began to flag. 'The Trout' received solid support all the way down the order and on reaching his century, promptly declared. His 102 was a valuable if laborious effort, which spanned 5 hours 30 minutes. DS de Silva's match figures of 10-188 are of interest only in that it was the last time an opposition bowler has taken 10 or more wickets in a match on the ground.

The declaration gave Sri Lanka no time in which to mount a real victory challenge. Wettimuny and Tennekoon put on 85 for the first wicket, profiting from a few undemanding overs from Javed Miandad and Parker, before both sides shook hands on a draw with 10 overs left and 110 still needed.

Despite the unsatisfactory outcome the *County Times* considered the fixture 'a blazing success' with 'both the bar and refreshment stalls...severely tested' by an appreciative crowd. The tourists may still not have beaten a county but they certainly won the hearts of many by their friendly and approachable manner. *Wisden* was even more effusive. Having mentioned how the Sri Lankan spinners 'fascinated us with their Eastern brand of bowling magic' and commenting how 'When battle was done, they went willingly to the nets at one end of this picturesque ground where Dr John Dew...had a band of keen youngsters anxious to have a close-up of this rare spinning science...not so long ago Parker was one of his keenest young hopefuls.' It was clearly a warm-hearted and thoroughly enjoyable occasion and would have done nothing to damage Horsham's aspiration to stage Championship cricket once again.

But where was all this leading? By the early 1980s Horsham had been without Championship cricket for 26 years. Were a handful of John Player matches and an assortment of one-off friendlies, however successful, really sufficient to persuade the hard-nosed power brokers at Hove to restore their Festival?

Chapter 8
RESTORATION TO MILLENNIUM: 1983-1996

1983: With Championship cricket returning to the town for the first time in 26 years, even the weather looked benevolently down on the Festival and it was fitting that Sussex captain John Barclay had strong local connections. Lancashire celebrated their first visit to Horsham since 1948 by winning the toss and declaring on 312/6. This owed much to an exhilarating 3rd wicket stand of 150 in less than even time between Frank Hayes and David Lloyd. The flaxen-haired Hayes was a graceful but enigmatic stroke player and his dazzling 149 included two 6s and 21 4s. In reply Sussex lost three cheap wickets on the first evening and their melancholia continue on the second morning until some late order resilience from Garth le Roux, Tony Pigott and 20-year-old Dermot Reeve lifted them from an anaemic 92/7 to 230. Medium-pacer Mike Watkinson caught the eye with six wickets. At the close the Red Rose was teetering uncertainly on 52/4, an overall lead of 134. The final day dawned fair and promised to be one of rich promise. And so it proved. Lancashire slipped initially to 82/7 but recovered to 172 all out, Pigott taking five wickets. This left Sussex 125 minutes plus 20 overs to make 255. Sadly, Colin Wells became the last Sussex player to date to complete a 'pair' and at 92/5 all hope seemed to have evaporated for the home side. Then in yet another twist, Paul Parker and le Roux came together in a lusty stand of 75 for the 6th wicket in only 40 minutes. Thoughts of an improbable Sussex victory were revived only to be dashed again when Parker was caught on the square leg boundary for 75. With only a draw to play for Reeve was adjudged lbw to the comfortably built off spinner 'Flat' Jack Simmons with only five overs remaining.

1984: Festival Week coincided with the controversial opening of an £8m Marks & Spencer store in Swan Walk – controversial in that it necessitated the demolition of the much-loved Capitol Theatre, a building woven deep in the Festival fabric. Sussex made hay on the opening day. There were centuries from opener Gehan Mendis (107) and Colin Wells, who atoned for his pair in 1983 with a flamboyant 127. Wells had made a double-century the previous week at Hove so was clearly in good nick and his innings here included 15 4s and four 6s. He and a more sedate Parker put on 200 for the 4th wicket in 158 minutes. Ironically Wells almost missed the match, having been hit in the eye by le Roux when warming up. Such enterprise enabled Barclay to declare on 358/4 before close on the opening day. Visitors Northants would have been seriously disappointed with their 200 all out (wickets here for Reeve and Barclay) and followed-on. The slide continued and they closed the second day on 59/3. There was no miraculous reprieve on the final morning. None of their side made 50 in either innings and on a wicket offering only modest turn their feeble 178 all out only asked Sussex to make 21.

1985: Sussex arrived at Horsham fresh from a most curious game at Hove. Having rattled up 303/5 declared they brushed Glamorgan aside for 58 and re-inserted them. This time the visitors made 447, setting a slightly surprised home side 206 for victory – which they promptly knocked off for the loss of one wicket in 39 overs. Visitors Surrey hadn't been seen at Horsham since 1939 and were expected to be made of sterner stuff. Both sides were led by stand-in skippers, Ian Gould and Trevor Jesty. Despite losing Mendis to the second ball of the game Sussex batted with great verve to declare on 391/7 after 94 overs. On his home ground Parker led the way with a fluent 107, reaching his century in the grand manner with a straight six. His stand of 187 with Allan Green was a new Sussex record for the 2nd wicket on the ground. Green made 90 and there were half centuries for Gould and Colin Wells. Forty runs were plundered from the final four overs as they accelerated towards a declaration. By stumps a demoralised Surrey had slumped to 37/3. They rallied strongly to 270 all out with Jesty unfortunate to fall to a stunning catch by Parker when on 99. Mendis and Green led off with 68 in eight overs second time round and having just missed out in the first innings, Green had reached a richly deserved century by stumps on the second evening. Still scoring at will, Sussex's pre-lunch declaration challenged Surrey to make 402 in 84 overs. The exuberant Monte Lynch (61 n/o) set out his stall but with Surrey's reply on 153/3 and 48 overs remaining, a familiar pantomime villain – sluicing rain – then put in an unwelcome appearance.

1986: Expectation was running high in the town at the prospect of Somerset's visit. Not only hadn't they been seen at Horsham since 1951, they also boasted three of the greatest draw-cards in the modern game in the forms of Joel Garner, Ian Botham and Viv Richards. However, the clerk of the weather was no respecter of persons. Relentless driving rain on the first and third days and an over-cautious approach by umpire Don Oslear on the second meant that for the one and only time at the Festival not a ball was bowled. It clearly wasn't meant to be for these two sides for the return fixture at Taunton was also ruined by the weather with only one of the four innings being completed.

1987: Arctic conditions welcomed neighbouring Hampshire to Cricket Field Road for the first time since 1952. They were one of the strongest batting sides in the country and Sussex – whose attack was among the weakest – were unable to prevent them declaring at 307/5. Skipper Mark Nicholas top-scored with an assured 147, his first century in two seasons. In bleak, cheerless conditions, West Indian fast bowler Malcolm Marshall was the last man one would choose to face. With the weather closing in, Sussex struggled for survival on the second day. Against a backdrop of howling winds, thunder and lightning, they had limped painfully to 79/4 from 45 overs when the heavens opened. For the second season in succession the weather had ruined the Festival. Just for good measure the return match at Portsmouth was also ruined by rain.

1988: Two mediocre sides were on show in 1988 and as so often happens they served up a thriller. Derbyshire, who last visited the town in 1954, were undeniably poor but Sussex if anything were even worse. A rain-affected opening day saw Sussex close on 247/6, Rehan Alikhan and Neil Lenham both making half-centuries, Alikhan's painstaking effort spanning more than four hours. Devon Malcolm (5/51) blew the home tail away on the following morning but in a curate's egg of an innings, Derbyshire replied with 250, a deficit of 22. Sussex's batting second time round was even more feeble – 155 all out with only Parker and Pigott earning plus marks. Allan Green 'enjoyed' the unusual distinction of being out first ball in each innings yet didn't record a king pair (he was run out second time round attempting a second run). All this left Derbyshire 50 overs in which to make

178. John Morris' 71 (highest innings in the entire match) put them in the box seat and at 162/6 the game seemed to be heading their way. At 170/9 however, the advantage was just with Sussex. The score stood at 176 when the final over was entrusted to Pigott. With five balls gone only two runs had accrued and Raj Sharma was on strike. He swung hard and the crowd howled with disbelief as the ball whistled through Green at slip for the fateful two runs.

1989: One important piece of transport infrastructure for visitors to the ground by road was Horsham's splendid northern bypass, newly opened just weeks before the match. The visitors couldn't have been more formidable - Essex, paying their first visit to the town since 1950. Led by Graham Gooch they were a powerful and well balanced side at the peak of their powers. On paper they carried far too many guns for a very average Sussex side. It was something of a shock when acting skipper Colin Wells asked them to bat and even more of one when they were skittled out at teatime for 185, Tony Dodemaide and Wells himself each picking up four wickets. Led by Ian Gould and David Smith, Sussex batted gamely to take a first innings lead of 100. At 76/4 Essex continued to toil but at last showed their true character on the final morning. Reserve wicket keeper Mike Garnham (90) and Derek Pringle (81) took the game completely away from Sussex with an unbroken stand of 174 in 112 minutes and a declaration then challenged Sussex to make 251 in a minimum of 50 overs. To their credit they went for it. Despite having to retire hurt when hit on the thumb early on, Smith made 71 and there were useful contributions from Alan Wells and Pigott. With five overs to go, 32 were needed with five wickets in hand but from 225/5 they collapsed with numbing rapidity to 240/9. In yet another twist the last-wicket pair of Ian Salisbury and Andy Babington survived the final 11 deliveries to earn their side a richly deserved draw in yet another compelling game.

1990: Draw specialists Lancashire were in town again in 1990 to try conclusions with a deeply troubled Sussex side destined to finish bottom of the Championship. The home side arrived fresh from having conceded 500 runs to Somerset at Taunton. With Parker again unfit, stand-in skipper Colin Wells would have been disappointed with 235 all out. Eight men made double figures, all ten wickets fell to catches and Dodemaide top scored with a grinding 70. Despite a characteristically watchful half-century from Mike Atherton and a more breezy one from Mike Watkinson, Lancashire had slipped to 224/8. Paul Allott then assisted Graeme Fowler (batting at No. 9 because of an injury sustained while fielding) in a 9th wicket stand of 100, a ground record. The persistent Dodemaide took 6/106. Trailing by 89 Sussex started brightly on the second evening but fell apart in sepulchral light the following morning to Phillip de Freitas and the fearsome West Indian Patrick Patterson. On a wicket of increasingly variable bounce they batted apprehensively, collapsing from 57/1 overnight to 108 all out, their lowest score of the season. Lancashire spent only five overs making the 22 needed for victory (Atherton 0 n/o).

1991: The powerful Essex side rolled into town again in 1991. They had finished Championship runners-up in 1990 and were to go one better this season, their fifth title in 13 seasons. Rain stalked the early stages of the match but Essex escaped from 73/5 to post 303/7 thanks in the main to a cleanly-struck and uncomplicated century from stand-in skipper Neil Foster, better known as a high-quality opening bowler. Alastair Fraser (younger brother of Test opener Angus) contributed a half-century to an unbeaten 8th wicket stand of 130, a record against Sussex on the ground. At one point Foster flayed local fast bowler Adrian Jones – who ended with a chastening 2/110 off 18 overs - for 30 in three overs. A despondent Sussex started confidently (Lenham 60), then collapsed and had just averted the follow-on before that old nemesis rain swept across the ground and washed away the final day. It was probably just as well...

1992: A little bit of history was made in 1992 with Championship newcomers Durham the visitors. It was a steep learning curve for the new boys and despite the presence of old hands such as Ian Botham and former Sussex favourite Paul Parker, the wooden spoon awaited. Following a troubled close-season Sussex arrived fresh from a humiliating 10 wicket defeat at the hands of Leicestershire. Rain ruined the first day but not before Parker rekindled memories of happier times when taking four boundaries off five balls from Jones. Durham declared late on the second afternoon on 303/8. Sussex started catastrophically, losing two wickets in the second over but with so much time lost to the elements it was always going to be a contrived match. They duly declared on 151/4 (Jamie Hall 81 n/o). Australia's Dean Jones then struck a powerful 89 as Durham rattled up 170/3 in only 35 overs (the luckless Adrian Jones conceding 72 from nine torrid overs). A third declaration challenged Sussex to make 340 in 65 overs. It was difficult to tell initially what their intentions were. Their early batsmen meandered along, provoking slow handclapping from a bemused crowd. Suddenly they exploded into action and it positively rained runs. Lenham anchored matters with a patient 118 while there were more spectacular contributions from Smith (67) and Martin Speight whose 49 included four sixes. Alan Wells and Franklyn Stephenson then smashed a further 75 in rapid order, including 18 off one over from David Graveney. Wells' 65 only took 37 balls. Eighteen were required off two overs, twelve off one. Channel Four TV pundit Simon Hughes was entrusted with it. Stephenson hit a towering six off the third ball and scooped the last one just out of reach of Briers for the winning runs as Graveney conceded 121 runs from 18 overs. A rueful Durham might have disagreed but despite the contrivances it was a wonderful advert for the modern game.

1993: Sussex and Leicestershire (who were visiting Cricket Field Road for the first time since 1930) were both destined to finish in mid-table. The home side arrived at Horsham on the back of a 10-wicket hiding from Surrey at Hove; and straight after it lost by an innings to Middlesex at Lord's. But as we shall see there was to be some interesting meat in the middle of this otherwise unappetising sandwich. The match was scheduled for four days, the first fixture of this duration to be played on the ground. It was also due to open on 20 May, the earliest start-date ever for a game at Horsham. But that old nemesis, rain, struck yet again and the whole of the first day was washed out. Despite the terrific soaking the ground had taken the pitch played well and a disappointingly thin crowd saw Sussex proceed in fits and starts. Alan Wells top scored with 78 as the innings closed on 271. Everybody except Nos. 10 and 11 made it into double figures as Foxes wicket keeper Paul Nixon held five catches. At stumps Leicester had progressed to 57/3 and the match was interestingly poised. It is difficult to account adequately for what happened next. In 79 minutes on the following morning the innings was all over, Leicester mustering just 97. It was a shockingly inept effort, even though the Sussex close catching touched the confines of brilliance. Stephenson took 4/45 and Eddie Hemmings 5/27 as eight men were caught and the other two stumped by Peter Moores. Disturbingly for Leicester, Hemmings – operating from the town end - was making increasing use of the rough created outside off-stump by visiting left-arm paceman Alan Mullally. Wells promptly sent Leicester back in - and their misery continued. At lunch Boon and Briers were already back in the pavilion with only 15 on the board. Afterwards Hemmings proved too much for his increasingly demoralised opponents. Their batting broke down totally and at 40/9 the lowest opposition score on the ground (Leicestershire's 51 all out in 1924) looked in very real danger. However, in the strangest twist yet, No 11 Mullally smote Hemmings for 18 in an over that contained two 6s. But, a mere 90 minutes into the afternoon session, it was all over. Leicester's two-innings total of 169 was the lowest ever made by a visiting side on the ground. Seventeen wickets had fallen on the day for 112 runs, but to their credit, Leicester cricket manager Jack Birkenshaw had no complaints. As he watched his charges fall to a third consecutive defeat he said they had simply batted badly. 'With stunning ineptitude' would be nearer the mark as the wicket was only ever helpful rather than treacherous. Hemmings wasn't fussed either way: the downy old bird adjusted his knee support and rolled gently back to the pavilion with 7/31 in the innings, 11 wickets in the day and 12/58 in the match, the best match return by a Sussex bowler on the ground since old George Cox's famous 17-wicket haul against Warwickshire back in 1926.

1994: Lancashire were playing their third visit to Horsham in 12 years and boasted one of the most powerful batting lineups in the land. For the most part Sussex's progress on a superb batting track was pedestrian yet this was transformed by the popular West Indian Franklyn Stephenson. He and Paul Jarvis put on 107 for the 7th wicket in better than even time and his century enabled Sussex to post 355. The crowd were particularly entertained by the rough treatment he meted out to world-class Pakistani all-rounder Wasim Akram. Clearly on a roll, Stephenson then bowled England captain Mike Atherton with his second delivery. Ed Giddins burst into life with four wickets in three overs as Lancashire slumped to

171/9 – only for skipper Mike Watkinson and No. 11 Peter Martin to put on 115 in two hours for the last wicket, Giddins ending with 5/81. Fortified by a healthy first innings lead, Lenham batted with rare freedom, blasting an off-colour Wasim for 20 in an over in the course of a lively century. He and Alan Wells put on 122 for the 3rd wicket before Speight and Moores rubbed further salt into the Red Rose's wounds. Joining in the fun, Stephenson hit Gary Yates for three sixes as the young spinner conceded over 100 runs for the second time in the match. Sussex's declaration left Lancashire the whole of the final day to make the little matter of 451. At tea they had reached 219/5 with little hint of what lay in store. The tall, left-handed Wasim, looking perhaps to atone for a first innings duck and lacklustre showing with the ball, then launched a sustained and withering assault on the Sussex attack that was to last long in the memory of those privileged to witness it. With the game seemingly going nowhere (141 wanted in 19 overs), he was rampaging along at 20 an over against spinners Salisbury and Hemmings. In 74 glorious minutes he struck 10 4s and no fewer than eight majestic 6s before being yorked by Hemmings when on 98. His innings had only lasted for 76 balls as his side fell a gallant 60 runs short. It was astonishing stuff even if some more cautious minded souls felt Lancashire should have settled for the draw. Horsham's first streaker only added to the entertainment.

1995: For both Sussex and visitors Surrey 1995 was to prove a disappointing campaign. With the talent available to both sides, their lowly Championship finishes must have been doubly frustrating. The ball swung around extravagantly from the off but at 116/3 Surrey must have thought they were through the worst. Jason Lewry then took three wickets in four balls as the visitors imploded to 139/9, only for Graham Kersey and Australian fast bowler Carl Rackemann to add 48 improbable runs in 21 riotous minutes, Kersey plundering 19 from one Giddins over. Nevertheless, 187 was a poor effort as Giddins and Lewry picked up four wickets apiece. Sussex took a first innings lead of 117, which at 193/2 should perhaps have been more. The highlight was a century stand for the 3rd wicket in better than even time from Alan Wells and Keith Newell. Second time round, Surrey's England Test stars Alec Stewart and Graham Thorpe combined in an exhilarating stand of 243 (in only 51 overs), the highest 3rd wicket partnership on the ground. Thorpe was finally bowled for 110 having a weary swipe at Lewry but Stewart went on to make 150 with one six and 23 fours. The explosive Alistair Brown was the last man a tired Sussex attack would have wished to see late in the day and he duly obliged with three enormous sixes off the spinners. Over 500 runs had been scored on the second day – which was 500 more than on the third as rain yet again put in an unwelcome appearance. Surrey accelerated towards a declaration on the final morning and their 501/9 was the highest score seen on the ground since 1927. Such enterprise challenged Sussex to make 385 off a minimum of 79 overs. Lenham and Hall led off with a run-a-minute opening stand of 128 against an innocuous attack but in an heroic 40 minute spell after tea Rackemann was virtually unplayable, taking five wickets for seven runs in six overs. Advantage Surrey, particularly with the prospect of Giddins and Lewry having to negotiate 21 deliveries for the draw. But negotiate them they did in yet another thrilling Horsham finale. Despite allegations of 'turning playing and missing into an art form', Lewry's unbeaten 11 spanned 100 minutes as the gallant Rackemann finished with 6/60.

1996: One long-standing omission was about to be rectified. Only two sides – Yorkshire and Middlesex - had never visited Horsham and the latter were the appointed visitors for 1996. Middlesex were alarmingly inconsistent while Sussex arrived fresh from a truly abject display against Warwickshire at Hove where they conceded 645/7 to lose by an innings and plenty. Slashing rain washed out the first day and the hosts ended a frustrating second on 216/3 thanks largely to a 3rd wicket stand of 150 between Bill Athey (77) and Alan Wells (92). With the third day also falling foul of the weather, what would skippers Wells and Gatting do? A deal was cooked up whereby Sussex were assisted to a declaration on 319/7, Middlesex forfeited their first innings and Sussex their second. Middlesex then capitulated for 85 with an embarrassing lack of resolve in only 24.2 overs. The final four wickets tumbled in a mere 14 deliveries and there were three cheap scalps for Giddins, Jarvis and Danny Law. A truly hag-ridden week also saw the Sunday League match abandoned without a ball being bowled. The irony of course was that when the sun did consent to shine at Horsham there were runs a-plenty.

In a second XI match later in the season against Notts over 1,200 runs were scored and only 21 wickets fell.

1997: Horsham's visitors in 1997 were Kent who, extraordinary as it seems, last appeared in the town 70 years previously. They were a powerful and well balanced side around this time who were often 'thereabouts' but never quite 'there'. Sussex were to endure a truly dreadful season winning only one Championship match and ending with the wooden spoon. Unusually both sides were captained by wicket keepers (Moores and Steve Marsh). Kent adopted far too cavalier an approach and despite scoring at four runs an over were dismissed for a below-par 245. Trevor Ward top scored with 67 but the visitors may have been unsettled when David Fulton had to retire hurt after the second ball of the game. Mark Newell (56) and Jarvis (55) put on 92 in 102 minutes to help Sussex to an unexpected lead of 19, Ben Phillips taking 5/47. Despite a forceful 83 from Ward second time round Kent were deep in the toils at 197/8. Then came one of the most extraordinary stands ever witnessed on the ground. Marsh (142) and Phillips (65 n/o) added an untroubled 183 for the 10th wicket in 191 minutes, the 6th largest last wicket stand in cricket history (Kent ironically already held the first) and highest ever against Sussex. Marsh was a nimble, quick footed player whose innings contained three 6s and thirteen 4s. Poor Vasbert Drakes conceded 152 runs, a new (but short-lived) Sussex record for the ground. It was a numbing experience. From a position of clear advantage Sussex were now fighting to save the game. At 289/4 and the Newell brothers from Three Bridges at the helm all seemed well but Kent's brawny Irish/Australian fast bowler Martin McCague rampaged through the breach with the new ball. Sussex collapsed with indecent haste to 317 all out, McCague ending with 7/82, the first time for over 40 years a visiting bowler had taken as many wickets in an innings. Keith Newell's unavailing 112 contained nineteen boundaries but to have competed so strongly for so long yet lose was a shattering experience.

1998: Visitors Derbyshire were riven by internecine strife more reminiscent of medieval Italy (or latter-day Hove) and did well to finish in mid-table. One of those to depart in their acrimonious close season was Chris Adams, who took over the helm at Sussex. One-day international duty with England kept him out of the match and in the event, it was probably a good one to miss. A little bit of history was made in that it was the first time that play in a Championship match at Horsham was scheduled for a Sunday. Buttressed by an unbeaten 135 from Mark Newell in over six hours, Sussex led off with 325. Derbyshire put this into context with a monumental 593, the highest score seen on the ground to date. Veteran skipper Kim Barnett made 162, Matthew Cassar (whose wife kept wicket for England Ladies) 121 and talismanic skipper Dominic Cork 102 n/o, while Phil de Freitas's flamboyant 87 included four 6s. Amer Khan's leg-breaks yielded 185 runs in a marathon 59 overs. Wasim Khan added 125 to his first innings 70 on the final day as Sussex fought hard to save the game. Australia's Michael Bevan also reached a century but when he was bowled for 127 the home side's batting broke down on a wicket accepting more and more turn. The last seven wickets fell for only 71, Mr Extras (37) being the third highest scorer after the two centurions. Derbyshire reached their victory target of 107 with seven wickets and 8.2 overs to spare. It was their first Championship victory over Sussex anywhere for six seasons and their hosts could have few complaints.

1999: This was a momentous season because after much debate it was decided that from 2000 the Championship would be formed of two divisions with promotion and relegation. Who went where would be determined by placings in 1999, so there was clearly much to play for. Visitors Worcestershire failed consistently to score enough runs and were destined by some distance not to make the cut. Sussex came into the match in good heart. Set 452 to win by Gloucester on the last day at Hove they reached their target with centuries from Michael di Venuto and Tony Cottey. The first day was washed out. Openers Toby Pierce (75) and Richard Montgomerie (66) made up for lost time on the second, racing to 100 off 25 overs, their fourth century stand of the season. Di Venuto bludgeoned the quickest Championship half-century of the season (34 balls) but from 223/1, 301/9 was disappointing. Worcester's reply was dismal: 124 all out as Lewry took 6/63 with his customary late swing. Following-on, four further wickets had fallen by stumps on the third day. Graeme Hick was one of the heaviest run-scorers of all time and moved almost inexorably to an imperious century – his eighth against Sussex and 105th in all –

as Worcester strove to avoid defeat. Hick would probably have been as surprised as the bowler when he fell to Adams for a majestic 134. His side had reached 255/9, an overall lead of 78 when heavy drizzle drove them from the pitch with 30 overs still remaining. They were destined never to return. Not for the first time at Horsham the elements had had the last laugh. Sussex could justifiably grumble that they had been robbed of victory and it was to cost them dear. Despite winning more matches than third placed Leicestershire, defeat in their final outing saw them slip to 11th place. Second Division cricket awaited them too in the new Millennium.

Chapter 9
THE NEW MILLENNIUM: 2000-DATE

2000: County cricket continued to evolve at a pace that must have astonished traditionalists. The year 2000 saw the introduction of a two-tier county Championship, but for Sussex and visitors Middlesex, it was to prove a disastrous campaign - the home side finished rock-bottom, their opponents, only one place higher. Australian Test opener Justin Langer won the toss for the visitors and batted. His side's 370 was probably about par for the course. Gritty wicketkeeper David Nash top-scored with an unbeaten 75, but the classiest knock was an untroubled 64 from Langer himself, with Jason Lewry and Robin Martin-Jenkins pick of the home attack. At the half-way point, Sussex were 284/9, thanks to a solid ensemble performance from their much-maligned middle order. The loss of the third day to rain was to have profound repercussions. Unlike the deal struck with Mike Gatting in 1996, spectators must have feared the worst when Umer Rashid and James Kirtley resumed the Sussex innings at the start of the final day. This was confirmed when a declaration came on 300, for it indicated that the match as a whole had been sacrificed in the quest for an additional batting bonus point. And so it proved. Who was to blame for what happened next depends on who you talk to. Sussex skipper Chris Adams blamed Langer for the failure to strike a deal; Langer blamed Adams. The bare facts were that Middlesex batted throughout the remainder of a completely meaningless day and ended up on 337/6. Langer himself was the worst offender, retiring into his shell for no obvious reason before emerging briefly to strike Rashid for three startling sixes in one over. But in ideal batting conditions, a sizeable crowd grew increasingly restless as it became all-too-evident that there would be no declaration and chase - the match had been condemned to a living death. Mike Roseberry came in for particular stick, his stodgy half century being greeted by a resounding silence as what remained of the crowd showed all too plainly what they thought of it. At 5.20pm, both sides trooped off to a chorus of jeers and catcalls. The reality was probably that neither man was to blame – it was simply too early in the season for teams to start gambling: better to pocket your bonus points and move on.

It may have rekindled the age-old argument about whether cricketers were there to win or entertain, but in a market-driven world, it was an undeniably shabby advert for the product and all the more regrettable because the first two days had been so keenly fought.

2001: 'We're looking forward to it' enthused Horsham C&SC chairman Kevin Barnes - the 'it' being a second visit in three seasons from Worcestershire. For Sussex, it was the start of their Renaissance. Bottom in 2000, champions in 2001 as the 'Adams Era' began to gather momentum. The fates were less kind to the visitors, whose lack of depth with both bat and ball, consigned them to a mediocre season. With Adams absent at his grandfather's funeral in Derbyshire, stand-in skipper Kirtley ignored the miserable conditions and elected to take first knock on winning the toss. He was soon to regret it. With the mood as gloomy as the weather, Sussex struggled to 137 all out on a cheerless, rain-plagued day. At one point, umpire John Holder actually uprooted the stumps before, in a sudden change of heart, permitting play to continue. However, as Worcester were to discover, what is sauce for the goose is sauce for the gander. Mark Robinson took three wickets in seven balls as they could only muster 183 (Kirtley 5/60), 18 wickets having fallen on the opening day. Then came an astonishing transformation. The sun emerged, Murray Goodwin (109) and Richard Montgomerie (112) made centuries, the tail wagged vigorously and Sussex's 372 all out invited the visitors to make 327. Goodwin and Montgomerie's opening stand of 212 lasted a little under four hours. At stumps on the third day, Worcestershire were interestingly placed on 173/3. At 262/6, Vikram Solanki and Stephen Rhodes were taking the game steadily away from the home side before, in a moment of carelessness, Solanki (89) slapped a full toss from Mark Davis straight to Goodwin. This was to cost his side the game. The final three wickets fell anticlimactically for one run as Sussex emerged victorious by 33 in an absorbing game of cricket which either side might have won. South African born Davis was the hero of the hour with 6/116, his first-ever five wicket haul for the county. It was all a far cry from 54/6 on the opening morning and dark mutterings about pitch inspections. This victory was to prove the catalyst for Sussex's season.

2002: Leicestershire were the visitors in 2002 and both sides were destined to finish just below mid-table in the top flight. In the previous match, Adams had scored a double-century against Lancashire, but had suffered a calf strain in the process, so Kirtley again led the side. A feature of the match was an extremely high wind blowing straight down the ground, which made life difficult for the poor devils bowling into it and wasn't much fun for spectators either. Skipper Vince Wells' unbeaten 86 anchored his side's 264 all out, Darren Stevens chipping in with an attractive 50. On his home ground, the tall, spare figure of Robin Martin-Jenkins took full advantage of the conditions, finishing with a career-best 7/51. Dr Dew was particularly delighted for his protégé, recalling a limited-overs competition down at Preston Park when 'RMJ' scored two centuries in the same day for Horsham under-13s. But what goes round comes round. Devon Malcolm may have been on the county scene for over 20 seasons and may also have been within a whisker of 40, but conditions such as this were tailor-made for him. Rolling back the years, the Jamaican-born fast bowler with the build of a heavyweight boxer, came storming in from the railway end like a runaway bull, the gale at his back. With wicket keeper Burns a disturbingly long way back, Malcolm simply blew away the Sussex top order like some splendid elemental force. They had crumbled alarmingly to 57/5, before opener Montgomerie inspired some belated resistance from the lower middle order. 'Monty' calmly set his stall out and batted, limpet-like, through the entire innings for an unbeaten 122. It was an innings of rare skill, technique and character, lasted a touch over four hours, and included one six and 17 fours. It was simple, effective and unfussy stuff, characterised by countless neat, unobtrusive tucks off his legs. To get the stats out of the way, it was the first time a Sussex player had carried his bat since Bill Athey against Kent at Tunbridge Wells in 1994; the third time such a feat had been achieved against Leicester; and the first time ever at Horsham. Emulating Martin-Jenkins' earlier effort, Malcolm ended with 7/76, taking his tally of first-class scalps to 997. Montgomerie's sterling effort had kept the deficit down to a manageable 17, but a patient, unbroken stand of 60 between Darren Maddy and former Sussex favourite Michael Bevan was turning the tide inexorably in Leicester's favour second time round when stumps were drawn. At the halfway mark, the score stood at 94/2 - advantage Leicester, but everything still to play for. What would the morrow bring? No-one knew it at the time, but that was the last ball to be bowled in the match. The morrow saw incessant rain join forces with the battering winds that were still sweeping across the ground. Things were so bad that the final day was abandoned an hour before the start, with the wicket ends sodden by a relentless overnight downpour. Yet another Horsham Festival had been ruined by the baleful weather.

2003: The summer of 2003 was among the driest on record. It and the next were to witness some long-standing batting records at Horsham not just broken but eclipsed. The visitors were newly-promoted Nottinghamshire, who had not been seen in the town since 1951. They were to endure a torrid campaign, with relegation awaiting at the end of it. Their batting was prone to truly frightening collapses – just before arriving at Horsham for example, they had spiraled to 8 for 7 against Kent. For Sussex, 2003 was the stuff of dreams – on a sun-dappled September afternoon at Hove, Murray Goodwin pulled Leicester's Philip DeFreitas to the mid-wicket boundary to clinch the Championship crown for the first time in their history. Not that they had it all their own way: they arrived in Horsham having been on the receiving end of centuries from Warwickshire's Jonathan Trott, Ian Bell and Jim Troughton; and in the match afterwards, it was the turn of Surrey's Ian Ward and Graham Thorpe to take tons off their perspiring attack. This time however it was Sussex' own turn. Adams won the toss and watched his men tot up a truly monumental 619/7 declared by tea on the second day, a new record for the ground and Sussex's highest-ever score against Notts. Montgomerie's 220 minute 105 ended a lean spell for him personally, but was his third consecutive century at Horsham and his 4th in seven matches against Notts. This simply cleared the decks for one of the most astonishing assaults ever witnessed at Cricket Field Road. With the score on 378, Matt Prior was joined by former Northants all-rounder Kevin Innes, a very useful player who was similar in content to Martin-Jenkins and therefore unable quite to cement a place in the side. The irony in what was to follow was that under a new ECB ruling, Innes had already been nominated by Sussex as the man to step aside should Kirtley not be required by England against Zimbabwe at Lords. Poor Innes sat with his pads on for an eternity, knowing that he would only bat if Kirtley – who in the event was released by England – didn't arrive on the ground in time. Kirtley left Lords at 11.15am, but was nowhere to be seen when Ambrose was dismissed. So in Innes went, enjoined by his captain to relax and enjoy himself. He and Prior needed no second invitation. They laced into an increasingly ragged Notts attack. An incredible 203 runs flowed in a memorable morning session, Prior being responsible for 124 of them. He smashed no fewer than six 6s and 15 fours in his 133, reaching his century in the grand manner with a straight six. In two amazing overs, he hit four 6s in moving from 98 to 133 in 11 balls. This included 22 in the final over before lunch from occasional spinner Bilal Shafayat. Innes duly became the third centurion of the innings – his maiden 'ton' and the first ever made by a 12th man - as he and Prior put on 157 for the 7th wicket. The situation was so unusual that the ECB computers and at least one national daily actually credited his runs to Kirtley! Innes' unbeaten 103 was made off 150 balls, lasted for 195 minutes and included two 6s and 13 fours. Australian leg-break bowler Stuart MacGill often outperformed the legendary Shane Warne when the two bowled in harness in Tests, but was reduced to impotence at Horsham, wheeling away – in the main from the town end - for 50 overs and ending with 3/172. A big spinner of the ball, MacGill was extracting turn but interspersed the testing deliveries with too much dross. On this showing, Adams' gamble on only batting once and bowling Notts out twice, was not going to be easily realised.

Despite a promising start, a shell-shocked Notts reply had slithered ominously from 109/1 to 139/4 on a slow but by no means impossible pitch. If the crowd thought it had already been richly entertained, they were to be transfixed by events about to unfold, for Kevin Pietersen then played an innings that simply took the breath away, making 166 off only 136 balls, with 17 fours and four 6s. He raced to his century off a mere 75 deliveries in an innings of almost transcendent quality. He and the beautifully wristy teenager Shafayat put on 193 in only 26 overs, a new ground record for the 5th wicket. The quick-footed Shafayat helped himself to three sixes off Sussex's new overseas signing Mushtaq Ahmed in his 71. Pietersen won a stirring, red-blooded duel with

Kirtley, smashing him for a six and three thrilling 4s in one over (including a top-edge into the tennis courts!). One stunning shot by Pietersen – who, in 2003, became the first man to hit a ball over the pavilion at Durham's Riverside ground - summed it all up. Bowling from the railway end, Martin-Jenkins dropped one short. In a flash, the South African deposited it lazily a full 40 yards beyond the leg-side boundary. It was heady, exhilarating stuff, but Mushtaq, despite sustaining heavy punishment, kept probing away. Despite going for 4-5 an over, he ended with 6/163 as Notts were finally dismissed for 421. With time running out, Adams had little option but to enforce the follow-on, but this required his men to take 10 wickets in a day on a pitch that had only seen 17 fall in the previous three. Ominously for Sussex, Darren Bicknell and Notts skipper Jason Gallian led off with a century opening stand, despite Bicknell being sorely handicapped by a calf strain which required him to use a runner throughout. His loss early on the final morning seemed to undermine the Notts resistance. They lost six wickets in an hour to Kirtley and Mushtaq on a wicket at last showing some signs of wear. Usman Afzaal and Pietersen tried to attack without really playing themselves in and paid the penalty – attractive cameos were all very fine, but not what their side needed. Sussex were not to be denied as Notts finally capitulated for 247 (Kirtley 4/74, Mushtaq 6/81). Mushy's match figures of 12/244 were the best by a Sussex spinner since Eddie Hemmings' 12/58, also at Horsham, 10 years earlier, while Tim Ambrose's seven scalps in the match equalled the ground record. Hoping against hope for a miracle, Notts opened the bowling with MacGill, but Montgomerie and Goodwin raced to their victory target of 50 amid a flurry of boundaries. In many ways, the key to the game had been the respective performances of the two world-class leg spinners on show, with Mushtaq comprehensively outperforming MacGill. Just for good measure, there were also runs galore in the return match, where centuries from Goodwin and Martin-Jenkins were counterbalanced by ones from Pietersen (again) and Russell Warren.

There had been 1,339 runs in the match, but astonishingly, this was as nothing compared with events in

2004: The year had opened badly for the town, with a shock announcement that the historic Kings Head hotel in the Carfax, which had played such a full role in the history of the Festival, was closing its doors for the last time. Visitors Warwickshire had provided the opposition in the sad final match in 1956, but hadn't been seen in Championship action in the town since. No-one was to know it, but it was to be a trial of strength between the reigning Champions and the Champions-elect.

Nick Knight won the all-important toss on a glorious summer morning and, ominously for Sussex, cracked the first ball from Pakistani fast bowler Mohammad Akram to the point boundary. This set the tone for the innings. By stumps, Warwickshire had reached 357/6, with Ian Bell unbeaten on 147. If Sussex thought this was bad, day two was even worse, for not a single wicket fell in the entire 83 overs bowled (the remaining 21 were lost to a late thunderstorm). On a low, slow wicket, Bell and wicketkeeper Tim Frost simply rewrote the record books. Their stand had reached 289 before Warwicks finally declared after 165.4 overs on 600/6, the second highest score ever registered on the ground. It was also a new record for Warwickshire's 7th wicket. By this time, 22 year old Bell had also obliterated the highest individual score (224, by Hampshire's Phil Mead back in 1921) in a blockbusting 262 n/o, which extended over 481 balls, contained 27 fours and six 6s and lasted ten minutes short of 10 hours. His partner Frost had progressed to 135, made in exactly five hours. Poor old Mushy conceded the highest-ever number of runs in an single innings on the ground (4/194 in 50 overs, including one over that cost 19 runs but also brought a wicket); while Kirtley's 28 wicketless overs cost him 130. All the more credit to wicket keeper Ambrose, who only conceded one bye. One sour note was that Sussex were penalised five runs for ball-tampering. Believing the match ball to have been scuffed and scratched deliberately, umpires Peter Willey and Barry Leadbeater intervened in the 66th over and ordered it to be changed. This was the first such offence since the new Law 42.3 came into force four seasons earlier. The offender wasn't named at the time, but was subsequently identified as Akram. It is difficult to know what was said in the dressing room after such a scourging, but to their very considerable credit, openers Ward and Montgomerie cast aside any physical or mental weariness. Despite the little matter of having to make 450 simply to avoid the follow-on, they opened up with a stand of 143 before the chunky, ex-Surrey left-hander was joined by Adams in a stand of 194 for the 3rd wicket. This came to an end when Ward finally fell for 160, an innings that lasted for 387 minutes and contained 19 fours and three 6s. Adams became the fourth centurion of the match, his spirited 144 coming off 183 balls and containing 17 fours and four 6s. At the close of another weary, foot-slogging day for the bowlers, Sussex had averted the follow-on, yet were still 136 adrift on 464/7. Talk in the pubs and clubs was whether Adams would declare overnight, and challenge his visitors to set Sussex a target. In the event, he didn't (or as *Wisden* censoriously put it, 'Adams made no attempt to open the game up, to the disappointment of a small crowd enjoying the sun, which for once smiled on the...festival'). He simply batted until his side were all out - which at least gave Mushtaq the opportunity of exacting a little retribution with the bat, chipping in with an expansive 62. Assisted by six dropped catches, Sussex eventually pulled up at the buffers on 562, their highest-ever score against Warwickshire, eclipsing their 546/5 at Edgbaston in 1937. With the game dead in the water, Warwicks meandered irrelevantly along in their second innings to 188/2 before declaring, Knight and Bell both notching half-centuries. Bell thus took his personal match tally to 324 without being dismissed. He recalled afterwards that he had scored a century on the ground some years previously (1999) in a 2nd XI match, so had been looking forward to renewing his acquaintance with it. With only 13 wickets having fallen on the first three days, it was difficult to see how a result could be manufactured without proceedings degenerating into farce. As with Middlesex in 2000, at this early stage in the season, it wasn't worth the gamble. Adams voiced the opinion of many in saying that the wicket was simply too benign. He too felt that a contrived slog and chase could only be founded on the premise of Warwicks batting Sussex out of the game first, leaving the home side with only a draw or a defeat to play for. Nor was this the end for a leg-weary Sussex attack. Their next match was down at Hove against Northants, who racked up the little matter of 570. But Sussex had obviously taken a liking to the Warwickshire attack, for in the return match, they posted 482/9. Nevertheless, with a dazzling One-day match that also broke all records, it had been an exhilarating week. With Warwickshire due to visit again in 2005, how could it possibly match up?

2005: We will never know. A rabbit was pulled out the hat all right, but it was hardly one that anybody locally either wanted or expected. The sorry story is briefly told. In the absence of a permanent groundsman, it became apparent during the close season that all was not well with the wicket. The club employed external contractors in an increasingly desperate attempt to put things right. In April, a fateful decision was taken to scarify the entire square, which resulted in the surface being covered in small, loose squares of turf. There was no way in which a pitch could be prepared in time for a four-day game. Had the match been played later in the season, there almost certainly wouldn't have been a problem, but sadly the die was cast so far as 2005 was concerned. Sussex head groundsman Derek Traill inspected the pitches, and the subsequent announcement 'that the surface of the square at Horsham is not conducive to first class cricket at the present time' was inevitable. Much hung on Sussex's rider that 'there is no reason why first-class cricket will not return to Horsham in 2006'.

2006: To their credit, the county were as good as their word, allocating Horsham a fixture against Middlesex. Sussex were unbeaten coming into the match and were to go on to win the Championship for a second time in four seasons. In stark contrast, the visitors were to endure a wretched campaign which culminated in relegation. Even so early in the season, it bore the hallmark of a 'top v. bottom' encounter – at least on paper. Adams won the toss and batted. Sussex proceeded in fits and starts to 231/7, but an explosive stand of 116 for the 8th wicket – a new ground record for the county - between Rana Naved (64) and Luke Wright (59) saw them up to 373. Middlesex's reply centred on the elegant Owais Shah. Despite being troubled increasingly by cramp in his hand, his poised 126 lasted for four hours and included four 6s and 15 fours. It helped lift his side to 208/3, but the middle order then evaporated for no obvious reason to a hugely disappointing 266 all out. Sussex took full advantage. Goodwin and Montgomerie led off with 114, Montgomerie continuing his prolific run of form at Horsham with 98. Adams and Prior tightened the screw with a century stand for the 3rd wicket and although falling away from 321/4 to 370 all out, this set

Middlesex the little matter of 481 for victory on a wearing pitch. Prior's 77 was a typically muscular affair, coming off only 57 deliveries and including three 6s and seven 4s. The visitors were never seriously at the races. Ed Smith completed the first 'pair' on the ground by a visiting player for over 50 years (and for good measure, followed it up with another duck in his next Championship innings). Dubliner Ed Joyce was the only man to show to advantage. He compiled an elegant and attractive 92 before being bowled through the gate by Mushtaq. At this point, Middlesex had slumped to 199/9, but the last rites were delayed by a rousing half-century stand for the last wicket. Chris Silverwood's 50 came off only 46 balls and included 44 in boundaries. Even so, the match was over 90 minutes into the final day, Sussex securing a 5th straight Championship victory. The popular 'Mushy', his beard now clearly flecked with grey, was roundly applauded for his 6/110 off 24 overs, the 10th time he had taken 10 wickets in a match for Sussex. Middlesex looked a thoroughly ragged outfit – yet in a tale of two Roses, they promptly won their next Championship game against Yorkshire, while at Liverpool, Sussex crashed to defeat in under two days against Lancashire.

2007: As Oscar Wilde might have said had he been in Horsham at the time 'to lose one's cricket Festival once might be regarded as a misfortune; to lose it again two years later looks like carelessness' – yet that is precisely what happened as the county apparently could find no space for a match at Horsham. The neo-Byzantine undercurrents that followed would have done credit to either Agatha Christie or Renaissance Italy, but mercifully a local company came to the rescue, so Horsham was back in business. The visitors were surprise packets Durham, who Horsham had the pleasure of welcoming when they first entered the Championship back in 1992. Their advance over the intervening 15 years could be measured by the fact that they were to contribute three home-grown players to the England team in 2007 (Paul Collingwood, Steve Harmison and Liam Plunkett). Following a thrilling contest with Lancashire, Sussex were to retain their Championship title, with Durham tiptoeing unobtrusively into runners-up spot. Stand-in skipper Dale Benkenstein opted to bat and was soon regretting it. If anything, Durham's approach was over-assertive and they found a variety of ways to lose their wickets – first and last to pacemen Rana Naved and Lewry; in the middle, to Mushtaq, who bowled 29 uninterrupted overs from the town end. Although given some rough treatment at times – especially by Kyle Coetzer and Ottis Gibson – 'Mushy' ended with yet another five wicket haul, his 99th in first-class cricket as Durham folded to a below-par 209. Coetzer, New Zealand Test all-rounder Scott Styris, Benkenstein himself, wicket keeper Phil Mustard and Gibson all got starts, but no-one stayed around long enough to play the big innings their cause demanded. Sussex started brightly. Local youngster Chris Nash had been playing club cricket on the ground since the age of seven and treated his home fans to a glorious 63 on a hard, dry pitch as Sussex progressively and pitilessly turned the screw. Clearly only wishing to bat once, Adams himself led the way with a characteristically robust 193 – surprisingly perhaps, the highest individual score by a Sussex batsman on the ground. It was his 48th first-class century, lasted for 4 hours 42 minutes, took a mere 202 balls and contained five sixes and 23 fours. He changed through the gears with increasing authority, some of his strokeplay between lunch and tea – including one monumental six over the tennis courts - being positively brutal. Yet there was always just enough in the pitch for him never to feel entirely in control. Adams received strong support from Goodwin and two ex-Horsham CC players – reserve wicket keeper Andrew Hodd and Robin Martin-Jenkins. Adams and Hodd (72) put on 158 for the 5th wicket; Adams and Martin-Jenkins a further 122 for the 6th as – shorn of the services of rangy fast bowler Harmison – an increasingly dispirited Durham attack seemed almost resigned to its fate. The end finally came on 517, with four expensive wickets apiece for Paul Wiseman and Plunkett. Sussex were without Lewry second time round, the veteran left arm swing bowler having broken a toe in the field during the Durham first innings. Even so, the visitors seemed to have no clear strategy as they embarked on their second innings 308 runs in arrears – and it showed. Wickets began to fall with depressing ease, Mushtaq again acting as tormentor-in-chief. At one point, he claimed three in 13 balls as the visitors ended the second day in near-terminal disarray. Benkenstein moved to a fluent half century, but the real fireworks came from 38 year old all-rounder Gibson. He launched a furious assault on Mushy, smashing five 6's and six 4's in a 76-ball 68. One six - into the tennis courts - caused a five minute delay while the keys were located. This clearly energised the veteran Barbadian, for despite going wicketless in this match, he was to take all 10 Hampshire wickets in an innings in the next. Entertaining though Gibson's efforts were, they were only delaying the inevitable. Mushy and Co. were not to be denied and with Harmison unable to bat, the end duly came early on the third morning, Sussex emerging victorious by a massive innings and 102 run margin. Almost inevitably, Mushtaq led the way with 4/77 (9-168 in the match), adding a further swathe of victims to the 18 he secured in Sussex's two innings victories over Durham in 2006. Although he had not received excessive assistance from a slow pitch, he was helped hugely by the naivety of many of the visiting batsmen. Another critical factor was that Sussex had adequate cover for the stricken Lewry, whereas Harmison's absence seemed to leave the Durham attack in disarray. It was Sussex's 11th win in 13 Championship matches over Durham, though the tables were to be reversed with a vengeance later in the season at Chester-le-Street.

And so, with all its twists and turns, ends the richly-woven tapestry that constitutes the first century of First-Class cricket at Horsham. The second is scheduled to open in 2008 with a visit from newly-promoted Somerset.

Chapter 10
ONE-DAY CRICKET

Prelude

Cricket had undergone many changes since Horsham was stripped of its cricket Festival in 1956. Not the least of these was the advent of the one-day game. Noting the success of the Rothman's Cavaliers matches the first of the county one-day competitions, the Gillette Cup, came into being in 1963.

It was an instant success. Looking to capitalise on this the next of this new breed of competitions to appear was the John Player Sunday League which commenced in 1969. The appeal of this was its simplicity. Each side batted for 40 overs and each bowler could only deliver eight of them. In the early days, BBC2 would televise a complete match live although because of Lord's Day Observance legislation play couldn't commence before 2pm. Although its biff-bang format never wholly won over all the purists, it had an undeniable popular appeal in that many spectators could have an early lunch, see an entire game of cricket and be home in time for their evening meal. And in around four hours playing time they were guaranteed a result.

The ill-feeling generated by what many locally felt to be Hove's hasty and ill-judged decision had long passed. By 1970 Sussex decided to dip its toes back in the Horsham water and, to commemorate the bi-centenary of cricket in the town, offered Horsham a John Player match in May 1971.

The Matches

1971: An estimated 5,000 spectators passed through the gates to see visitors Leicestershire – captained by England skipper Ray Illingworth - defeat Sussex by 29 runs. Big-hitting Rhodesian Brian Davison (78) anchored Leicester's innings while Ted Dexter's one and only appearance at Horsham ended in disappointment. He injured his back so badly in the field he was unable to bat. The match was a runaway success but for reasons of their own Sussex decided not to return until...

1977: ...when a crowd estimated at anywhere between 5,000 and 8,000 packed in for the visit of cricket's one-day kings,

Lancashire. After Harry Pilling and Clive Lloyd had set the early pace for the visitors, it ended in thrilling fashion with John Spencer needing a boundary off the very last ball of the game to win the match for Sussex. He swung as much in hope as expectation, the ball flew off a thick edge to the boundary and Sussex were home. The only sour note were concerns expressed by Sussex skipper Tony Greig about the state of the pitch and a lack of organisation. Against the advice of local groundstaff, Greig insisted on playing on the reserve strip rather than the one specially prepared – and then castigated it!

1978: Somerset were the visitors with Vivian Richards among the ranks. The weather was bleak and cheerless, the game one sided. Somerset couldn't cope with a tight seam attack splendidly led by Imran Khan, posted a mediocre target and Sussex cantered home by six wickets with oodles of time to spare, despite unsung seamer Kevin Jennings taking two for nine off his eight overs. Horsham squash club member John Barclay top-scored with 47.

1979: Because of yet more inclement weather this match (against Surrey) descended into farce but ended in high drama. Led by Alan Butcher, Surrey posted a challenging total in their 25 overs. With Javed Miandad to the fore Sussex went for it with gusto. More rain fell. The pitch simply oozed moisture and the match was further reduced to 10 overs per side. With one of them remaining – to be bowled by the fearsome Sylvester Clarke - they required 17. Horsham's Paul Parker and Giles Cheatle could only manage 14, leaving Surrey victors by three runs.

1980: An astonishing match against Worcestershire. A crowd of between 4,000 and 4,500 witnessed Parker make 106 n/o in 84 balls and Imran 73. These two put on 156 for the 3rd wicket in 17 overs as Sussex racked up an astonishing 293/4. New Zealand Test opener Glenn Turner made a valiant attempt to win the match off his own bat for the visitors. He smashed 147 in 138 minutes but when he was last out - caught in the deep with 33 needed - the game was up for his gallant side.

1981: A disappointing match with table-topping Sussex resoundingly thumped by Warwickshire. Their stop-start 198/9 never looked remotely enough and England opener Dennis Amiss took full advantage with eight 6s in an undefeated 117.

1982: More disappointment as Worcestershire gained early revenge for 1980. Despite Parker's flamboyant 73, Sussex's 206 on a pitch battered by overnight hailstones was again neither fish nor fowl. Nevertheless, Worcester were behind the clock for most of their reply in an absorbing and even contest until Phil Neale and John Inchmore launched a furious assault late on against Tony Pigott.

1983: Lancashire again but this time it was a thriller. A crowd of between 5,000 and 6,000 saw Sussex post yet another something-and-nothing total. A see-saw reply with the balance tilting first one way and then the other saw the visitors require 13 off the last over, bowled surprisingly by skipper Barclay. Amid scenes of general chaos last man Ian Folley was run out off the penultimate ball to leave his captain John Abrahams stranded on 79 and his side two runs short.

1984: Despite Alan Walker's 3/12, Sussex took full advantage of Northants' decision to select only four front-line bowlers. Parker yet again led the way with his fifth consecutive one-day half-century on his home ground. Supported by Alan Wells (49), his 77 saw Sussex to a healthy 236/8. Northants started brightly but despite David Capel's efforts ran out of steam to leave Sussex comfortable victors.

1985: A corker against Notts in front of the BBC2 cameras. Sussex's 196/7 (Imran 72) seemed below par, particularly when Clive Rice (67) and John Birch (49) left their side requiring only eight from the final two overs. Ian Waring then bowled the over of his life – leaving five from one, with Tony Pigott to bowl it. The over went: .w1w1 when, with an involuntary squirt down to straightish third man, Eddie Hemmings registered the three runs needed for victory off the final delivery, causing non-playing skipper Barclay to reflect on the irony of a match at Horsham – a ground known on the county circuit as one of singles and boundaries - being decided with a three.

1986: The Championship match with Somerset had been a complete washout and the baleful weather cast a shadow over the One-day fixture. Giant West Indian fast bowler Joel Garner was impossible to handle on a damp, green wicket as Sussex struggled to a sorry-looking 108/9. Anchored by Viv Richards' explosive 42 n/o, Somerset eased home by eight wickets with time to spare.

1987: Another thriller. Paul Terry made 75 and Chris Smith 54 as Hampshire posted 216/7. Colin Wells made a robust 70 before ceding centre-stage to the massive flaxen-haired South African, Garth le Roux. Le Roux smote about him hip and thigh until 12 were required from the final over with two wickets in hand. With 10 needed off the final two deliveries it looked like 'game over' for Sussex but le Roux hit the first for four and the second high into the crowd for six to earn his side a one-wicket victory. His own 83 had been scored off just 55 balls. The victory roar could be heard all over town and the excitement was such that the local St John Ambulance Brigade had to deal with two suspected heart attacks.

1988: Another nerve-jangler. Sussex were in control for most of the Derbyshire innings but 53 off the final five overs allowed the visitors to post 213/8, poor Tony Pigott again being subjected to the long handle. A start of 8/3 had little to commend it and the 'ask' became 100 off 10 overs. Parker made 80 as Bruce Roberts retired from the fray with five overs, 2 for 53. Pigott and Neil Lenham then put on 57 for the 8th wicket in 24 minutes. With 84 scored off nine, 16 were required from the final over. This became eight off two deliveries before Pigott holed out with five wanted.

1989: An injury-stricken Sussex side containing three wicket-keepers was no match for Graham Gooch's ruthlessly efficient Essex. Despite Ian Gould's perky 63, 154/7 was never going to be remotely sufficient as Don Topley conceded a beggarly 11 runs from his eight overs. And so it proved. Despite the loss of a couple of late wickets (including that of Australian Mark Waugh), Essex strolled home with time and wickets to spare in a functional, low-key display.

1990: The presence of the 'Sky' television cameras had no effect on the clerk of the weather. Relentless rain meant the fixture against Lancashire was the only match in the country to be abandoned without a ball being bowled.

1991: Further sluicing rain meant that for a second successive season the match – this time against Essex – never got off the ground. It was perhaps appropriate that one of the umpires was Mr Dickie Bird.

1992: Yet another last-ball finish, this time against Championship new boys Durham. Wayne Larkins made 86 and

Australia's Dean Jones was unbeaten with a high-tempo 74 as the visitors set Sussex a Herculean 276 to win. Yet again poor Pigott received a mauling (1-65 off eight overs). With 18 overs to go the omens weren't good – 161 runs needed and half the side out. But Jon North then made a half-century in only 24 balls leaving last man Andy Robson – who ironically hailed from Durham – needing to hit the final ball of the match for six. It was not to be but Sussex's 270/9 was their highest Sunday League total of the season.

1993: A comfortable win over Leicestershire. A disappointing crowd of 2,000 saw coloured clothing on the ground for the first time – Sussex resplendent in bright yellow, blue and red; their opponents in lime green and scarlet. And that wasn't all. The start had been moved back to mid-day and the duration of the match extended from 40 overs to 50. Martin Speight and Alan Wells both made half-centuries as the Sussex innings closed on a daunting 283/8, poor Gordon Parsons' 10 overs yielding 72 runs. Leicester were never in the hunt. Their tactics puzzled friend and foe alike and they never made any real effort to hit out until it was far too late. Once again Pigott was in the wars – 0-69 off 10 overs this time – as the visitors closed on 220/7.

1994: The 'Sky' cameras were again present as a crowd of around 4,500-5,000 settled back to watch Sussex take strike against Lancashire. Some of the experimentation with the format introduced in 1993 had been abandoned – it was back to 40 overs and a 2pm start. A dense swarm of bees seemed to unsettle the home side and 229/9, while not to be wholly despised, was less than par on a very flat track. Jamie Hall (69) and Speight (45) were the main contributors but the last six wickets fell for 16, three in the final over alone. Sadly, Sussex's bowling was ragged throughout and Lancashire coasted home with ease. Future England captain Mike Atherton moved effortlessly to a century in 102 balls. Rubbing yet further salt in the wound, he and Jason Gallian added an unbroken 121 for the 3rd wicket in only 61 minutes.

1995: Another close run thing before the television cameras. The match against Surrey was reduced to 37 overs per side but a disappointingly low crowd resulted in an uncharacteristic lack of atmosphere. All the Sussex top order got starts but Mr Extras with 48 top scored as the home side closed on 222/7 – healthy but not compellingly so. Despite England left-hander Graham Thorpe's half-century, Surrey pulled up just short on 212 as Ian Salisbury – who was to move to Surrey in 1997 – derailed the latter part of their innings with three wickets in four balls. It was just as well for Sussex bowled 19 wides, Jason Lewry's opening over alone lasting for 11 balls.

1996: For the third time in seven seasons the Sunday League match – this time against Middlesex on their first-ever visit to Horsham – was completely washed out. Alan Wells would have particular cause for regret – he had chosen it for his benefit.

1997: Sussex came into the match against Kent having played four, lost four; by contrast, their opponents had played three, won three. And the inevitable happened as Sussex emerged victorious – but only just. With two umpires named Holder to ensure that the proprieties were observed, Kent seemed too intent on playing big shots. Their 220/9 was probably 20-30 below par. Matthew Walker top scored with 60, former Sussex favourite Alan Wells made 45 and Amer Khan took 5/40 with his leg-breaks. A streaker with only a mobile phone for cover added to the entertainment. Bill Athey and Keith Greenfield added 100 for the 2nd wicket in 61 minutes to set Sussex on the right road but then Kent's second-string attack succeeded where their main men couldn't. Thankfully Athey kept a cool head. His unbeaten 109 in 112 balls was a textbook display of how to keep the scoreboard moving as the home side squeezed home with three balls to spare.

1998: A dismal defeat against Derbyshire in a Sunday League match played on a Monday. Kevin Dean exploited the heavy atmosphere early on as Sussex crashed to 148 all out, losing their first three wickets for 11 runs and their last three for only one. This never remotely troubled their opponents. Australian opener Michael Slater (66) led them home by six wickets in a swagger. One to forget…

1999: For the first time since 1976, the county declined to allocate Horsham a Sunday League match.

2000: A crowd of around 3,000 came to see if Sussex – still to win a Sunday League Division One game – could upset visitors Leicestershire who had yet to lose one. The duration of the match had changed yet again – this time to 45 overs. On a very flat track

Sussex's 219 all out was disappointing. Skipper Chris Adams top-scored with 52 but it was a stop-start effort. With skipper Vince Wells in the vanguard, Leicester set off like an express train but Sussex steadily clawed their way back into it. By sheer tenacity they held their nerve fractionally better than their visitors to edge home by 11 runs. This was hard luck on Wells (81) but the two sides had tied at Grace Road earlier in the season so a close finish was not wholly unexpected.

2001: An inglorious effort. Visitors Worcestershire posted a useful but by no means unassailable 210/6, with half-centuries for Graeme Hick and Vikram Solanki. Pick of the home attack was Mark Robinson who only conceded 17 runs from his allotted nine overs. The pitch was uncharacteristically slow and Sussex had trouble adjusting throughout. Their innings proceeded fitfully and eventually imploded totally. Five wickets fell for six runs in 35 balls to leave Worcester easy victors.

2001: A bonus match in the shape of a 50-over Cheltenham & Gloucester Trophy 3rd round contest between the Sussex Cricket Board and Gloucestershire. The Board XI was only formed in 1996 and was to be disbanded in 2002, the idea being to bring together all forms of recreational cricket in the county. The visitors were one of the leading exponents of knockout cricket in the country and on paper it was a complete mismatch. In the event class did tell but the Board XI gave their more illustrious opponents plenty to think about during the first half of the game. Gloucs were made to work hard for their 238/9, Matt Windows top-scoring with 82. At 37/5 the Board's reply was in total disarray and it says much for their resilience that they rallied to 143. Horsham CC contributed two players to the Board side – Carl Hopkinson and future Notts star Dave Hussey.

2002: With the Championship match a week earlier against Leicestershire ruined by the weather the groundstaff performed prodigies of valour to get this one under way promptly. They were amply rewarded. At 95/5 Sussex would have settled for 240 all out as Matt Prior took 22 off an over from Essex medium-pacer Graham Napier en route to a 55-ball 73. Essex weren't daunted by a start of 4/2. Promoted to No. 3 Napier made a half-century and despite increasingly heavy rain Zimbabwean Andy Flower and England's Ronnie Irani blazed away in the gathering gloom. The light was sepulchral as Essex's final wicket fell with 32 still wanted.

2003: The Championship match just ended had seen a veritable *runfest*. If the sizeable crowd expected more of the same they were in for a grievous disappointment. Usman Afzaal held the Nottinghamshire innings together with 83 and there was an explosive cameo from Kevin Pietersen. However, the real fireworks were supplied by New Zealand all-rounder Chris Cairns who rushed straight to the ground from Heathrow Airport following an 8,000 mile flight from Sri Lanka. His brutal assault on the Sussex attack at the death enabled his side to post a daunting 258/6. Rain had been threatening all afternoon and to make things worse the dreaded Duckworth-Lewis method then came into play. It was all too much for a shell-shocked Sussex who subsided to 150 all out with scarcely a whimper.

2004: Horsham's candidate for the greatest One-day match of all time. The Borough band entertained a 3,000 crowd before the start with the theme tune to 'The Great Escape' but there was to be no way out for Sussex. Adams must have watched in mounting horror as, having given Leicestershire first use of a sublime batting track, the visitors took full advantage. They ended their 45 overs with a staggering 324/4, the highest score ever made against Sussex in the competition. Australia A all-rounder Brad Hodge made a quite breathtaking 154 off 122 balls – again the highest individual score ever made against Sussex in the competition - moving from 100 to 150 in just 17 deliveries. With Darren Maddy (95 off 92 balls), Hodge put on 165 for the 2nd wicket, yet another record. Mohammad Akram took 1/63 off his nine overs while James Kirtley's eight cost 75. Sussex fought back stronger than any side in the history of the competition. Ian Ward struck a sparkling 136 off 120 balls and incredibly they found themselves requiring 29 to win from the final two overs. Thirteen came from the first of these with Mike Yardy on strike for the fateful last act. With two deliveries left the 'ask' stood at 10. The first of these was paddled to the fine leg boundary while the second was lofted high, straight down the ground. To Sussex's mortification it landed just inside the playing area to leave their visitors victorious by one run. Adams' reaction to such a fabulous match? 'We did not deserve a win. I was very disappointed with the way we bowled and...fielded.'

2005: To the amazement of many the pitch was deemed unfit and the scheduled four and One-day matches against Warwickshire moved at short notice to Hove. For reasons explained elsewhere, this decision was probably correct and there was sadness but no arguments from Horsham C&SC.

2006: This was Sussex's first-ever Cheltenham & Gloucester Trophy match at Horsham, on Whit Monday against Somerset. Sadly the rain ruined it. After several downpours and inspections Somerset put together a competitive total which was revised several times under the Duckworth-Lewis method through a damp and depressing afternoon. Despite losing four wickets with the score on 16 Sussex finally overhauled it at the death thanks to some explosive and uncomplicated hitting from young all-rounder Luke Wright (32 off 17 balls), supported more prosaically by Robin Martin-Jenkins. Many spectators actually went home, believing (erroneously) that there would be no further play.

2007: A belated decision to restore Horsham's four-day match did not extend as far as the One-day one. For the third time in nine seasons there was no One-day cricket on offer at Cricket Field Road.

With Worcestershire due to visit in 2008 the only sides still to be seen in One-day action at Horsham are Glamorgan, Middlesex and Yorkshire.

Chapter 11
TO SEE OURSELVES AS OTHERS SEE US

Part of the charm of the Horsham Festival is its timelessness. In 1913, a newsreel film was made showing crowds making their way down The Causeway to the ground. If these same people could be transported to the early part of the 21st century they would find this part of their journey remarkably unchanged.

In June 1912 the influential periodical *Cricket: A Weekly Record Of The Game* painted an equally engaging picture. In the context of a feature speculating how Kent's tradition of holding Cricket Weeks around the county may have been a factor in their recent run of success, it went on, '*Other county committees have perceived this and the number of weeks has increased largely of recent years...Given fine weather, the latest Week of all, that at Horsham, seems assured of success. The West Sussex town is just the place for a Week; the smaller towns around send in contingents of enthusiasts for whom the Hove ground is too distant...Emerging from the station, the visitor sees before him a broad highway, gay with banners and bunting. This leads him to the clean little town – sleepy some may say, but spacious and pleasant. Past the Town Hall and through what looks like a cathedral close he goes, crosses the youthful Arun – not much of a river here – and finds himself on a ground that can give points to Tonbridge for charm. And if, once there, he cannot enjoy himself, he must be very hard to please... Shift your eyes from the middle, and have a glance at the lovely country around – watch the trains passing on the line hard by, and note how travellers lean from the windows for just a glimpse of the cricket as they pass. '* This description has a certain period innocence but is eminently recognisable almost a century later and must have been just the sort of boost a fledgling Festival needed.

Ten years later the veteran Gloucestershire slow left-armer George Dennett proclaimed it 'the prettiest ground he had ever seen'. Mind you, he had just arrived from the grimy vastness of the Oval and had also just taken seven wickets in his side's unexpected victory, so perhaps he had reason for such generosity.

The 22 June 1929 edition of the opinion-forming *Cricketer'* magazine enquired of its readers: *'Is there any more charming ground in England than Horsham? Others have more obvious, more stately, beauty, Canterbury and Maidstone for example, but Horsham is more truly "the country" than any of them. The approach is perfect – round the corner of a church, down the churchyard, across a wooden bridge, over a smooth, limpid water, and up a little path to the marquees at the top. Looking across towards the pavilion, the country is wide and generous, thick woods and sloping fields. It is all very quiet and very English and the progress of even the most important county match is always liable to be interrupted by a wobbling procession of quacking ducks; and in the outfield one can sometimes see one or two meditatively scratching hens.'* Once again not the least interesting aspect of this is that 79 years on, the description – less perhaps the ducks and hens – is instantly recognisable today.

Sussex and England captain Arthur Gilligan loved playing at Horsham. Writing in his 1933 history, *Sussex Cricket*, he leaves us the following vignette: *'I can safely say there is no ground in the whole of England that has a more delightful and rural aspect than Horsham. It is a real country ground, possessing every attribute of real sylvan glades and surroundings. A fine rustic pavilion graces the west part of the ground; a large marquee, which acts as a tea tent, is to be seen at the north end with the pretty church spire towering in the background, and there are some glorious trees on the eastern edge, under which Sussex farmers, postmen, labourers and all branches of honourable pursuits are seated. The Southern Railway lies away in the south-east corner, and cricket is always suspended while the trains go past the screen.'* A touch romantic perhaps, but even when at the pinnacle of his career Gilligan spent much time in the town during Festival Week giving homely and much appreciated lectures to the YMCA and other groups such as the Victory Road Old Boys' Association.

The deep-seated need to reach back to a Golden Age is nothing new. In 1936 one of the London dailies informed its readers: *'I know of few grounds where cricket can be better enjoyed than at Horsham, where the game is played, as it should be, on a village green. One of the drawbacks of cricket…is that matches tend to become spectacles in an arena rather than games on a field and the character of the game changes with its surroundings. If ever I had to explain to a foreign visitor what cricket meant to English people (an impossible task by the way) I should take him to Horsham rather than Lord's.'*

The social and personal turmoil caused by war accentuates this human need to look back. The distinguished poet and scholar Edmund Blunden's elegiac 'Cricket Country' was published in 1944. Blunden – who went to Christ's Hospital – recalled how he kept wicket at Cricket Field Road for the Invalids, a bohemian touring side put together by JC Squire and immortalised in AG Macdonnell's *England their England*. Even if a match had to be abandoned because of the weather, Blunden writes, *'I am still glad to have been once again setting foot on that ground...There, from wooded knoll to wooded knoll, from leaning spire to lime tree avenue, a swift and beautiful phantom is my master. Looking one way from the ground I fall into dreams with the dreaming spire, which leans as though in very truth it were sinking gently to sleep;... beyond it, you discover the quiet streets of cool exquisite houses...and then all those good old shopping quarters and stores and craftsmen's establishments... The umpire has meanwhile called 'Over ball' and next by change of ends I can look past the railway bridge, a footbridge which does not disturb the scene of the ages before the railway, at the rising ground of Denne, with its wide-spreading boughs and occasionally spiky oak...'*

With hope and optimism coursing through the land in the first post-war season, Robertson-Glasgow caught the *Zeitgeist* when contributing the following to the 1946 Festival programme: *'Words, few or many, could not describe the beauties (geographical and otherwise) of Horsham, appointed by nature for Cricket Festivals... When I was last fortunate enough to play here – I will say it! – Somerset won. May they do so in this year's match; but by only one run or one desperate wicket, as the sun westers and the old familiar silence waits upon every ball.'* The charming but ultimately tragic Robertson-Glasgow knew the Horsham area well. He played a large part in Somerset's victory there in 1925 and in 1930 turned out for the Old Malvernians in the marvellous country house cricket festivals staged in nearby St Leonard's Forest by Mr JT McGaw and his family.

This same hope and idealism is captured by the author and broadcaster Dudley Carew. His book *To the Wicket* was published in 1946 and contains yet another beautifully crafted piece about Horsham. Acknowledging the snare and then tumbling headlong into it, he wrote *'Cricket literature is perhaps inclined to babble overmuch of green fields, and the sun on the ale house at times shines a little too strongly, but for all that, Horsham is a ground which tugs at the heart and the memory....Round one side of it runs a railway, and every now and then a train, which is doubtless prosaic and much like any other train, but somehow contrives to seem oddly primitive and unreal, puffs round and causes the bowler to pause in his run. There is a little wooden pavilion square with the wicket, a number of appropriate tents and an atmosphere which contrives to hold the spirit of a country festival and of a game not too far removed from the village green by averages and sophistication.'*

However nominally, David Sheppard was a playing member of Horsham CC and his family had lived in the nearby village of Slinfold since he was eight years of age. The chillier post-war winds of financial austerity prompted him to write in the 1953 Festival programme that *'there is a certain almost sleepy charm about Horsham which puts it at the top of many people's list of favourite grounds'*. Living so locally, Sheppard was better placed than most to appreciate how Horsham *'has been in danger of losing its week to the demands of an anxious treasury'.*

By 1956 however, the demands of Sheppard's anxious treasury were about to overwhelm the Festival. The programme that year carried a piece by Maurice Tate that was all the more poignant because by the time it saw the light of day Tate was in his grave. Interviewed at his pub at Wadhurst, Maurice was naturally saddened to learn that county cricket would no longer be seen at *'one of the finest natural surroundings'* he had ever played at. He recalled fondly the joys of *'the famous Christ's Hospital school band playing in the interval – the marquees and that most hospitable tea tent where...us players all ate too much chocolate cake, etc. It was truly one of the social successes of the year and many a time we would exceed the tea interval time because of it.'* Another to lament the passing of the Festival was Northants' George Tribe. He told John Dew that nowhere else on the county circuit could he simultaneously play cricket and watch a herd of

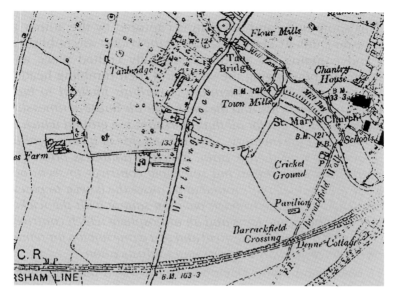

16. Here in 1898 there is no trace of the present-day Cricket Field Road, while the pavilion – presented to the club by the Lucas family of Warnham Court in 1878 – is situated by the railway close to the Barrackfield crossing.

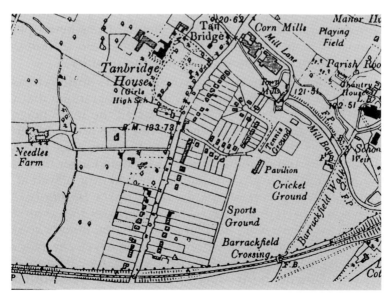

17. By the 1930s it is much more recognisable.

18. The legendary Jack Hobbs played six times at Horsham between 1909 and 1934. In 1912 he and his veteran partner Tom Hayward put on 50 in the first half hour.

19. Charlie Oakes (20 matches). Born in the groundsman's cottage in 1912, he made a century for Horsham CC at the age of 16. Made his County debut at Horsham in 1935. Three years later (v Surrey) made his only century on his father's wicket. Lived to be 95.

20. At the age of 20 Charlie's brother Jack (11 matches) scored 157 for Horsham against Christ's Hospital. A lively, ebullient character he and fellow local boy George Cox hold the County's record 6th wicket partnership on the ground.

21. Only Maurice Tate has taken more career wickets for Sussex than Warnham's George Cox senior (22 matches) and only Tate and Jim Cornford have taken more at Horsham. Yet George's 9/50 in 'Cox's match' in 1926 is not the best individual performance on the ground.

22. Old George's son young George (27 matches) made 50 centuries for Sussex but only one of them on his home ground – and he was 41 years old when he managed that. Yet only the Langridge brothers, Ted Bowley and Jim Parks senior have scored more runs at Horsham than George Cox junior.

HORSHAM AND WEST SUSSEX
COUNTY CRICKET WEEK

SUSSEX v. OXFORD UNIVERSITY,
June 24th, 25th and 26th,

SUSSEX v. SURREY,
June 27th, 28th and 29th.

The above matches will be played on the

Horsham Cricket Ground.

A Band will play during each Afternoon.

Tea will be generously provided by Ladies of West Sussex and many parts of Surrey, and sold by them in and outside the Enclosure for the Benefit of the County Club.

TEA (including, Cake, and Bread and Butter) 6d outside the Enclosure.
LUNCHEONS will be supplied on the Ground each day by the Caterer, Mr. A. STREET, at 2/6 and 1/- per head.

Admission to the Ground, 6d.

Tickets 1s. each for either Match may be obtained from the following, if taken before the day of the Match.

BILLINGSHURST, Mr. W. Joyes.	CRANLEIGH, Mr. Elliott.	RUSPER, Mr. W. Martin.
" Mr. Argent.	ITCHINGFIELD, Mr. Peskett.	RUDGWICK, Mr. Cowdery.
BROADBRIDGE HEATH, Mr. Richardson.	LOWER BEEDING, Mr. Edwards.	SOUTHWATER, Mr. J. Burchett.
CRAWLEY, Mr J. Baker.	PARTRIDGE GREEN, Mr. G. Mitchell.	SLINFOLD, Mr. J. Spence.
" Mr H. Melling.	PULBOROUGH, Mr. L. N. Corden.	WARNHAM, Mr. F. W. Freeman.
COWFOLD, Mr. W. Sprinks.	ROFFEY, Mr. F. Passell.	WEST GRINSTEAD, Mr S Tidey.

HORSHAM—Mr. A. Peirce, 12, Station Road ; Mr. J. Foreman, East Street ; Mr. A. Street, The Nelson ; Mr. Huntley, West Street ; Messrs. Hunt Brothers, West Street

The L.B. & S.C.R. are kindly issuing Cheap Tickets each day up to three o'clock.

EVENING ENTERTAINMENTS

At the KING'S HEAD ASSEMBLY ROOMS. "KIPLING DETECTIVE," by Arthur C. Oddie, J.P., will be presented Monday, Tuesday and Thursday evenings, and The "HAMS" MINSTREL TROUPE will appear Wednesday and Friday.

Late trains will be run to Brighton via Steyning, Guildford and Three Bridges, stopping at all Stations, provided sufficient passengers are guaranteed. Particulars apply to Mr. C. Hunt, 2, West St , Horsham.

For Further Particulars see large Bills.

"West Sussex County Times," Horsham.

23. The Oxford University attack at the 1912 Festival was described as being so ineffective as to positively invite punishment, Sussex winning by an innings and plenty.

24. A contemporary matchday view looking towards the tennis courts and St Mary's Church.

25. Action from the first morning's play against Worcestershire in 2001.
Michael Yardy has just been dismissed and Murray Goodwin defends watchfully against Andy Bichel. Non-striker is Bas Zuiderent.
The scoreboard fell victim to arsonists in February 2003.

1939
PROGRAMME

The present Cricket Ground about 80 years ago
(From a Painting in possession of Wm. Albery)

HORSHAM COUNTY
CRICKET FESTIVAL

26. The much sought-after Festival programmes were produced between 1931 and 1956 by local journalist Bob Green. That for 1939 proudly boasts 'the present ground provides a rural charm unequalled in the country.
That is what we in Horsham think and our visitors invariably agree with us.'

27. Carl Hopkinson plays club cricket for Horsham CC and made a half-century in his one County appearance to date at Cricket Field Road.

28. John Dew never played County cricket on his home turf but as Horsham CC captain for 10 seasons and club president for over 40 more, he has probably spent more hours on the ground than most. He is now 88 and a former GP in the town.

29. Another playing member of Horsham CC, reserve wicket keeper Andrew Hodd also scored a half-century on his only first-class innings on the ground, helping skipper Chris Adams put on 158 for the 5th wicket v Durham in 2007.

30. Yet another 'Dewdrop', Chris Nash has been playing cricket at Horsham since the age of seven. He too made a half-century on his only first-class appearance to date on home soil.

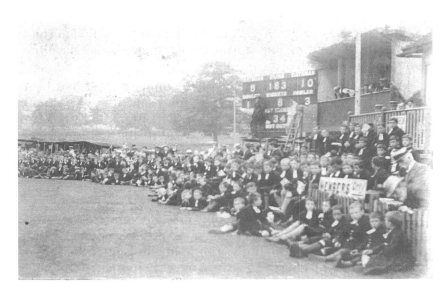

31. One from the archives. Serried ranks of scholars from Christ's Hospital watch attentively as Surrey's first innings draws to a close in 1909. 'Shrimp' Leveson Gower is the 'last man 34'.

32. Oh dear! Durham's opening bat Mark Stoneman is comprehensively bowled by Rana Naved-ul-Hasan in the second over of his side's second innings in 2007. It was Stoneman's first-class debut.

Friesian cows. Of course the fact that he regularly scythed through Sussex's fragile batting line-ups of the time might also have had something to do with it...

A brief clerical interlude. By 1986, county cricket had been restored, but sadly the clerk of the weather saw fit to visit rain of near-Biblical proportions on the town. This prompted the Rev'd Derek Tansill, Vicar of Horsham, to write to the *County Times*: *'with reference to the caption to your gloomy picture of Horsham cricket ground and equally gloomy silhouette of the parish church',* commenting that *'we occasionally pray for good weather in St Mary's, but never "to the fates". Who are they?'*

John Vinicombe was a well known Sussex pressman who in 1962 took over from the legendary Jack Arlidge as chief sports correspondent for the Brighton *Argus*. The perils attendant upon membership of the Fourth Estate are never better illustrated than in the following recollection from the 1993 county yearbook: *'Once when Horsham's pavilion was built on very short stilts, there was enough space for a man to crawl underneath. It came to pass after one long and very hot day that Archie Quick, of the Sunday Pictorial, decided to sleep off the effects of a heavy lunch and sought the only available shade on the ground. Dear old Archie squeezed his not inconsiderable girth underneath and fell into a blissful sleep and awoke the next morning... In Horsham's refurbished clubhouse, the Press occupy a sort of passageway from the dining area which is separated by a door, and the men's and women's lavatories. There is also a little room at the end of the passage where the physiotherapist can examine patients. Very rarely do all the doors remain shut through the hours of play. Through the door opening out onto the ground stretch long queues of both sexes, some with legs tightly crossed and wearing pained expressions. Doors bang, cisterns flush in a constant symphony of cascading water and wood knocking on wood. Sometimes a thin curtain is suspended between writers and the great chattering throng, but more often than not, this is clawed aside to afford a better view of "those Press people"'.*

By this time concerns over the capriciousness of the Horsham wicket had long evaporated. It was known round the county circuit as being one where batsmen might feast like panthers. Sussex skipper Alan Wells wrote a personal diary of the 1994 season, which was published as *The Captain's Year*. In this he observed that *'Horsham is a ground on which you hope to win the toss...It offers bounce and turn for the bowlers and short boundaries with the ball coming on for the batsman. I... was looking for the classic four-day scenario: bat first, post a large total, and bowl them out twice.'* In a memorable encounter that year against a Wasim Akram-inspired Lancashire, Wells' strategy was vindicated – but only just...

In 1997 this reputation for heavy run scoring was endorsed, a touch ruefully, by incoming chief executive Tony Pigott, who remarked that *'Horsham is always a good cricket wicket, though I can't say I enjoyed too much success with the ball. Batsmen usually made hay.'* Pigott enjoyed a lengthy county career with Sussex and also played club cricket for Horsham CC but a glance at the statistical section of this book (alas) bears out his melancholy recollection.

Martin Speight was a talented wicketkeeper/batsman who never perhaps did himself full justice in the 1990s for either Sussex or Durham. He was also a talented watercolourist. In his book *Cricketer's View* he wrote, *'Horsham is a great place to play cricket. Matches here are often-high scoring, there is always a festival atmosphere with good crowds and the pavilion a delightful place to sit out and watch cricket. I started playing league cricket at Horsham as a teenager and have enjoyed coming here year on year ever since.'*

Brian Halford used a full colour shot of the ground looking towards St Mary's church as the front cover for his 2004 book *Year of the Bear* a blow-by-blow celebration of Warwickshire's Championship success. He observed that the side were obliged to stay at the *Holiday Inn* at Crawley because Horsham lacked a hotel large enough to accommodate a modern-day cricket team and its retinue. He made one or two general remarks to the effect that while headquarters grounds may possess the kudos and grandeur, outgrounds also capture the spirit of the game – even if players and spectators do have to 'rough it' a bit. Halford felt that with nets plonked down on the outfield, rows of trees and rows of marquees, Horsham in a word was 'gorgeous'. He described Ian Bell's record knock of 262 not out as 'masterful batting in a beautiful location.'

But let the final – and extended – word rest with national journalist Alan Lee. Throughout the summer of 2001 Lee ran a feature entitled 'The Good Grounds Guide' which awarded marks out of 10 to a number of county grounds against ten different criteria. Trent Bridge with 78 held a narrow lead over Durham's Riverside (77), with Grace Road at Leicester bringing up the rear. In full (more or less) this is how Lee perceived Horsham: *'The character of Horsham is revealed on leaving the cricket ground by the quaint back gate, crossing the river by the wooden footbridge and passing through the churchyard of St Mary's into a civilised and very English street called Causeway. Amid immaculate and venerable residences, the landmarks last week were a shop selling Aga cookers and the campaign centre for the local Conservative Party.*

Horsham is true to the popular perception of typical Home Counties, that land of teashops and tennis parties and Tory voters. Its pedestrianised centre is overseen by a Victorian bandstand and a cheese shop ('picnic baskets filled to order'). Its cricket ground is one of the surviving delights of the county circuit.

Every county used to have its outgrounds, those once-a-year venues that added variety and vitality to the programme. Now, almost half never leave their headquarters. Driven by hard economics, to the exclusion of the missionary spirit, this is a worrying trend for all who prefer cricket in its most natural habitat.

First used in 1851, (Horsham) remains a well-used venue, partly by being so endearing but also through its position. Solicitous roadsigns usher traffic from the A24, missing the town centre and nipping down an inconspicuous side street to the entrance. The one drawback is that Cricket Field Road (it really is called that) is extremely narrow, causing inevitable problems at start and close of play. Space is not a problem inside, for a colts ground provides a convenient and ample car park, supervised by stewards wearing Festival polo shirts.

Not the least of Festival ground pleasures is the attitude of the staff. Generally, they are club members, volunteers working for a beloved cause, and it is amazing how much cheerier and more helpful this makes them than the jobsworth professionals. Plainly, too, Horsham is a thriving club. There are tennis courts at one end and squash courts in an extension to the low-slung pavilion, an unprepossessing structure softened by hanging baskets and rows of chairs on a tiered terrace. Inside there are three dartboards and a notice board detailing functions. There was a music workshop last night, a jazz night this evening.

Counties increasingly resist such venues, claiming that their routines are derailed, but Sussex and Horsham clearly co-exist contentedly. The public address system mixed club and county news and grew quite active after a post-prandial lull in early afternoon. Two club scoreboards operated efficiently. Sussex, meanwhile, distributed their simple but informative Scorecard Extra sheets, in which the team news of the day is explained along with items of general interest. A miniature version of the county shop was selling its replica kit and merchandise alongside an extensive second-hand bookstall.

Further round, in the nets area near where the rail line to Victoria thunders past, spectators were invited to pay £2.50 to have their bowling speed measured by a radar gun. There was a mobile betting booth and the sort of beer tent you might find at a village fete (though sadly lacking any real ale). What there was not is any proper catering for the general spectator.

A burger van next to the betting shop was the sole provision for the appetites of those itinerants who might just have fancied a day watching cricket...and this, alone of the ground's features and facilities, left a poor impression. It is not good enough to claim that members could eat in the pavilion. To prosper, cricket must go out of its way to attract as many as possible who have not already paid their county subscriptions. For those with the correct accreditation, the pavilion fare was well above average...

The nicest place to watch from...is in front of the tennis courts. Here, perched on one of hundreds of loose chairs, the play feels close and is visually enhanced by a backdrop of mature trees on lovely downland slopes.

There are no stands at Horsham, little shelter and few public facilities. Yet it is a ground with soul and atmosphere, a ground to which people will still hurry after work to watch an hour's cricket in the evening sun. It is a reminder of what has been lost and what county cricket must never completely surrender.'

For the record, Horsham in 2001 scored 8 for access, 8 for car parking, 6 for comfort, 6 for catering, 7 for bars, 9 for staff attitude, 8 for aesthetics, 7 for communications, 6 for scoreboards and 5 for viewing and shelter. Total 70, equal with Bristol.

It is a question of playing to one's strengths. As a club ground Horsham, like Guildford and Southgate, can never hope to provide a full range of headquarters facilities. Yet that is its appeal – that is precisely why people visit and record their experience in such glowing terms. It reminds them of a time – and values – long vanished. In descriptive terms Lee has visited a ground that would be recognised by Arthur Oddie and old George Cox, by Arthur Gilligan and Bob Green. Despite the financial imperatives that increasingly define whether a commodity endures or not, the challenge for those in charge of cricket in Horsham is to ensure that the essence of this gossamer-like charm is not lost in the hurly-burly of 21st century life.

182

Chapter 12
PROFILES

The British are a strange, obsessive race. They are forever talking about the weather. Or forming clubs. Or compiling lists. In considering potential members of the Horsham Festival 'Top Ten' it is disturbing how many high-quality candidates cannot be accommodated. No room for example for Bob Green, that great hearted local journalist who kept the flame of the souvenir programme burning bright from 1931 right through to 1956. On the playing front there is no room for locally produced favourites such as Paul Parker, who also played rugby for Horsham; or, from a much earlier era, Crabtree's Tim Killick, who learnt his cricket under a lamp-post in the Normandy when a pupil at Collyer's Grammar School before it moved to Hurst Road. Off the field, no place either for unsung heroes such as Mike Beckwith (who sadly died while this book was in preparation); Barry Peay, who started his playing career with Horsham CC in the early 1960s and is still going strong; and the ever-genial Chris Hoskins, each of whom have spent countless hours ensuring that all goes well. Or long-serving groundsman Bill Ford, whose misfortune it was to have his tenure of office largely coincide with the dark years when the county eschewed Horsham. Bill could at least be consoled with the memory of a day when the great Australian fast bowler Graham McKenzie told him that his had been the quickest wicket he had played on all season.

So, having given a flavour of those who were unable to cement their place in the hall of the greats, who have been admitted to full membership? Lacking the courage to place them in anything other than chronological order, step forward

ARTHUR ODDIE

Arthur Campbell Oddie, the son of Henry Hoyle Oddie of Coney Park, St Albans, was born at Tilgate Forest, Crawley in 1856. He was educated at two comparatively obscure schools: Seigar's preparatory in Stevenage and Beaumont College, Old Windsor. It is not known what brought him back to Sussex but as a man of independent means he had settled at North Lodge, a large house set in its own grounds in North Parade (close to the present-day White Horse Close) by 1881. He soon became an integral part of the social fabric locally. Oddie had a strong artistic streak and as a young man studied painting in Belgium and Italy. He had a particular penchant for amateur dramatics, directing and taking many leading roles in local productions and was also a playwright. A man of many parts, he was president from its inception of the annual town Carnival which, under his energetic influence, was soon to forge strong and enduring links with the cricket Festival. As with many men of his social class he was also a local JP, prominent Conservative and keen supporter of the local Primrose League. He married in 1876 and his wife Hilda – a most interesting woman in her own right – bore him two sons, Francis in 1879 and Neville in 1882. But it is as a sportsman and sporting administrator that he has the greatest claim on our time. Oddie was a keen devotee of bowls, croquet, tennis, shooting and fishing but cricket was indubitably his greatest love. A playing member of Horsham CC for 22 seasons (1881-1902 and occasionally thereafter), he was club captain and hon. sec. from 1886 until 1899. Primarily an opening bat with an adamantine defence, he played in over 320 matches, scoring 4,500 runs at a respectable average and carrying his bat on three occasions. His highest score came on a June afternoon in 1893 – 103 v. the delightfully named Wandering Screws. Oddie was also a member of the county committee at Hove for more than two decades and chairman from 1908 until 1910. He was very much alive to Horsham's sporting traditions and became almost fixated by a desire to bring county cricket to the town on an enduring basis. A dynamic, restless visionary with a finger in umpteen pies, he died at home in October 1914 at the early age of 58, a grievous loss to the local community.

Ten years later the 1924 Festival was overshadowed for many by the shocking death just before the start of the season of

GEORGE BENJAMIN STREET

On the morning of 24 April George Street had attended pre-season training at the county ground. He was motorcycling home along the Old Shoreham Road when he swerved to avoid a stationary lorry at the Southern Cross crossroads at Portslade and accelerated into a wall. He was found bleeding from the head, nose and mouth and pronounced dead at the scene 11 minutes later. He was 34. By a supreme irony, a man with whom George had served through most of the Great War was also killed at the very same location the previous week. George Street was born just over the Surrey border in Charlwood in December 1889 but was very much a Sussex man, living virtually all his life in Warnham just round the corner from his brother in law, George Cox. He made his Sussex debut against Cambridge University in June 1909 and it was obvious from the outset that here was a ready-made replacement for the veteran wicketkeeper Harry Butt, though he wasn't able to nail down a regular spot until 1912. George scored one century for Sussex – 109 v. Essex at Colchester in 1921 – hitting JWHT Douglas for five fours in one over in the process. But as a wicketkeeper he had few equals in the country at the time of his death and might very well have added to his solitary England cap, earned as a replacement for Hampshire's Walter Livsey on the 1922/23 MCC tour to South Africa. In all he accounted for 419 batsmen (304 ct, 115 stumped), 97 of them in the 1923 season alone, having seen off a determined challenge to his place from the bespectacled mathematics teacher RA (Dick) Young. But for the Great War, which, courtesy of a delayed demobilisation also caused him to miss the entire 1919 season, there is no telling what heights George Street might have scaled. With tragic inaccuracy, *Wisden* prophesied in 1922 that 'Street is young and has plenty of time before him.' A carpenter by trade George was also a keen footballer, playing for both Warnham and Horsham. During the War he served with the 6th Cyclists Battalion, rising to the rank of sergeant-major and seeing service in Mesopotamia and India. Despite wretched weather, hundreds of mourners attended his funeral at Warnham parish church, anxious to pay a last farewell to someone who was very much part of the village. The pallbearers were his old pals Joe Vine, Maurice Tate, Ted Bowley, Joe Stannard, Tich Cornford and Bert Wensley. Virtually the entire Sussex team and officials were present as well as Captain Cornwallis and fellow stumper Jack Hubble from Kent. A popular, friendly man, George Street left a wife and four-year-old son. He also left a gaping hole in the lives of all who had known him.

We remain in the village of Warnham for our next profile.

GEORGE COX (SENIOR)

At the end of the 1928 season George Rubens Cox decided his

old legs could take no more and finally hung up his boots. Born at Friday Street, Warnham in November 1873, he was thus almost 55. After an apprenticeship served in local village cricket, Horsham CC and the Sussex Colts and 2nd XIs, his first-team debut arrived in 1895. Between 1893 and the early part of 1895 he was a regular member of Horsham CC, taking 80 wickets at 7.5 apiece in 1895 and 160 at 10 apiece in all. His professional career was slow-burning rather than meteoric, but as *Barclay's World of Cricket* noted in 1980, he 'became a formidable left-hand bowler. In 1905 he was spoken of by some who should have known better as the equal of Rhodes and Blythe. That he never was, but at his best, he was a fine bowler.' Fine enough indeed to take over 1,800 wickets at 23 apiece, score over 14,500 runs at 19 apiece and hold over 500 catches – a prodigious record by any yardstick. His highest score was 167 n/o v. Hampshire at Chichester in 1906, while he helped Harry Butt add 156 for the 10th wicket v. Cambridge University in 1908. His bowling is studded with startling analyses, including 5 for 0 in 6 overs v. Somerset at Weston-super-Mare in 1921 and 7 for 8 in 16 overs v. Derby at Hastings in 1920. He was also on the Lord's groundstaff for many years and in 1907 took all 10 wickets v. the Royal Navy. He was awarded the plum fixture against Yorkshire at Hove in 1914 for his benefit only to see it cancelled on account of the Great War. George was always interested in coaching making four visits to South Africa and one to India during his playing days and becoming county coach for a while in retirement. He was a gruff, genial character, popular wherever he went but as historian John Marshall also made clear, he 'was a nuggety old warhorse with splashes of grey in his military moustache and a tongue that belied a pair of kindly eyes.' Squat and thickset, he was not known as 'The Guv'nor' for nothing and chased the young pros in the Sussex dressing room as relentlessly as any sergeant-major. If possible he was an even greater terror to his own son, to whom, for fear of accusations of nepotism, he is said to have scarcely ever spoken an encouraging word. Even in retirement, he found it difficult to unbend. In 1939 young George made 232 at Kettering and 182 at Hove on successive days. On returning home – and no doubt feeling just a little bit pleased with himself – the old man simply growled 'what's the matter with you then? Gone mad or something?' A tough cookie no doubt, but them were different days...Old George was the quintessential embodiment of a good old county professional and for many years was 'senior pro' in the Sussex dressing room where he was of inestimable value to Arthur Gilligan and others. Indeed Gilligan described him as 'one of the finest gentlemen professional cricketers ever to step into a pair of boots' and he was deservedly made an honorary life member by the county in 1937. George Cox was a simple man who set and lived by simple, old fashioned values. Straight as a die, he never deviated far from his country roots and died in March 1949 at the age of 76 - ironically while visiting his daughter in Dorking Hospital.

Horsham was fortunate in the calibre of its cricketing administrators and we look now at another of these who took over the reins after the Great War following the untimely death of Arthur Oddie.

REV'D EDL HARVEY

The Rev'd Edward Douglas Lennox Harvey OBE, DL, JP was pre-eminent in both local and county politics. Son of William Harvey, DL, of Carnoustie (Angus), Douglas Harvey was born in 1859 and educated at Harrow and Trinity College Cambridge, where he won a soccer Blue. He had an equally distinguished brother, Colonel Sir George Samuel Abercrombie Harvey, who saw service in the Middle East and during the Great War was Provost Marshal for Cairo, Upper and Middle Egypt. Harvey was ordained into the Church of England by the Bishop of Dover and spent seven years as a curate in Croydon, following which he became rector of Downham Market in Norfolk. He moved to the splendid mansion of Beedingwood House (off the Forest Road near Colgate) in the 1890s and appears to have relinquished his clerical duties around this time. A man of independent means – his family were connected to the famous Bristol-based sherry firm – he married Constance Annie Hills in 1885. Three years after her death he married again, this time to Emma Jessie Thornton, daughter of Philip Rawson JP of Pease Pottage and widow of Edward Thornton, a diplomat who had been stationed in Central America. Harvey became involved in an astonishing range of activities in his public life: to give just a flavour of these, he sat on West Sussex County Council for 40 years, becoming chairman of the Finance Committee in 1928 where he was said to be 'a born financier with a great grasp of figures'. The development of the new Horsham Hospital was due largely to his driving energies and this was an abiding interest. In addition he was – inter alia – chairman of Collyer's School, the local Conservative Association, the local bench of magistrates and the Crawley & Horsham Hunt, the latter another abiding passion. Just for a change he was president of the Horsham branch of the YMCA and of the county agricultural show. He was deputy lieutenant of the county and a long-time member of Horsham Rural District Council and the Board of Guardians. How he found time to assume the presidency of Sussex CCC in 1935 is anyone's guess but he had been closely involved with the town's cricket Festival since its inception and contemporary newspaper coverage confirms that his was an active presence. Contemporary comment has it that 'probably no other person in West Sussex has such a wide interest in public affairs.' Indeed so. That is the public face of the man: conscientious, industrious – almost obsessively so some might think. But privately – and the two may very well be linked - Harvey's life was touched by great sorrow, for only one of the five children by his first marriage survived him. One daughter (Marjorie) drowned at the age of eight in May 1897; at the age of 13, youngest son Ian died of pneumonia while a pupil at Eton in April 1908, only months before the death of his first wife. Two other sons were killed in the first few months of the Great War at Messines: Douglas on 3 November 1914, aged 22; while Frank had been reported missing a few days earlier. A few days after the marriage of a son from his second marriage in early July 1938, Harvey himself died at home at the age of 79 – his death hastened, many felt, by a relentless, self-imposed burden of work and duty. Douglas Harvey was buried four days later in a simple ceremony in Colgate, his coffin being borne to the church from his estate on a simple farm wagon.

He has been referred to probably more often than any other person in the preceding pages. Time finally to look at the life and times of

ALFRED (JOKER) OAKES

After 44 seasons faithfully tending his beloved square and ground, Alfred Oakes decided, at the age of 72 to call it a day at the end of the 1954 season. Son of a Horsham family of gunsmiths –

his father had a shop in Market Square - Alfred was born on 20 April 1882 ('Hitler's birthday' he used to remind folk). Soon after the turn of the century, he was on the groundstaff at Beaumont College Windsor before, in 1905, taking up a similar appointment at Christ's Hospital. In February 1911 he took over the reins at Horsham and lived for the remainder of his long life in a little cottage at the river end of the ground. 'Joker' was a very good cricketer himself, starting his career with the Volunteers, playing for Horsham CC as a teenager and scoring his first century against long-defunct West Grinstead in 1901. He completed the 'double' for Horsham in 1921 ('a dry season and good for run-getting' he recalled). In all he scored almost 10,000 runs for the club at 29 apiece and took over 1,000 wickets at 13.5 with a highest score of 143 n/o v Horley in 1923. Alfred was also a fine footballer playing for 18 seasons up to the Great War for Horsham FC (captaining the side for the final two) and being awarded his county colours in 1908/09. Several professional sides were apparently interested in him, including Queen's Park Rangers. He joined the 9th Battalion, Royal Sussex Regiment in 1914 and after being invalided home when a trench collapsed on him was transferred to the Durham Light Infantry. Alf sired four sons – Charlie, Jack, Arthur and Alfred (who predeceased him) - and two daughters, Dorothy and May. In what was a real family enterprise, all would pitch in and help in some capacity or other during Festival week (along with his wife). The girls would clean each cricketer's boots and pads for sixpence. Jack recalled having to take the Festival week off school as a young lad to help out. 'Dad was a very hard man to work for. Everything had to be just right...I must have got the sack about once a week'. As with old George Cox, Joker was hard on his boys even when they made it into the county side. Again Jack was to recall late in life how 'It really worried mother if we didn't do well because she would then have to bear the full brunt of dad's temper'. A man of conservative habits, Alfred was no great lover of modern technology. The story is told that after being required to trade in his old horse for a mechanised motor mower, his initial efforts to master 'the new-fangled mechanical thing' almost foundered at the first fence when the machine somehow got into gear and lumbered round the stable with Alfred lunging at the controls while cursing and swearing in a manner quite remarkable even for him. Of his wickets, John Marshall remarked generously in 1959 that they were 'true enough so that the strokemaker could make plenty of runs, even if the ball did sometimes tend to fly a bit'. John Dew recalls telling Alfred how a (completely fictitious) complaint had been received that his wickets in a club match weren't pitched in a straight line and what was he going to do about it. Apparently it took some hours for tranquility to be restored. At the end of the 1954 season a benefit match was staged for 'Joker' which saw Horsham CC entertain a star-studded Invitation XI captained by EW Swanton and including many of the current Sussex side along with Bob Barber and AH Kardar of Pakistan. At the end of the game Alf was presented with a huge cake in the shape of a cricket pitch, complete with wickets, pavilion and scoreboard. In retirement he served as bar steward until late 1959 but was always to be found by his wide circle of cronies for a chat over old times at his cottage. Alfred Oakes died in Horsham Hospital on 16 August 1965 at the age of 83 and his ashes were strewn on the ground on 3 October. His funeral in the parish church was a unique cricketing occasion and why not - his was a record of selfless and devoted service to a club and ground he loved that is truly breathtaking. Apparently he was nicknamed 'Joker' because of a startling capacity for grumbling at anything and everything connected with work. O rare Alfred Oakes! Club president John Dew recalled a wonderful story-teller who was universally liked 'and as he mellowed with age…became a father-figure for all who sought advice and encouragement.' The *County Times* was surely right in remarking that 'Horsham is not so rich in characters…that the death of one can be allowed to pass without genuine regret'.

Having looked at the father, time perhaps to consider two of his sons…

CHARLIE & JACK OAKES

The close of the 1954 season saw Horsham's own Charlie Oakes play his final match for Sussex. Charlie was born in the groundsman's cottage in August 1912 and hit his first century for Horsham CC against Bristol Wayfarers at the tender age of 16. The following season, he shared in an unbeaten 3rd wicket stand of 265 against Cheltenham. In all he scored almost 3,500 runs for the town club at an average of 43, with six centuries, 14 fifties and a highest score of 138. Talent such as this couldn't be long confined but although joining the Sussex groundstaff in 1930, he had to wait until 1935 before making his first-class debut – at Horsham (where else?) against Northants. One of many who lost their best years to the war (where he served in the RAF), he was nevertheless to play 286 matches for Sussex, scoring over 11,000 runs at 25 apiece. A forceful bat, the highest of his 14 centuries was 160 against Glamorgan at Priory Park, Chichester in 1950. Charlie also bowled slow leg breaks and googlies well enough to take 450 wickets at 31 apiece, though writing in the 1998 county yearbook his sometime skipper Robin Marlar remarked mischievously that his leggers 'tended to deceive by holding line rather than deviating'. In reality he lost the ability to bowl the basic leg break and relied on a mix of top spinners and googlies which hummed audibly in flight. His best bowling figures of 8-147 came against Kent at Tonbridge in 1939. Charlie's benefit season in 1954 was an anti-climax in that although it realised over £4,000, he was injured for virtually all of it and only played one match. At his best Charlie Oakes was a fine all-round cricketer – an attractive strokemaker with a wide range of shots, a teasing slow bowler and an outfielder of the highest quality. He was also a thoroughly nice bloke, a charming, laid-back man who often dropped off to sleep while waiting to bat. For a number of seasons he spent the winter months coaching at a school in Cape Town and in 1958 accepted a coaching appointment at Stowe School. Sadly, Charlie went blind in later life and died at Tunbridge Wells in December 2007 at the ripe old age of 95.

His younger brother John Ypres (Jack) was also born in the groundsman's cottage - in March 1916 - and was educated at Oxford Road school. He made his debut for Horsham CC at the age of 15 in 1931 and was to score 2,650 runs for the club in a brief but meteoric career at an average of 30.7. The highest of his four centuries was 157 against Christ's Hospital in 1936. It wasn't long before he too came to the notice of the powers-that-be at Hove and in 1937 he made his county debut at the age of 21. A bluff, burly, cheerful character who gave the ball a real whack, Jack Oakes was a handy man to have in any side. He played 128 matches for Sussex, scoring 4,400 runs at 22.2 and taking 166 wickets at 39 apiece with his off-breaks, picking up 7-64 against Warwickshire in 1947. He was also a superb fieldsman close to the wicket. The higher of his two centuries was 151 v. Cambridge University at Hove in 1950, but he also smashed 99 in 100 minutes against Kent at Tunbridge Wells in 1949, the year he was awarded his county cap. Always a snappy dresser, Jack was a lively and ebullient character - a popular, balding, moustachioed figure who, perhaps too often for his own good, gave the impression of dealing in explosive 40s rather than measured tons. His jolly disposition had sometimes come across misleadingly in some quarters as betokening a lack of resolve and he resigned in 1952 following allegations from the county committee that he wasn't trying in a 2nd XI match against Hampshire. If he did harbour any resentment it would surely have been at having to make way in the school holidays for gilded amateurs. He went on to play as a club professional in Norfolk and Chester before moving in 1954 to Northumberland. He played Minor Counties cricket there until 1960 when – following in his father's footsteps - he became groundsman at Tynedale CC. Jack Oakes died at Hexham in July 1997, aged 81.

Whilst on the subject of fathers and sons, time now to look at

GEORGE COX (JUNIOR)

In the 1956 *Playfair Cricket Annual*, Gordon Ross referred to 'The effervescent George Cox; a ruddy faced man who loved his cricket, and cricketers loved him.' This was no more than the truth for at the close of the 1954 season George left his beloved Sussex to take up a coaching position at Winchester College – but not for long. He missed life on the county circuit too much and returned to Sussex in 1957 at the age of 46, scored his 50th first-class century and finally hung up his boots in 1960 after a spell captaining the 2nd XI. George was born in Warnham in August 1911 and was captain of both football and cricket at Collyer's School. He made a quite brilliant double-century for Horsham CC in 1933 but his obvious ability had already been spotted. He had already made his debut for Sussex in 1931, though his early years produced more lean than fat. Nevertheless, Sussex had the far-sightedness to recognise that talent will eventually out and he was awarded his county cap by Alan Melville in 1935 (allegedly in the gents toilet at Leicester railway station!). Another who lost his best years to the war, George played in 448 matches for the county, scoring around 23,000 runs at 33 apiece. The highest of his four double-centuries was 234 n/o against India at Hove in 1946. An attractive, quick-footed batsman who was always easy on the eye, George scored 1,000 runs or more in a season on 13 occasions with a best of 2,369 in 1950. The previous season he and Jim Langridge compiled an unbroken 326 for the 4th wicket against Yorkshire at Headingley, still a club record. George Cox was also a handy medium pacer with a best return of 6-125 v. MCC at Hastings in 1946. His benefit in 1951 realised £6,600, a record for the county at the time. George recalled a match against Northants at Rushden in 1952 when Jim Cornford had taken the first nine wickets to fall. George was put on to bowl against last man Ken Fiddling because he was reckoned the least likely member of the eleven to take a wicket – which to everyone's chagrin was what he inadvertently proceeded to do! Pretty much to the end of his career George was also one of the best cover fielders in the land. He was also an excellent soccer player, a goalscoring centre forward who played initially for Horsham FC but who, in November 1933 at the age of 22, signed professional forms for Herbert Chapman's Arsenal. His opportunities at Highbury were limited and in May 1936 he was transferred for £150 to Fulham and later moved on to Luton Town. George Cox was county coach from 1961 until 1964 and was to serve for a number of years on the county committee until resigning in 1978. Like his father he was very much part of the local sporting scene, a modest and unassuming man who was much loved and admired. The celebrated author AA Thomson was one of these admirers. In an affectionate tribute in the June 1961 edition of The Cricketer he referred to George as being among those 'so gifted, so dazzling...that you wonder what little devil of malicious fortune has kept snatching an England cap away from them', a man 'whose gay batting gave pleasure alike to the connoisseur of beautiful strokes and the cheerful chap in the wooden seats who likes to hear the scoreboard rattle'. Thomson loved to hear George reminisce ('I have rarely heard a more beguiling conversationalist') but was all the more impressed because 'George Cox has not only humour but humanity.' He was always in great demand as an after-dinner speaker and in retirement acquired a 'country' property at Wivelsfield which possessed a paddock. This was swiftly transformed into a cricket ground to which he invited teams of boys, often from deprived backgrounds. George Cox died at Burgess Hill on 7 May 1985 at the age of 73 and was universally mourned.

Next in line is a man whose involvement with Horsham cricket can be traced all the way back to 1908 and earlier.

HC HUNT

On 6 March 1954 the death occurred at his Wimblehurst Road home of a man who, together with Arthur Oddie, was responsible for bringing county cricket to the town. Hastings Cyril Hunt was 78. Born in 1875 he joined Horsham CC in 1894 and in a career that stretched intermittently through to 1927, scored 5,000 runs at 21.7 apiece with seven centuries (the highest being an unbeaten 149 in 1905) and 25 half-centuries. He served as hon. sec. between 1904 and August 1907 and again during the War years (1941-45). Never one to shirk responsibility, he was club captain in 1919 and 1920 and treasurer between 1936 and 1945. Cricket was clearly in his blood for his great-grandfather played for the club in 1842, while brother Stanley was a wicketkeeper who also played for a similar length of time as Cyril. But, like Oddie and Douglas Harvey, Cyril Hunt was a man of many parts. He joined Horsham FC in 1894 skippering the side for 10 seasons and was prominent in the club's move from West Sussex to County league football in the 1920s. He ultimately rose to become club president, resigning in 1951 in protest at their decision to join the semi-professional Metropolitan league and away from a policy of playing local men. Cyril Hunt was also a proficient golfer, billiards and snooker player and represented Sussex at chess. With his brother he helped run the prominent departmental store (Hunt Bros) that traded for many years in West Street and which was founded by his father in 1865. Needless to say Cyril somehow found time to play a full part in the civic, commercial and business life of the town. He was a member of the influential Horsham Club from 1896 and of the Town Council from 1905 to 1925, becoming chairman between 1920 and 1922. He was captain of Horsham's volunteer fire brigade and a warden for many years at St Mary's church. It is a pretty fair bet that whatever was going on in the town Cyril Hunt would be part of it, yet his main claim to our attention is the time he devoted not simply to bringing county cricket to Horsham but for nurturing and retaining it. He left a widow, two daughters and a son Geoffrey. The latter was a master at Aldenham school in Hertfordshire and yet another talented cricketer who captained (briefly) both Horsham CC and Sussex CCC.

My final profile is of a person who for many is the living embodiment of Horsham cricket.

DR JOHN DEW

Couple Horsham with cricket and the first name on the lips of many will be John Dew, for the two are synonymous. For many he simply is Horsham cricket...John Alexander Dew was born in the town in May 1920. He was educated at the now defunct Manor House prep school off The Causeway; thence to Tonbridge where he was vice-captain of the cricket 1st XI and captain of rugby, his second great sporting love. He played both at St Catherine's College, Cambridge before moving on to the London Hospital in Whitechapel, where he served as a houseman after qualifying as a physician in late 1944. He applied unsuccessfully to join the RAF but served in the Royal Naval Reserve as medical officer aboard the Atlantic cable ship *Monarch* from 1947 until 1950. He applied unsuccessfully for a post as a doctor at Rugby School before, in 1952, heading back to Horsham and joining the old North Street medical practice headed by his father, Dr John Westcott Dew, who for many years had been a well-known sporting physician in the town. 'Young' Dr Dew remained one of the town's most eligible bachelors until his marriage in 1961 to Rosemary, sister-in-law of Canon Gillingham, vicar of St Mary's. This union was to last until Rosemary's death in 2006. In time, John became senior partner at what was by now the Park surgery in Albion Way, before retiring in 1985 at the age of 65. He acted as a locum to most surgeries in the town for some years thereafter and to all outward appearances seemed every bit as busy as before. Outside cricket and rugby his greatest interests are classical music and the church. He joined the choir at St Mary's in 1952 and remains a churchwarden there to this day. In 1978 he was co-founder of the West Sussex Philharmonic Choir. But it is of course for cricket that he is justifiably celebrated. He saw his first matches at the town ground while in his pram, played for Sussex during the War; and also twice in the county championship as an amateur in 1947 though he found it impossible to combine both careers. Writing in his history of Sussex cricket in 1950, Sir Home Gordon referred to 'the Light

Blue wicketkeeper JA Dew from Tonbridge, (who)...came from time to time to prove he only needed opportunity to be ranked among the very best, and his keenness added to the satisfaction he afforded.' Like his father before him John was an attacking wicketkeeper batsman in the true amateur tradition. He captained the town XI for nine seasons from 1951 and again in 1961 before in 1971 increasing back trouble compelled him to retire for good. He saw service on several county committees and has been president of Horsham CC for in excess of 40 years. All this would be sufficient for most men but John Dew isn't most men. His most enduring legacy is the flourishing network of colts and junior sides that is the envy of the county. Conceived late in 1959, its apogee surely came in 2005 when John was present at Lord's to witness a team comprised largely of lads he had groomed win the coveted National Club Championship. Ever courteous, ever friendly, John Dew even into his mid-80s retains a wonderful zest for, and interest in, life. 'Much loved' is an overworked epithet in a throwaway age when praise is cheap. But John Dew is not simply much but greatly loved by thousands in Horsham and the 'nursery' ground at Cricket Field Road is quite deservedly named after him. Some years ago a friend of mine had to visit 'the doctor' professionally. He was welcomed warmly into the surgery, his family enquired after and a lengthy debate about cricket ensued. At length John rose – mindful perhaps of his other patients – shook my friend warmly by the hand, said how wonderful it was to see him again and hoped he wouldn't leave it so long next time. It was only after he was in the car park that the penny dropped: my friend had completely forgotten whatever it was that had occasioned him to go there in the first place! As Alan Lee put it in the September 1988 edition of *The Cricketer* '*John Dew must rank as one of the most delightful hosts on the summer round. To watch him, in his avuncular, disarming manner, encourage and exhort his young charges to greater effort, is a heart-warming experience.*' A civilised, compassionate and humane man, John Dew's may be the final Profile but his name is arguably at the head of Horsham cricket's Pantheon of Fame. So let us leave the last word with the man himself: '*Perhaps the most pleasant of all my memories at Horsham has been the sight of our ground on fine summer evenings, alive with activity, from end to end until dusk, when the last few boys glumly pull up stumps and wander dreamily home.*'

Chapter 13
UMPIRES

Umpires, like lamp posts, are as much sinned against as sinning. Yet in the rich and colourful pageantry of a cricket match their role is almost as significant as that of the protagonists. Like Solomon in their wisdom and Daniel in their handing down of justice, mighty deeds may hinge on their decisions. Yet for all their sagacity and valour these men remain curiously vulnerable figures. And like Chaucer's pilgrims they are as susceptible to the frailties and vagaries of the human flesh as any other disparate group.

In first-class matches, 97 different umpires have 'stood' at Horsham, 22 of whom also played there. In One-Day cricket the respective equivalents are 36 and six. These include some of the greatest officials of all time including HD 'Dickie' Bird, Syd Buller, Frank Chester, Bill Reeves, David Shepherd and Alec Skelding (it almost goes without saying that Bird's solitary appearance at Horsham was bedevilled by rain). Virtually all these men had played county cricket while a number were of sufficient stature to have 'stood' in Test matches. Some (Joe Hardstaff senior, Ken Palmer, Fred Price, Tiger Smith and Peter Willey) both played and officiated in the Test arena. Chester holds the appearance record – he 'stood' on seven occasions at Horsham between 1925 and 1955. Frank Chester officiated in over 1,000 First-Class matches (including 48 Tests) after a promising playing career with Worcestershire was cut short when he lost part of his right arm during the Great War. He once no-balled Hedley Verity at the Oval for bowling an underarm delivery without notifying the batsman (Verity was making a silent protest at the pitiless perfection of the pitch).

Yet behind the white coat lies any amount of life, colour and human interest. The little-known AJ Atfield (1920, 1923) was clearly a man of some personal courage. The same day as he got married at fashionable Hanover Square, he slipped off to Lord's and scored a century for the Cross Arrows. Many of these men were all-round sportsmen. WAJ (Bill) West (four occasions from

1908) was ABA heavyweight boxing champion in 1885, while former Gloucestershire wicket-keeper Barry Meyer's professional soccer career was ended by gout. Staying with soccer, 15 September 1975 saw Chris Balderstone (1992, 1993) in the field for Leicestershire against Derbyshire at Chesterfield during the day, before dashing 30 or so miles north-eastwards to Belle Vue, arriving just in time to help Doncaster Rovers to a 1-1 draw with Brentford in a Division Two fixture.

Humour of course was rarely far from the surface. Bill Reeves (1937) once told a bowler that the only person he knew who appealed more than he did was Dr Barnardo. With his snowy hair, foghorn voice and trademark white boots, Alec Skelding (four visits 1933-1953) was an irrepressible humorist. It was his invariable custom at close of play to remove the bails with an exaggerated flourish and announce, 'And that, gentlemen, concludes the entertainment for the day.'

Yet there were darker shades too. Syd Buller (1952, 1954) dropped dead at Edgbaston in August 1970 while umpiring in a Warwicks-Notts match, while Albert Trott (1912, 1913) was a tragic figure. A top-class all-rounder who played Test cricket for both Australia and England, he is seen on the cinefilm of the 1913 match v. Lancashire smiling and with flat cap pushed back on his head, idly tossing a ball in the air while strolling to the wicket. Yet within a year he had blown his brains out in his seedy digs in Willesden, tormented beyond endurance by a combination of ill-health, alcoholism and poverty. Four years after umpiring at Horsham in 1923, Derbyshire's Harry Bagshaw was buried in his umpire's coat, ball in hand.

In between you have a full range of human behaviour and emotions. Frank Lee (three visits in 1950s) no-balled South African fast bowler Geoff Griffin at Lord's in 1960, while in his playing days, Hampshire's Jack Newman (1934) was sent off the field at Trent Bridge in 1922 by his own skipper for indiscipline when he first refused to bowl and then kicked over the stumps when directed to do so. At Taunton in 1919, Surrey's Alf Street (1926-1928), ruled Sussex's HJ Heygate out under the two-minute rule as, with his side nine wickets down, he struggled to reach the wicket. Heygate, grievously stricken with rheumatism, had previously declared himself unfit to bat. At Canterbury, Bill Reeves was said to have inadvertently signalled to a beer tent rather than the scorers. Warwickshire's John Jameson (1984), a rumbustious opening bat, was run out three times in his first four Test innings but in 1976 scored a century before lunch on the first day of his final county match. Former fast bowler Allan Jones (three visits, 1988-1997) wrote his name into the record books by becoming the first player since the qualification regulations changed in 1873 to appear for four different counties.

With all their eccentricities, quirks and foibles this band of brothers would have been easily recognised by Shakespeare. While attention is rightly focussed on the players, let us not wholly lose sight of those who also serve.

Chapter 14
PITCH AND GROUNDSMEN

Pitch

Rather like Longfellow's little girl with the little curl, it was said that when the pitch at Cricket Field Road was good, it was very, very good but when it was bad, it was horrid.

As with many uncovered country wickets the weather often held the key. In his autobiography *46 Not Out*, RC Robertson-Glasgow described the 1925 wicket as 'fast and uncertain'. In his pen-portrait of Ted Bowley he went further, reflecting that Horsham 'used to have a pitch which, in a dry summer, could make a batsman mind his whiskers. The chemists hadn't got at it.'

Part of the problem was Alfred Oakes' aversion to anything mechanical. In 1926 the club had bought a motor mower 'owing to the horse...having got too old and slow.' The horse was duly sold (for the princely sum of £4) which meant that 'Mr Oakes can spend more time on the wicket' (what Mr Oakes made of this isn't recorded).

This reputation for pacy, not to say fiery, behaviour was hard to shake off. Before the Gloucestershire match in 1932 Alfred Oakes opined that 'In all probability it would be the fastest wicket the Sussex team has played on this season. There was a chance that the sun might cause it to crack and cake out on top and rain in the meantime would certainly affect it to a great extent (he was right: Sussex won by just two wickets chasing less than 80). In 1934 the legendary Nottinghamshire pace attack of Harold Larwood and Bill Voce, one of the most formidable pairings in cricket history, unleashed their thunderbolts on 'a good sporting wicket'. In 1939 ex-England skipper Bob Wyatt was so badly knocked about by Jack Nye he had to retire hurt in each innings.

Things improved briefly after World War II with the 1949 wicket playing 'fast and true throughout', though all the old doubts came flooding back in 1951 with an enigmatic remark from an unattributed source at Horsham CC denying that the wicket was 'sporting'. 'I wouldn't say it was sporting. It's a "fair" wicket. We have had no complaints about it from the players. In fact several of them have said that they wished there were more like it.' This was the Festival in which not one of the five completed innings reached 200, so we can hazard a pretty shrewd guess that it wasn't the batsmen who wished there were more like it. Seventeen wickets fell on the opening day of the 1952 Festival where the wicket was described, again a touch enigmatically, as 'fast and true...apart from the occasional low 'un'.

At the risk of repetition, one of the visitors in 1956 was Northants who were expected to include Frank Tyson in their starting line up. In what sounds suspiciously like whistling in the dark to keep one's spirits up, the Sussex attack is 'ideally suited for the sporting type of wicket Horsham provides'. Nothing was said about what havoc Tyson might wreak 'on this natural green wicket (where one) can expect the ball to fly'. In the event Tyson didn't play but Sussex were still bowled out for 125 and 63 in a match which saw a meagre 377 runs scored and 31 wickets fall as 'experienced bowlers used a hostile pitch' to advantage.

And things were to get worse before they got better. Although he enjoyed the atmosphere at Horsham, Sussex skipper Tony Greig was highly critical of the pitch and facilities for the One-day match against Lancashire in 1977. With a number of the Lancashire players also unhappy (England opener Barry Wood described it as 'bumpy'), word was that a grumpy Greig reported it as not fit for purpose.

That was the nadir. From then on it was undiluted praise pretty much all the way. Warwickshire's England opener Dennis Amiss told Bill Ford in 1981 that he would like to take him back to Edgbaston for his wicket was 'perfect for the type of game we were playing' and Bill had the satisfaction of picking up several awards from Lord's before his retirement in 1990.

The accolades continued to mount. In 1992, Test umpire David Shepherd said 'it had pace and bounce and was an excellent cricket wicket...I am always happy to visit Horsham.' Three years later Surrey and England's Alec Stewart commented, 'It's the best four day wicket we have played on this year.' Even in 2001 when 18 wickets fell on the first day, Worcestershire skipper Graeme Hick was quick (in large part) to exonerate the pitch.

Apart from 1993, when a feeble and dispirited Leicestershire were bundled out for 97 and 72, the story over the last 15 years or so has been of a wicket that if anything is *too* good. Indeed some criticism was levelled at the pitch in 2004 to the effect that how could a result be expected in four days on a surface designed to last for 10? (they had a point: 1,350 runs were scored and only 18 wickets fell). In 2003, 1,339 runs were scored.

This was the opening salvo in a bizarre sequence of events. In 2004, 1,350 runs were scored; for reasons explained elsewhere the pitch was unfit to stage first-class cricket in 2005; while in 2006, rather than use the specially prepared strip, Sussex decided - with Lord's blessing – to play the Championship fixture on a rain-affected track that had only a few days previously, been used for a One-day fixture (and the decision was justified for over 900 runs were scored in three innings). Nowadays batsmen grin broadly, bowlers howl and lament, while a succession of delighted groundsmen walk away with 'Outground Groundsman Of The Year' awards and the like. It is all a far cry from the years when batsmen had to mind their whiskers.

Robertson-Glasgow once described a Festival wicket at Southend in the 1920s as being 'like Jezebel – fast and unaccountable'. Was the Horsham wicket ever that capricious? The balance of evidence suggests not. In almost 100 games there have only been 21 completed innings totals of under 100 and many of these appear attributable as much to a lack of batting competence as a tricky wicket. Only five of these – out of 39 completed innings - have occurred since 1994. By comparison there have been 81 scores in excess of 300, 32 of which have been posted since 1983. All but two of the record wicket stands put together by opponents have taken place post-1983, along with 34 (in 23 matches) of the 93 centuries scored. Seven of the eight most expensive analyses on the ground by Sussex bowlers have occurred since 1995 but interestingly only one by their opponents (Stuart MacGill's 3-172 for Notts in 2003). The highest individual scores for and against Sussex have both been registered since 2004.

This same disparity is evident in the incidences of seven wickets or more being taken in an innings. Of the 13 occasions this feat has been achieved by Sussex bowlers only three have taken place since World War II; whereas for opposition bowlers, the incidence is six out of nine. That said, no opposition bowler has taken 10 wickets in a match at Horsham since Northants' Jack Manning back in 1956.

So what are we to conclude from this welter of evidence? One, that over the past decade or so the Horsham wicket has been as good as any in the country. And two, that in the more distant past the many perfectly passable totals posted suggest it was not routinely dangerous and probably no worse than any other outground.

Groundsmen

These are the men whose skill and knowledge can make or break a Festival. When county cricket first came to Horsham, the groundsman was Alfred (but known as Roger) Etheridge. He was appointed as a professional ground bowler in 1902, the same year he took over from his brother Bobby and W Charman as groundsman. Roger Etheridge was a formidable club cricketer. He took 990 wickets for Horsham at 11 apiece and scored 3,350 runs. He captured 100 wickets on four occasions and in June 1904 took 10-29 in a 12-a-side game against Knepp Castle. Roger Etheridge remained in post until the end of the 1910 season when he took a tenancy of the 'Stout House' in the Carfax. He offered to continue tending the ground on a part-time basis but his overtures were somewhat brusquely rebuffed by the Horsham committee.

His departure opened the door for Alfred Oakes' extended tenure of office. Alf's life and times are chronicled elsewhere but he had joined Horsham CC as a youngster in the 1890s and at the time of his appointment had been groundsman at Christ's Hospital School for five years. He succeeded Roger Etheridge in February 1911 and remained in post for 44 years.

There was a brief interregnum after Alfred left office in the 1950s but the next major appointee was Bill Ford in 1971. Bill – who today lives quietly in retirement in the town - came to Horsham from the groundstaff at Parham House in 1964. He remained in post until 1990 when Jeg Francis (and his cat 'Wickets') took over. Jeg seemed to almost live on the ground and was much missed when he moved to Sherborne School at the close of the 1998 season.

David Fitch was at the helm from 1999 to 2002 but the weather interfered with three of his four games. Lawrence Gosling - formerly No. 2 at Hove – took over in 2003 and produced what some saw as a heavily over-prepared wicket in 2004 (in fairness, Lawrence was also responsible in 2004 for a pitch which staged one of the greatest One-day matches ever played, Sussex failing by one run to chase down a Leicestershire score of 324/4 in 45 overs. This match witnessed the highest individual One-day scores on the ground, both for (Ian Ward) and against (Brad Hodge) Sussex. Roger Ward broke new ground in 2006 by being the first 'absentee' groundsman. Roger runs a company specialising in sports ground maintenance in Oxted and having charge of Horsham was the fulfilment of a personal dream for him.

The groundsman's cottage, so long associated with the Oakes family, has not been used since 2000. Talks have been ongoing with Horsham District Council for some while regarding its renovation and it is hoped that these will bear fruit in the not too distant future.

Chapter 15
TEA LADIES

The act of purchasing tea and other refreshments at the Horsham Festival today is a commonplace commercial transaction of no transcendental significance whatever. Yet it was not always so.

A century ago the antecedents of the unromantic retail outlets on the ground today were a formidable roll-call of fashionable Edwardian society. Those seeking a humble cuppa in the big marquee at the town end of the ground were likely to be served by Lady Alexander, Mrs Applewhite-Abbot, Mrs Boyd-Wallis, Lady Bell, Mrs Cazenove, Mrs Clifton Brown, Lady Harben, Lady Hutton, Mrs von Hartmann, Lady Stirling-Hamilton, Mrs Hunter-Jones, Mrs Duncan-Knight, Lady Loder or the Misses Lee Steere. To further enhance the ambience teas were served 'in a delightfully-arranged and artistically decorated enclosure'. In those class-conscious times the entire experience must have been something of a revelation to the clientele of yeoman farmers, clerks and urban artisans.

Even after the Great War one of the advertised features in 1920 was the 'charmingly decorated tea enclosure between the field of play and the placid Arun...Roses, crimson ramblers and sweet peas were tastefully and artistically utilised for the adornment of the tables, a delightful effect being produced.'

In 1923 Mrs Douglas Harvey 'found an ample outlet for her untiring energy in making all the arrangements for the teas.' Local villages each had their own stalls and teams of helpers, with 'the feminine touch...seen in the splendid floral decorations at the tables.' The Rusper table for example was staffed by Lady Blake, Mrs Haviland, Mrs Holroyd and Lady Bell; Lady Dunning took her turn replenishing the urn and sugar lumps on the Lower Beeding stall; while Lady Georgina Corser supervised proceedings on the Horsham Town stall. It strains credulity to believe that local pride was not on the line here, with each village striving to outdo its neighbours in the magnificence of its local arrangements.

However, there is a more serious point to all this. At a time when ground admission was more affordable than today these tea stalls were serious money-spinners for the cash-strapped town and county sides, thanks to an arrangement brokered by Arthur Oddie back in 1908 in which the ladies met virtually all the expenses themselves. In 1925 for example, gross gate receipts for the week were £451, out of which the usual expenses had to be met. Yet the tea account showed a profit of £120 on gross receipts of £166.

Nor was this a one-off. The following year gross gate receipts were shown as £407, while the tea account profit was £114. In 1927 the story was broadly the same – gross gate receipts £481, profit on tea account, £131.

The aristocratic tea ladies of Horsham, bustling about in their bosky domain in elegant long dresses, are now long gone, swept away by World War II and the changing face of contemporary society. But as you drink your overpriced burger van beverages of indeterminate provenance from polystyrene cups, which would you rather have, given the choice?

Chapter 16
THE FESTIVAL PROGRAMME

Although the souvenir programme only really came into being in 1931, that man-for-all-seasons Arthur Oddie produced an attractive, 20 page commemorative brochure as far back as 1912. It sported an intensely blue cover, two photographs of the ground during Surrey's visit in 1910, the 1911 county averages and pen portraits of the Sussex squad. Horsham was proclaimed 'The Capital of North West Sussex' and – ambition clearly vaulting – Oddie felt that, in entertainment terms, it should strive just a little harder 'to show that we can hold our own with Canterbury, Tunbridge, Bournemouth and other centres of our neighbouring counties.'

Nineteen years and one World War later, the idea was revived by local journalist Bob Green, an engaging and highly talented man who loved cricket and the town of Horsham in equal measure. A man of many talents, he frequently contributed not just prose and poetry to the programmes but also pen and ink drawings, cartoons, etc. An eminently approachable individual, he was frequently to be seen around the town and always had time for a chat. The debut edition in 1931 retailed at 6d, ran to 64 large pages and carried a lovely cream and maroon cover featuring the figures of an elegant, top hatted, Fuller Pilch-like cricketer accompanied by a graceful Gainsborough lady – complete with the spire of St Mary's in the background. Inside was to be found a wealth of cricketing information, details of social and other activities on offer in the town, cartoons by Fred May and adverts from all over the country (Derby, Sheffield, Coatbridge, Cardiff, etc). Via the medium of this programme, it is possible to recreate the full organisational structure that underpinned the Festival.

Production survived an early scare in 1933 when a falling-off in Festival receipts generally was ascribed to a 'partial failure of the programme'. A wide-ranging internal report by Horsham CC found that it 'had not achieved anything like the success of past years due to a heavy fall off in advertisements. The whole question of the production of the programme another year should be considered very carefully.'

Looking to make the most of its reprieve, the 1937 programme sought to capture the public mood by carrying a patriotic Coronation cover. There was a poignancy about the 1939 issue, when in his Envoi, Bob Green wrote, *'Horsham welcomes all its visitors...particularly our neighbouring friends from over the Surrey border, and we wish them a full week of sunshine, plenty of good cricket and, on leaving, happy memories.'* The crowds had all three in abundance but nobody departing the ground on those deliciously warm, sun-dappled evenings could have guessed just how long those memories would have to sustain them.

The programme price had been reduced to 3d before the War and this remained in force until 1951. It then doubled to 6d and doubled again (to one shilling) for the final issue in 1956. Cost was clearly an ever-present spectre at the feast. There is no record of the programme appearing at all in 1949, though normal service was resumed the following season.

The 1948 programme was typical of many. In addition to the usual pen portraits of both teams and the social attractions on offer, it contained a number of interesting features. John Langridge recalled how he had been awarded his county cap at Horsham and, in a nice aside, mentioned how Alfred Oakes is 'very proud of his two boys...although he tells them they ought to do better'. Sussex coach Patsy Hendren confided how many good things he had heard about Horsham during his playing days; and having now visited the ground for the first time (in 1947), he understood what all the fuss was about.

But the grains of sand were fast ebbing away. The 1956 edition boasted a startling blood-red cover, with a batsman doffing his cap and St Mary's church in silhouette in the background. By then the decision to strip Horsham of its Festival was in the public realm. Bob Green must have been mortified but despite his hurt, was determined to sign off with a flourish. His final edition ran to a staggering 90 pages. In his welcoming address, Horsham CC president Philip Mair found it 'difficult to be convinced that what had been right for 48 years – and for 10 since World War II – should suddenly be found to be so no longer.'

Regret, heavily tinged with nostalgia, was the theme of Bob Green's own address. He likened the decision to a batsman who plods along loyally trying to keep his wicket intact and the score ticking over suddenly being faced with a change of bowling 'which has but one intention – the break-up of a fairly fruitful partnership.' Horsham now looks impotently on as 'the heavy roller of economy lumbers across the pitch.' Green also selected his all-time county eleven from Horsham & District, which for the record, was FM and MP Lucas, David Sheppard, EH Killick, Dr RB Heygate, HL Wilson, both George Coxes, George Pearce and the two Oakes brothers, with George Street to keep wicket. 12th man was Colonel AC Watson. An excess of either emotion or talent (or both) had clearly caused him to miscount.

There were contributions too from Arthur Gilligan, Cyril Hunt and Miss FM Aldersmith, doyenne of the local amateur theatrical scene and now hon sec of the Horsham Music Festival. But it was John Dew who summed it all up for many with his customary elegance in another personal perspective. 'County cricket in Horsham has been an incalculable stimulus to the game north of the Downs' he wrote. 'With its loss, something intangible will also be lost, not just from the confines of our cricket field.'

It is only fitting that the final word should rest with Bob Green. *'To us in Horsham' he wrote, more in sorrow than anger, 'this drawing of the County stumps for the last time amounts to a darkening, eventide veil drawn over an hitherto sunlit scene...and we are bound to say that we would rather it had not happened. Up here at Horsham we like our cricket and the game will go on unhindered, but through the gloom of the County Club's edict of "No more play", we see some of the sunshine of the past, and, reflecting upon it, we feel we can say Horsham has not failed its County Cricket...We shall miss these County Weeks – who wouldn't, after nearly 50 years of it – and we have no illusions on that point, but as we take this "Rap on the pads"...we think of the immortal lines "Be cheerful, wipe thine eyes. Some falls are means the happier to arise".*

And he was right. Bob Green was dead by the time county cricket returned to Horsham in 1971, but no-one surely would have been better pleased than he to witness how in 2004 – albeit for one season only - energetic new Festival organiser Kevin Barnes oversaw the production of an informative, all-colour souvenir programme. In concept and execution this was remarkably similar to the one Green himself had single-handedly conceived over 70 years earlier. There can be no finer epitaph.

Chapter 17
A NIGHT AT THE THEATRE

It was always part of Arthur Oddie's vision for the Festival that it include an enduring theatrical component, mindful no doubt of the popularity of the 'Old Stagers', who had proved such a successful part of Canterbury Week since the 1840s.

In this, not only was Oddie playing to his own artistic strengths, he was also building on a solid theatrical foundation already in existence in the town. In January 1874 at the *King's Head* Assembly Rooms, Miss Sarah Thorne (late of St James' Theatre and manageress of the Margate Theatre) presented a 'Grand Comic Pantomime', while in December 1876 a short-lived Horsham Amateur Dramatic Society made its debut. Their chosen work was not Shakespeare or some other heavyweight dramatist but an altogether fluffier piece entitled 'A Kiss in the Dark'. The local newspaper was not impressed: 'we learn that practical joking of a nature tending to jeopardise the success of the performance on the second night was carried out by one whose duties and position in the society ought to have made its success his first consideration. We forebear to mention his name, but we hope he will meet with the censure his breach of trust deserves.'

The *Assembly Rooms* was clearly the premier theatrical venue at this time. It has long vanished and at the time of writing, the old-established town centre hotel to which it was attached – the *King's Head* – could very well follow. In the years running up to the Festival the *Assembly Rooms* staged performances by professional touring companies.

By the turn of the 20th century local amateur thespian talent had already been enlisted intermittently to raise funds for Horsham CC. In November 1905, for example, Mr A Bromley-Davenport directed two performances of Jerome K Jerome's 'Woodbarrow Farm' at the *King's Head*. It proved to be highly popular and among the company was a name we will encounter later, Mrs Eden Paget.

The first Festival plays ('A case for eviction' and 'Old Cronies') were performed for one night apiece in 1910 and were low-key affairs. It was only in 1912 that the theatrical tradition really began to flower. 'Kipling: Detective' was described as 'an original play in three Acts by Arthur C Oddie JP (and) produced under the direction of Mr HS Goodwin and the Author' – who, for good measure was also among the many 'well-known Amateurs' taking part. It ran for three nights at the *Assembly Rooms* with the "HAMS" (the Horsham Amateur Minstrel Society), giving Christy Minstrel entertainments for the other three. Ticket prices ranged from 5/- down to 1/-. It can't have been too bad for we are told that it 'drew such a crowd that a great number had to be turned away.' Oddie had been involved for many years previously in organising smoking concerts and the like in aid of Horsham CC funds and 'has a reputation as an amateur actor. But as a playwright, he had never previously made a public appearance.'

He clearly enjoyed the experience for his offering the following season ('Modern Slavery') was even more rapturously received. 'The seating capacity of the largest hall of which Horsham can boast…was found more than usually inadequate. So much so that a row of chairs were placed to face the footlights at a nearness which must have been disconcerting to both those on as well as off the stage.' It again shared the limelight with a vaudeville performance by amateur Pierrots but a pattern can already be discerned. Among the cast were Miss Marjorie Aldersmith, whose father held a senior position on the medical staff at Christ's Hospital, and Mrs Eden Paget. Stage Manager was Mr HS Goodwin, also of Christ's Hospital. These three were to be intimately connected with the Festival productions pretty much until their demise.

The euphoria continued in 1914 with 'Milord', again from the fruitful pen of Mr Oddie. 'An original farcical comedy, this play is full of life and cannot fail to amuse and delight from start to finish'.

Death had stilled Arthur Oddie's prolific pen by 1920 so the town had to make do with 'Mrs Dot' a lesser-known offering by Somerset Maugham. 'All the actors played with a verve that verged on professional standard' and the indefatigable Mrs Eden Paget was presented with a bouquet for her efforts. In a speech that I'm sure sounded more felicitous then than it reads now, Harry Goodwin reminded everyone what a debt of gratitude they owed to Mrs Paget 'who had worked like a dog from start to finish.'

The general fare on offer was undemanding, consisting in the main of either farces or light drawing-room comedies with romantic overtones. This was not to everyone's liking. In 1923 the *West Sussex Guardian* complained of the chosen piece that 'it was a pity...a comedy with a little more substance was not chosen', though it appears to have played to full houses. The producer now was Mr Carol Fane, alias Mr Milnes-Hey of Broadbridge Heath.

By now the venue was the old Capitol Theatre, situated between Swan Walk and Albion Way (where Marks & Spencer's now stands). In 1924 'there was not a moment of boredom' for the comedy drama 'Mrs Gorringe's Necklace', when 'laughter and pathos throughout are cleverly balanced'. But there was one unusual problem. 'Had not the heat been almost tropical, no doubt larger bookings would have helped the funds'.

In 1926, there was a cost-driven decision to switch venues once again, this time to the New Hall. Top seats now cost 3/6 (less than in 1912), but it clearly wasn't a success, so it was back to the Capitol in 1927 for a three-night run of Ian Hay's domestic comedy 'The Sport Of Kings'. After the final performance 'the curtain was rung up again and again to repeated applause'.

Arthur Gilligan attended the final performance of the 1928 offering "Tons Of Money" a well known farce which had been played in the town professionally earlier in the year. Responding to an invitation from Rev'd EDL Harvey to say a few words, he went one better, congratulating the actor who had played the gardener 'and amidst applause and laughter, presented him with some carrots and a cucumber'!

The intervals of these productions were enlivened by spirited orchestral music from a 12, sometimes 15, strong group of local musicians under the baton of Mr A Harrison Carter, another pre-Festival veteran.

The new decade showed little sign of this by-now tried and tested formula losing its appeal. Quite the contrary, in fact. In 1930, 'all the artists were in splendid form and the whole production was most highly spoken of by one and all. The comedy was just the right sort of thing for Cricket Week, being brim full of bright and sparkling incidents and causing good fun throughout.'

The actor-director now was Major Green, who 'is always clever on the stage and his acting...left nothing to be desired.' Miss N Bright 'delighted her audiences at every turn' while – surprise, surprise – 'in the exacting role of Jennifer, Mrs Eden Paget displayed great histrionic ability. It is always a pleasure to see this lady...her acting is quite up to the standard of many professionals'.

By now the organising committee had acquired a pretty good idea of the sort of fare to lay before their patrons. 'After witnessing the 'stern realities' of a County Championship struggle for supremacy, it is pleasant' the *County Times* informed its readership in 1931 'to be transported into a world of riotous make-believe, where nothing really matters so long as we are being amused.' And amused the audiences certainly were, despite the plot of Ian Hay and PG Wodehouse's offering being 'of little account'.

With its cricketing undertones, the exploits of EW Hornung's aristocratic burglar 'Raffles' appeared a safe enough choice in 1933 but darker forces were already at work. An internal report commissioned by Horsham CC actually questioned whether it was worthwhile running a play at all when the weather was so hot in the evenings (Hornung's family, incidentally, lived at Compton's Lea, a landed estate to the north of the town).

For whatever reason there were no performances between 1934 and 1936, leading to concerns that the Festival's tradition of amateur dramatics had been lost forever. It was wounded but not – as yet – mortally. Thankfully, normal service was resumed in 1937 with 'Leave it to Psmith', 'a comedy of youth, love and misadventures', by those old Festival standbys, Ian Hay and PG Wodehouse. Dare I say it but the prime mover in the revival was another old Festival standby, Miss MB Aldersmith, with Mr Goodwin again doing duty as stage manager. In what I'm sure was not a case of art imitating nature, Miss Aldersmith herself 'gave a perfect character study (of) an interfering spinster' in this 1937 production.

The final pre-War attraction was 'the Bat' – which had nothing whatever to do with cricket, but was instead 'a play of mystery involving a criminal mastermind...whose personality permeates the whole of the play'. In 1947, the theatrical tradition returned in a modified form when Miss Aldersmith produced three short plays at yet another venue, the Court Royal theatre in the Carfax.

1949 was a bleak year all round for the Festival, but what was billed as a gala performance of RC Sherriff's slightly musty cricketing farce 'Badger's Green' was on offer at the Court Royal. But the Christ's Hospital mafia was beginning to lose its grip on the amateur dramatics – the octogenarian Harry Goodwin was by this time president of Horsham CC and had other things on his mind. This production took place courtesy of the Sussex Theatre Company.

The sand was by now coursing through the neck of the hourglass. After all the enjoyment the amateur dramatics had given, it was depressing to watch it die by degrees. The only live theatre during Festival Week in the early part of the 1950s was brought to the town by the Westminster Repertory Company as part of its standard commercial repertoire. Its assistant stage manager at this time was a 20 year old novice called Maurice Micklewhite whose stage name was Michael Scott. A decade or so later, Scott was to find international fame and fortune under yet another *nom de stage* – Michael Caine. Caine never forgot his grounding in Horsham though there was no mention of him in either of the 1953 cricket week offerings. However a fortnight later he 'never convincingly dons the years as a fashionable physician' in HA Vachell's 'Case of Lady Camber'. The *County Times* could be quite rough with its theatre reviews around this time. Under the headline 'Oh What A Silly Play This Is', their critic lambasted the Westminster Rep's production of 'March Hares' with the terse observation, 'They have much talent – here, sadly wasted.'

The curtain finally fell in the seismic season of 1956 – and even this had a tinge of bathos. The town had reacted defiantly to being stripped of its cricket Festival and in the close season, local thespians decided to resurrect the good old Festival tradition by persuading HAODS – the Horsham Amateur Operatic and Drama Society (happily still with us) – to turn back the clock and put on one final cricket week play at the Capitol. Sadly HAODS had already committed itself to a production in April and another so soon afterwards was deemed out of the question. However, the Cowfold Players ('a most competent company') expressed their readiness to fill the breach free of charge. They duly staged Agatha Christie's well-known thriller 'The Hollow' and were rewarded for their pains by the *County Times* observing that the success of this piece is 'not easy to explain, for certainly better plays have been seen there.'

And so the footlights were extinguished for the final time and the flame of Festival Week amateur dramatics, which had burned so brightly for so long, departed the land. With hindsight there was a certain inevitability about its passing – but at its zenith it brought light, colour, spectacle and laughter to the lives of many in a local community which doubtless had a sufficient portion of drabness and austerity. There have been worse legacies...

Chapter 18
THE CARNIVAL AND OTHER CRICKET WEEK ATTRACTIONS

Part of Arthur Oddie's 'Grand Vision' was that Horsham's Cricket Week should be able to stand comparison with any in the land. It was always his intention that cricket during the daytime should be complemented by a full programme of social, artistic and cultural events in the evening. At their zenith these activities generated a life of their own to the point that the cricket almost appeared incidental. They took over the town to a degree that can scarcely be imagined today.

We have already looked at the tradition of amateur dramatics. This in fact was preceded by the Carnival, which had been organised in quasi-military fashion by Oddie and others since the 1890s. Traditionally it was held on early August Bank Holiday Monday, so did not usually form part of Cricket Week. Often too it was combined with the town's sports and athletics tournament. Yet its track record was curiously patchy. Often held in Springfield Park, the Carnival was actually cancelled in 1905 'because there was no meadow.' In 1906 around 3,500 spectators attended the athletics at the cricket ground while around double that number turned out in the evening for the Carnival, which was held 'in meadows off the Bishopric'. In 1907 masquerades were prominent and revellers were also promised 'London Star Artistes', a Great Naval Spectacular, torchlight procession and – clearly a much-anticipated climax – a 'Battle of Confetti.' By 1913 however, Oddie had so managed things that the two events coincided though this was not always the case. Held this time in Horsham Park and captured on cinefilm, the highlight was a 'Grand Cavalry Display by the 11th Hussars (Prince Albert's Own).' There were also tent-pegging displays, an 'Al Fresco Concert by the Lyric Entertainers' and those old standbys, the grand torchlight procession and confetti battle in the Carfax (plus equally-obligatory fireworks display).

A key feature of the Carnival was, of course, the procession. In 1931 around 150 folk 'arrayed in a striking variety of costumes and a number of decorated cars' set off in procession from the Bishopric'. The following year a huge crowd took advantage of a lovely warm evening to line the streets as the procession left the football ground en route to Horsham Park. The attractions there were many and varied – stewards in period attire, fancy dress, historical and other tableaux (including an eye-catching 'Negro Wedding'), a spectacular flying display given by the Surrey Auto Club which culminated in 'bombing a motor car' with flour and a large floodlit ring set aside for dancing. In 1933 the number of revellers in the Park was said to be numbered in thousands.

Nevertheless the local Chamber of Trade considered the 1935 Carnival to be a 'broken hearted affair altogether'. The weather was brutal, there was no trademark procession and very little evidence of sideshows or revelry, despite possibly the only appearance at Horsham of 'Eddie Wenstob, the Famous Canadian Cowboy Boxer (who) will give exhibition bouts with Ginger Hauxwell.'

The Carnival was back with a vengeance in 1936. Around 160 entrants assembled in Denne Road, headed by Town Crier Mr Smith and the obligatory bands, for a procession to the football ground where there was a funfair. In 1938, 2,000 tickets were sold for the afternoon funfair while a mammoth procession moved off at 7pm, led by a local squadron of the legion of frontiersmen and the massed ranks of the silver and military bands. Prominent among the fancy dress entrants was one from the local branch of the International Friendship League. Nine hours of revelry concluded with the traditional firework display and confetti battle at midnight which 'brought to a close a day in which King Carnival reigned supreme.'

Although perhaps the most popular and accessible, the Carnival was by no means the only attraction on offer. The social highlight in 1908 and 1909 was a *Café Chantant* in the grounds of Mr GF Stanford's house off Worthing Road. In 1908 the whole Worthing Road façade of Mitchell's Brewery was illuminated with coloured electric lamps, while the windows and doors were outlined with roses. An attractive stage, lit temporarily with floodlights and Chinese lanterns, had been erected on a lawn covered by builder's boards. In the meadow beyond dancing was kept up until about 11pm to the strains of a small but effective band. Sadly, rain curtailed the programme on the second night though everyone rose gallantly to the occasion – none more so than Mr W Jackson Byles (accompanied on the piano by Mr Bevan), who 'received an encore, notwithstanding that his first piece had to be performed in almost total darkness, the electric light suddenly indulging in one of its occasional vagaries by going out.'

This charming tableau was repeated in 1909 complete with promenade concert at 8.15pm. The 'comic songs and sketches in character' performed by Mr Grogie Blackburn – billed elsewhere as 'the Sussex comedian' - were said to have 'proved irresistible'. To prevent *ennui* setting in there was a complete change of programme for each of the three nights, which must have been great for the audience but pretty hard going for the artistes. 'In an adjoining meadow, to the music of Mr Harris' band, a delightful programme of dancing was joined in by many couples'.

Another perennial Cricket Week feature was the brass band. The Town and Recreation silver bands were in action at the ground on matchdays while in 1913 Mr ER Cook's Orchestra was to be found at the illuminated bandstand in the Carfax in the evenings and this popular musical tradition persisted for many years..

By 1920 the range of attractions had expanded to include an evening fete in the grounds of Manor House (which in the event had to be deferred by a week on account of the weather); a fancy dress dance with prizes for the most historic, comic, original and artistic costumes; a 'grand display of daytime fireworks'; a Maypole dance by the girl guides; and an open-air whist drive. The prominent outfitters Chart & Lawrence advertised 'Cricket Week – correct wear in dainty frocks and millinery.' Another feature was a best-dressed shop window competition. In 1928 this attracted 80 plu entries and was adjudicated by no less a luminary than the chief window dresser to the HMV Gramophone Co Ltd (and was won by a display in West Street in the form of a tomato store).

In 1921 there was a torchlight tattoo at Horsham Football Club's Queen Street ground. Between 1,500 and 2,000 turned up to listen to a stirring programme of music from the 4th Royal Sussex Regiment. At 11.30pm they concluded their performance by marching dramatically off to their camp at Roffey Park to the strains of 'Bubbles', 'Sussex by the sea' etc, with the sound of bugles, fifes and drums resonating round the quiet streets. Nor was that all. In mellower vein there was a display for two nights of 'Ballet, Fancy and National Dancing, all in costume' by a company of almost 50 pupils of Miss Doris Haygarth. Miss Betty Taylor sang two songs, Mr Figgis of Rusper 'gave amusing pianoforte selections', while it appears that the dancing of Miss Joyce Pratt 'brought down the house.' Miss Haygarth's mother took centre stage in 1922 with two performances of her original ballet 'the Fisherboy's Dream'. Even as late as 1938 Miss Beryl Munro Higgs, principal of the Horsham School of Dancing, arranged two performances of 'Ballets, Songs and divertissements.' Over 600 parents and others bore witness to 'an artistic and beautiful production from a cast of 60 children.'

In 1924 there was the first appearance of a fancy dress carnival ball with the curious and somewhat self-defeating caveat ('fancy dress optional'). Depending on where one's fancy lay, there were also a whist drive, dance and concert at which 'a Bluther grand pianoforte will be used.' Not to be outdone, there was also the alluring prospect of a session with '"Madam Palmis", who will, by Palmistry, peep into the future for you'. With Worcestershire's unexpected capitulation earlier in the day, it didn't require much of an effort on Madam Palmis' part to foresee a day off for both sides as their immediate future. In 1931 the first post-war Carnival to be held during Cricket Week included a 'display of huge figures as seen at Nice…never before seen at Horsham' – or as the *County Times* put it more picturesquely, 'forty figures bearing heads of grotesque proportions such as might well figure in a phrenologist's nightmare.'

A point that strikes even the most casual observer is the extent to which the whole town joined in these celebrations. Among the local organisations participating in 1932 were the football and rugby clubs, fire brigade, rotary club and round table, boy scouts, local NFU, Blue Star Harriers and Horsham players.

By the late 1920s the County Ball had become an established

feature of the Festival. More often than not players from Sussex and their opponents would be among the attendees. In 1930 for example 'it was a pleasure to meet them and chat about doings on the field of play. It is evident that the cricketers are good dancers as well as highly skilled in the popular summer game. The stage had been artistically prepared to represent a scene of the cricket field'. In 1928 there was a 'Splendid programme of music given by the Missouri Orchestra' at the Drill Hall, where the 'brilliantly lit ball-room, delightful in its artistic features and natural proportions, requires little adornment.' The County Balls were highly decorous affairs, the dancing in 1933 being 'composed entirely of fox trots and waltzes.'

However, a lack of interest led to its cancellation in 1934. In 1935 an attempt was made to broaden its appeal and run it along different lines from its predecessors. Ticket prices were substantially reduced, the outcome being a 'pleasant informality …that increased the enjoyment.'

In their heyday the County Balls were glittering social occasions with the cream of county and local society out in force. In 1931 there were over 300 guests at the New Drill Hall, headed by the Duchess of Norfolk, Duke of Richmond, Earl & Countess Winterton, Countess Rosslyn, Lord & Lady Cowdray, Lord & Lady Leconfield, Lord Hailsham and Lord Woolavington. KS Duleepsinhji, PGH Fender, Arthur and Harold Gilligan were also there, along (for good measure) with the entire cast of 'A Damsel in Distress'. In 1932 'A large number of distinguished people has agreed to patronise this event'.

Listing just some of the ensembles providing the musical accompaniment for the County Ball is like peeping into a lost world – Gibson's Orchestra from Haywards Heath, the Orion Orchestra from Brighton, the Pips Medlars Orchestra, Cecil Sapseld and his Savona band, the Harmony Aces from Hastings.

The Ball was unashamedly exclusive. The 'Other Ranks' were catered for by the Cricket Week Dance. Again in 1931 over 400, dare I say it, more ordinary folk attended this less exalted function, among them Maurice Tate, Ted Bowley and Jim Langridge, along with Nottinghamshire's Arthur Carr, Joe Hardstaff, Harold Larwood, Bill Voce and the Staples brothers. The

'Cricketer's Dance' was to prove one of the more enduring Cricket Week traditions.

Another enduring attraction was the whist drive, one of the prime organisers in the 1930s being George Pearce's mother. In 1936 there were no fewer than 41 tables while by 1947 the number had increased to 50. On at least one occasion it was held away from the usual town centre venues, at Roffey.

The range of attractions conjured up by an increasingly ingenious organising committee seemingly knew no bounds. In 1929 the Festival coincided – by accident or design – with the long-established annual exhibition of the Association of Sussex Artists, while there was an All Star Boxing Programme at Horsham FC. In 1938 the grounds of Holbrook House were opened to the public for the first time by Horsham CC president Ernest Neathercoat. An estimated 1,000 people 'took the opportunity to see this lovely corner of West Sussex at its best', with the ubiquitous silver band again on hand to perform a selection of popular music.

Dancing was a central component of the pre-war Festivals with the Drill Hall being the most popular venue. In 1937 there were no fewer than three separate terpsichorean functions, one of which was organised by the vicar of Horsham and his '21 Club' in honour of local boy Charlie Oakes' first appearance for the county. 'Everyone knows how popular the Vicar's ...dances always are, and this one will be no exception to the rule'. Another variation on the theme was a supper dance (until 2am) at the *King's Head* (this was an 'evening dress' do). In the late 1940s/early 1950s there were a number of popular – but doubtless exhausting - non-stop dances.

However, by the troubled summer of 1939 the nation had other things on its mind. There was no Carnival and no Cricketers Dance. Although Hugh Bartlett (Sussex) and Monty Garland-Wells (Surrey) were present, the dance floor at the King's Head ('one of the best in Sussex') 'was filled to capacity without being overcrowded' for the County Ball.

The Festival flame remained alight during the difficult years immediately after World War II. In 1947 the Urban District Council assumed responsibility for putting together the social programme and bravely rolled out an ambitious itinerary of events which included a swimming gala, Christ's Hospital pupils performing selections from 'A Midsummer Night's Dream' (in the event, under overcast skies and light drizzle) and a gymnastic display. The Council relinquished this role in 1948 and the cricket club turned to the Chamber of Trade for help. By now, only the Cricketers Dance and whist drive remained afloat. The County Ball had been scrapped for lack of interest, likewise a proposed motor-cycle gymkhana.

After an absence of several years the Carnival made a surprise re-appearance in 1951, complete with a 'Health and Beauty' display and torchlight run. Carnival King (duties unspecified) was George Cox. The *County Times* did its bit, talking the occasion up for all it was worth. 'Flowers, Flags for Town's Go-Gay Week' exclaimed the headline and readers might have been forgiven for imagining they were in Rio de Janeiro, as 'Carnivals, Flowers, Festival, Fun' were promised in a town donning its gayest garb, with streets ablaze and 'Banners, bunting and flags flying.'

It was illusory. There was a brief return to the good old days in 1956 when a County Ball and a Cricketers Dance were staged, but these were as much the defiant gestures of a town still smarting from the decision to strip it of its Festival and looking to cock a snook at the powers that be at Hove. The winds of change were blowing ever stronger through post-war Britain and Horsham wasn't the only community unable to stand against it. The advent of television and a gradual lessening of the grip of the old symbols of authority meant that even in sleepy Horsham a new generation was growing up that had no real interest in reviving moribund institutions that had been good enough for their parents. Nor was there the same spirit of civic pride in a more materialistic land: it all seemed so anachronistic. The town no longer took pride in being *en fête*. When county cricket returned to the town in the 1970s it was no longer part of a week-long Festival. The Carnival persisted for many years as a stand-alone event but even that has now gone to the wall. There was even less appetite for organising County Balls, *Café Chantants* and the like in Mrs Thatcher's Britain. Yet as the cricketers come to town nowadays there are still those who close their eyes and recall a less knowing, less cynical, time when it was oh so different...

Chapter 19
THE FUTURE

So, having reviewed the past in some detail, what price the future? Will there still be a Horsham Cricket Festival in five, 10, 100 years time?

The answer to that depends on who you speak to. As we have seen, Horsham has been fortunate historically in producing committed and dynamic men from Arthur Oddie and Cyril Hunt down to Mike Beckwith, Barry Peay and Kevin Barnes, men who have been prepared almost to shed their life's blood in bringing first-class cricket to the town and then keeping it there. But cricket's own changing face and a much harder-nosed commercial climate govern these things in the 21st century. The simple answer is that all the while it makes financial sense for Sussex CCC to continue coming to the town, they will do so. The powers-that-be at Horsham must concentrate their efforts on putting together an irresistible business case that forces the county to pose the same question in reverse – 'can we afford not to go to Horsham?'

The neo-Sicilian manoeuvrings in 2006/07 introduced a subtle twist to the mix in that in addition to putting together a five-day package, it has to be the *right* five-day package, with the county always reserving the right to cream off the best pickings to place before the faithful at HQ. Why, for example, have Yorkshire never played at Horsham? There appears to be little room in their thinking for a missionary role – in taking their product out to the shire rather than remain anchored at Hove and expecting the shire always to come to them. You might be able to get away with this approach in the good times but at what longer-term cost? Yet this is a difficult balance. There are heavy standing costs maintaining a headquarters establishment (particularly a heavily under-utililised one such as a cricket ground) and it flies in the face of commercial logic to decide wilfully not to maximise such use.

That said, the fate of Horsham's Festival remains to some extent – as it always has done – in the town's own hands. But in addition to getting the commercial package right, it must also continue to throw up charismatic, resourceful, innovative and self-sacrificing men (and women) who are prepared to 'go on the stump' chasing up local sponsorship from a town and district that (with the odd exception) all too often gives the impression of being apathetic.

Other factors also come into play. There has been a steady reduction since the war in the number of Championship fixtures being played. Although this has been counterbalanced by an upsurge in variations on the One-day theme (including, most recently, the phenomenally successful 20-20 competition), the advent in 2000 of a two-tier Championship means that each county only has eight home fixtures. Despite being a comparative newcomer to the county cricket scene, Arundel has a more alluring ground even than Horsham and a resilient and well-established commercial infrastructure. Should the time ever come that there was only room for one West Sussex outground, Arundel must be strongly fancied to outperform Horsham.

There is also the as yet dormant threat from the east. In times past Hastings and Eastbourne both had popular and well-established Festivals. To the regret of many, the old Central Ground may be no more but although parking is a concern, Hastings' new and well appointed Horntye ground is perfectly capable of staging county cricket and in 2008 is hosting a One-day match. Strenuous efforts supported by the local Council are also being made to upgrade the wicket and facilities at the attractive Saffrons ground. There is still some way to go but it would be naïve to assume that neither town will ever again host Championship cricket. With so few home games on offer anyway, the county may very well take the view sometime down the line that they wish – for political, strategic or commercial reasons – to return to the east. And via some unwritten Faustian pact, the price to be paid for this may be to sacrifice one of the two West Sussex venues. Fanciful perhaps but not wholly unimaginable…

Conversely, the county might equally take the view that with the major investment taking place at Hove at the time of writing, they need to move away from outground cricket altogether. Where is the commercial rationale for investing so heavily in a fixed and depreciating asset and then not fully utilising it? As Manuel in *Fawlty Towers* might have put it *'Ees crazy!'*. Couldn't happen, do I hear you say? Why ever not – the county ceased to smile on Horsham in 1956 and 2007 and could easily do so again, further fuelling long-standing suspicions locally that when push comes to shove Sussex CCC has always really stood for Sussex *Coastal* Cricket Club.

Yet by the same token one would have thought the county could ill-afford to be too cavalier in the way it treats Horsham. As one of Sussex's premier club venues it is much in demand for county 2nd XI matches and the like. These too take time, money and local goodwill to stage. As well as showing the flag locally, using outgrounds for such matches eases the burden on the overworked square at Hove. But however compliant they may have been historically, logic suggests there must be some form of quid pro quo on offer, or Horsham C&SC may simply decide to take away their bat and ball and let the county look elsewhere.

I believe the county to be sincere when they say they would like to continue playing at Horsham. But equally I believe that the threat to disinherit Horsham is all-too-tangible. One 'given' is that everyone locally must pull vigorously in the same direction if the town is to have any chance of retaining its Festival. This does not appear to be the case at present. The District Council is bound to be a key – perhaps pivotal – player in the survival of the Festival, yet – again depending on who you speak to – there is a disturbing difference in perception locally as to how far they would really be prepared to go to save it if push really did come to shove. Yes, they would make all the right noises but with at least one eye on their electorate, would they really man the barricades/die in the last ditch? Viewed another way, how realistic is it anyway to expect them to? Why should they be standing at the ready with rictus grin and blank cheque? Is buttressing a minority interest sport an appropriate way of disbursing Council taxpayer's money? Their dealings with the now homeless Horsham Football Club have been described variously as cynical, devious, Laodician and Machiavellian – but again is favouring them any part of their remit? If, as is claimed, the cricket Festival confers wider commercial benefits, why don't more of these beneficiaries put their hands in their pockets?

There are no easy answers and the fact that Horsham has a rich cricketing heritage butters no parsnips in a wintry commercial world. Other, more deeply entrenched cricketing Festivals – not least in my own home town of Folkestone – have perished for one reason or another. At the risk of ending on a gloomy note, for a number of local Jeremiahs, the real question isn't if Horsham will lose its Festival permanently, but when.

Thank you for staying the course. Appendices apart, over and out.

APPENDICES

A) - SUSSEX'S PLAYING RECORD AT HORSHAM
(FIRST-CLASS MATCHES)

	Played	Won	Drawn	Lost
CHAMPIONSHIP	87	33	26	28
OTHERS	9	4	3	2
TOTAL:	96	37	29	30

(the match in 1986 was abandoned without a ball being bowled; the match scheduled for 2005 was played at Hove)

RESULTS
1908 Sussex (298) drew with Essex (2-0)
1909 Surrey (187 & 355) drew with Sussex (146 & 291/5)
1910 Surrey (295 & 160) lost to **Sussex** (331 & 129/9) by 1 wkt
1911 No Game
1912 **Sussex** (414/8d) beat Oxford Univ (186 & 81) by an inns & 147 runs
1912 **Surrey** (281 & 178) beat Sussex (254 & 127) by 78 runs
1913 **Northants** (154 & 115) beat Sussex (59 & 160) by 50 runs
1913 Lancashire (236 & 112) lost to **Sussex** (81 & 332) by 65 runs
1914 **Hampshire** (396 & 82/8) beat Sussex (146 & 329) by 2 wkts
1914 Cambridge Univ (173 & 102) lost to **Sussex** (266 & 10/1) by 9 wkts
1920 Sussex (287 & 215) lost to **Kent** (261 & 242/3) by 7 wkts
1920 Gloucs (201 & 129) lost to **Sussex** (351) by an inns & 21 runs
1921 Hampshire (260 & 411) drew with Sussex (359 & 182/5)
1921 Leics (189 & 303) lost to **Sussex** (519) by an inns & 27 runs
1922 **Gloucs** (320 & 245) beat Sussex (273 & 155) by 137 runs
1922 Surrey (294 & 109/4) drew with Sussex (248)
1923 Notts (94 & 121) lost to **Sussex** (79 & 137/3) by 7 wkts
1923 Glamorgan (86 & 91) lost to **Sussex** (447) by an inns & 270 runs
1924 Leics (186 & 51) lost to **Sussex** (233 & 6/0) by 10 wkts
1924 Worcs (280 & 57) lost to **Sussex** (155 & 184/5) by 5 wkts
1925 **Sussex** (255 & 179) beat Hampshire (124 & 184) by 126 runs
1925 **Somerset** (199 & 230) beat Sussex (213 & 140) by 76 runs
1926 Warwicks (257 & 177) lost to **Sussex** (261 & 174/5) by 5 wkts
1926 Gloucs (144 & 146/5d) drew with Sussex (163 & 54/7)

1927 Sussex (515) drew with Warwicks (318 & 201/4)
1927 **Sussex** (160 & 292) beat Kent (250 & 172) by 30 runs
1928 Surrey (226 & 156) lost to **Sussex** (387) by an inns & 5 runs
1928 Hampshire (199 & 214/6d) drew with Sussex (232 & 55/1)
1929 Sussex (248 & 106) drew with Essex (194 & 53/2)
1929 Sussex (306 & 147) lost to **Glamorgan** (101 & 408) by 56 runs
1930 Leics (254 & 156) drew with Sussex (362 & 13/4)
1930 Derbyshire (203 & 192) lost to **Sussex** (429) by an inns & 34 runs
1931 **Surrey** (195 & 255/8d) beat Sussex (113 & 325) by 12 runs
1931 **Sussex** (309 & 310/4d) beat Notts (185 & 126) by 308 runs
1932 Gloucs (229 & 191) lost to **Sussex** (335 & 86/8) by 2 wkts
1932 Worcs (88 & 153) lost to **Sussex** (343) by an inns & 102 runs
1933 Hampshire (157 & 224) lost to **Sussex** (277 & 106/2) by 8 wkts
1933 **Essex** (259 & 297/6d) beat Sussex (150 & 112) by 294 runs
1934 Sussex (312 & 180/4) drew with Notts (331)
1934 Surrey (280 & 224) lost to **Sussex** (452/5d & 54/1) by 9 wkts
1935 Northants (124 & 109) drew with Sussex (124)
1935 Sussex (383) drew with Hampshire (144 & 20/0)
1936 Sussex (233 & 109) lost to **Warwicks** (104 & 239/5) by 5 wkts
1936 Surrey (386/7d) drew with Sussex (174/7)
1937 **Sussex** (443 & 75/5) beat Gloucs (230 & 287) by 5 wkts
1937 **Derbyshire** (342 & 311/3d) beat Sussex (243 & 129) by 281 runs
1938 Sussex (362 & 80) lost to **Surrey** (438 & 8/0) by 10 wkts
1938 Sussex (227 & 165) lost to **Hampshire** (209 & 184/9) by 1 wkt
1939 Warwicks (217 & 167) lost to **Sussex** (179 & 206/6) by 4 wkts
1939 Sussex (265 & 309) lost to **Surrey** (354 & 221/1) by 9 wkts
1946 **Glamorgan** (265) beat Sussex (35 & 127) by an inns & 103 runs
1946 Somerset (150 & 146/5d) drew with Sussex (95 & 145/7)
1947 Sussex (301 & 228) lost to **Warwicks** (406 & 124/4) by 6 wkts
1947 **Derbyshire** (217 & 193/4d) beat Sussex (198 & 113) by 99 runs
1948 Northants (342 & 43/3) drew with Sussex (123 & 418/9d)
1948 **Lancashire** (354/7d) beat Sussex (158 & 132) by an inns & 64 runs

1949 Sussex (275 & 265/7d) drew with Cambridge Univ (229 & 275/8)

1950 Essex (274 & 166) lost to **Sussex** (363 & 81/2) by 8 wkts

1950 Sussex (226 & 225/6) drew with Notts (213)

1951 **Sussex** (163 & 123) beat Somerset (178 & 89) by 19 runs

1951 Notts (149 & 154) lost to **Sussex** (185 & 120/5) by 5 wkts

1952 **Northants** (166 & 334/7d) beat Sussex (135 & 247) by 118 runs

1952 Sussex (178 & 214) lost to **Hampshire** (300 & 96/2) by 8 wkts

1953 **Sussex** (306 & 106/6d) beat Warwicks (181 & 188) by 43 runs

1953 Glamorgan (239 & 48/0) drew with Sussex (305/7d)

1954 Sussex (322/5d) drew with Cambridge Univ (126 & 354/6)

1954 **Derbyshire** (213 & 85) beat Sussex (148 & 74) by 76 runs

1955 **Sussex** (251 & 179/5d) beat Northants (203 & 154) by 73 runs

1955 Sussex (361/7d & 135/5d) lost to **Cambridge Univ** (232 & 267/6) by 4 wkts

1956 Sussex (125 & 63) lost to **Northants** (186/7d & 3/1) by 9 wkts

1956 Sussex (201 & 81) lost to **Warwicks** (194 & 91/6) by 4 wkts

1957-1970 No Matches

1971 Sussex (299/9d & 231/5d) lost to **Cambridge Univ** (272/4d & 260/7) by 3 wkts

1972 & 1973 No Matches

1974 Oxford Univ (71 & 169) lost to **Sussex** (181 & 60/3) by 7 wkts

1975-1978 No Matches

1979 Sussex (180 & 283/8d) drew with Sri Lanka (248 & 106/2)

1980-1982 No Matches

1983 **Lancashire** (312/6d & 172) beat Sussex (230 & 200) by 54 runs

1984 **Sussex** (358/4d & 21/0) beat Northants (200 & 178) by 10 wkts

1985 Sussex (391/7d & 281/6d) drew with Surrey (271 & 153/3)

1986 Match Abandoned without a ball being bowled (v Somerset)

1987 Hampshire (307/5d) drew with Sussex (79/4)

1988 Sussex (272 & 155) lost to **Derbyshire** (250 & 178/9) by 1 wkt

1989 Essex (185 & 350/6d) drew with Sussex (285 & 240/9)

1990 Sussex (235 & 108) lost to **Lancashire** (324 & 22/1) by 9 wkts

1991 Essex (303/7d) drew with Sussex (176/8)

1992 Durham (300/8d & 190/3d) lost to **Sussex** (151/4d & 340/6) by 4 wkts

1993 Sussex (271) beat Leics (97 & 72) by an inns & 102 runs

1994 **Sussex** (355 & 381/9d) beat Lancashire (286 & 390) by 60 runs

1995 Surrey (187 & 501/8d) drew with Sussex (304 & 230/9)

1996 **Sussex** (319/7d & forfeit) beat Middlesex (forfeit & 85) by 234 runs

1997 **Kent** (245 & 440) beat Sussex (264 & 317) by 104 runs

1998 Sussex (325 & 374) lost to **Derbyshire** (593 & 107/3) by 7 wkts

1999 Sussex (301/9d) drew with Worcs (124 & 255/9)

2000 Middlesex (370 & 337/6d) drew with Sussex (300/9d)

2001 **Sussex** (137 & 372) beat Worcs (183 & 293) by 33 runs

2002 Leics (264 & 94/2) drew with Sussex (247)

2003 **Sussex** (619/7d & 52/0) beat Notts (421 & 247) by 10 wkts

2004 Warwicks (600/6d & 188/2d) drew with Sussex (562)

2005 Scheduled match against Warwicks transferred to Hove

2006 **Sussex** (376 & 370) beat Middlesex (266 & 256) by 224 runs

2007 Durham (209 & 206) lost to **Sussex** (517) by an inns & 102 runs

SIDES PLAYED MOST FREQUENTLY

12 Surrey
9 Hampshire
8 Warwickshire
7 Northants
6 Essex, Notts & Derbyshire
5 Lancashire, Cambridge University, Gloucestershire & Leicestershire
4 Worcestershire & Glamorgan
3 Kent, Somerset & Middlesex
2 Oxford University & Durham
1 Sri Lanka

(Sussex have never played Yorkshire at Horsham)

B) - GENERAL PLAYING RECORDS (FIRST-CLASS MATCHES)
HIGHEST INNINGS TOTALS

FOR: 619-7 dec v. Nottinghamshire, 2003
AGAINST: 600-6 dec by Warwickshire, 2004

LOWEST INNINGS TOTALS
FOR: 35 v. Glamorgan, 1946
AGAINST: 51 by Leicestershire, 1924

HIGHEST INDIVIDUAL SCORE
FOR: 193 by CJ Adams v. Durham, 2007
AGAINST: 262* by IR Bell for Warwickshire, 2004

BEST BOWLING IN INNINGS
FOR: 9-50 by GR Cox v. Warwickshire, 1926
AGAINST: 9-35 by V Broderick for Northamptonshire, 1948

BEST BOWLING IN A MATCH
FOR: 17-106 by GR Cox v. Warwickshire, 1926
AGAINST: 12-133 by GE Tribe for Northamptonshire, 1952

MOST MATCHES PLAYED: 39 by Jim Langridge

MOST MATCHES PLAYED BY OPPONENT: 6, by EWJ Brooks, A Ducat, RJ Gregory & JB Hobbs (all Surrey)

MOST RUNS SCORED: 1878, by John Langridge

MOST WICKETS TAKEN: 150, by MW Tate

HIGHEST NUMBER OF CENTURIES: 4, by EH Bowley & JH Parks

NUMBER OF CENTURIES SCORED:
For Sussex: 51
Against Sussex: 41

RECORD WICKET STANDS
i) For

1st	258	John Langridge & JH Parks	Surrey	1934
2nd	187	AM Green & PWG Parker	Surrey	1985
3rd	200	EH Bowley & TER Cook	Warwickshire	1927
4th	200	GD Mendis & CM Wells	Northamptonshire	1984
5th	158	CJ Adams & AJ Hodd	Durham	2007

6th	141	G Cox & JY Oakes	Nottinghamshire	1950
7th	175	AE Relf & HS Malik	Leicestershire	1921
8th	116	LJ Wright & Naved-ul-Hasan	Middlesex	2006
9th	178	HW Parks & AF Wensley	Derbyshire	1930
10th	60*	SC Griffith & JH Cornford	Northamptonshire	1948

ii) Against

1st	187	WW Keeton & CB Harris	Nottinghamshire	1934
2nd	166	AE Alderman & TS Worthington	Derbyshire	1937
3rd	243	AJ Stewart & GP Thorpe	Surrey	1995
4th	254	KJ Barnett & ME Cassar	Derbyshire	1998
5th	193	KP Pietersen & BN Shafayat	Nottinghamshire	2003
6th	145	IR Bell & GB Hogg	Warwickshire	2004
7th	289*	IR Bell & T Frost	Warwickshire	2004
8th	130*	NA Foster & AGJ Fraser	Essex	1991
9th	100	G Fowler & PJW Allott	Lancashire	1990
10th	183	SA Marsh & BJ Phillips	Kent	1997

MOST EXPENSIVE BOWLING ANALYSES

i) For

31-1-125-4	Douglas M Smith	Surrey	1938
32-4-129-2	ESH Giddins	Surrey	1995
39-4-152-4	VC Drakes	Kent	1997
59-12-185-2	AA Khan	Derbyshire	1998
31-5-132-1	UBA Rashid	Middlesex	2000
37.1-3-163-6	Mushtaq Ahmed	Nottinghamshire	2003
50-6-194-4	Mushtaq Ahmed	Warwickshire	2004
28-3-130-0	RJ Kirtley	Warwickshire	2004

ii) Against

54.3-17-125-4	H Dean	Lancashire	1913
39.3-2-187-6	WE Astill	Leicestershire	1921
32-3-137-5	AS Kennedy	Hampshire	1921
32.2-1-149-5	RES Wyatt	Warwickshire	1927
44.1-11-125-5	CWL Parker	Gloucestershire	1932
43-9-131-5	DS de Silva	Sri Lanka	1979
50-12-172-3	SCG MacGill	Nottinghamshire	2003

SEVEN WICKETS OR MORE IN AN INNINGS

i) For

9-50	GR Cox	Warwickshire	1926
8-18	MW Tate	Worcestershire	1924
8-30	MW Tate	Glamorgan	1923
8-56	GR Cox	Warwickshire	1926
8-68	MW Tate	Kent	1927
7-17	JH Parks	Leicestershire	1924
7-28	EH Bowley	Gloucestershire	1932
7-31	EE Hemmings	Leicestershire	1993
7-44	MW Tate	Hampshire	1925
7-46	MW Tate	Nottinghamshire	1923
7-51	RCS Martin-Jenkins	Leicestershire	2002
7-52	DJ Wood	Hampshire	1938
7-53	RG Marlar	Northamptonshire	1955

ii) Against

9-35	V Broderick	Northamptonshire	1948
7-51	JH Mayer	Warwickshire	1936
7-53	GE Tribe	Northamptonshire	1952
7-60	CE Benham	Essex	1908
7-60	G Brown	Hampshire	1925
7-63	J Lawrence	Somerset	1951
7-69	GE Tribe	Northamptonshire	1955
7-76	DE Malcolm	Leicestershire	2002
7-82	MJ McCague	Kent	1997

10 WICKETS IN A MATCH

i) For

17-106	GR Cox	Warwickshire	1926
13-68	MW Tate	Nottinghamshire	1923
12-58	EE Hemmings	Leicestershire	1993
12-114	MW Tate	Worcestershire	1924
12-148	MW Tate	Kent	1927
12-244	Mushtaq Ahmed	Nottinghamshire	2003
11-101	RG Marlar	Northamptonshire	1955
11-108	AE Relf	Lancashire	1913
11-157	JH Cornford	Cambridge Univ	1949
10-87	MW Tate	Hampshire	1925
10-202	Mushtaq Ahmed	Middlesex	2006

ii) Against

12-133	GE Tribe	Northamptonshire	1952
12-135	WC Smith	Surrey	1910
11-132	WC Smith	Surrey	1912
11-154	CWL Parker	Gloucestershire	1932
10-80	J Lawrence	Somerset	1951
10-91	MS Nichols	Essex	1929
10-93	JS Manning	Northamptonshire	1956
10-95	SG Smith	Northamptonshire	1913*
10-104	GJ Thompson	Northamptonshire	1913*
10-104	MS Nichols	Essex	1933
10-114	JH Mayer	Warwickshire	1936
10-126	W Huddleston	Lancashire	1913
10-132	FE Woolley	Kent	1920
10-154	V Broderick	Northamptonshire	1948
10-157	RO Jenkins	Worcestershire	1947
10-188	DS de Silva	Sri Lanka	1979

(* In 1913, Messrs Thompson & Smith bowled unchanged throughout both innings)

PAIRS OF SPECTACLES

i) For

1926 – EH Bowley v. Gloucs
1947 – DJ Wood v. Worcs
1983 – CM Wells v. Lancashire

1929 – J Langridge v. Glamorgan
1954 – DJ Wood v. Derbyshire

ii) Against

1920 – LJ Corbett, Gloucs
1924 – EH Bryant, Worcs
1926 – WG Peare, Warwicks
1932 – SH Martin, Worcs
1932 – JA Rogers, Gloucs
1935 – GC Perkins, Northants
1950 – IJ Skinner, Essex
1953 – CW Grove, Warwicks
2006 - ET Smith, Middlesex

1923 – FW Mathias, Glamorgan
1924 – HO Rogers, Worcs
1928 – EWJ Brooks, Surrey
1932 - FD Ahl, Worcs
1935 – TA Pitt, Northants
1937 – RA Sinfield, Gloucs
1951 – J Redman, Somerset
1956 – RE Hitchcock, Warwicks

CENTURIES SCORED
i) For

193	CJ Adams	Durham	2007
176	EH Bowley	Warwickshire	1927
175*	JM Parks`	Cambridge University	1955
174*	DS Sheppard	Glamorgan	1953
170	HW Parks	Worcestershire	1947
160	John Langridge	Surrey	1934
160	IJ Ward	Warwickshire	2004
153	AE Relf	Leicestershire	1921
151	VWC Jupp	Kent	1920
144	CJ Adams	Warwickshire	2004
142	MW Tate	Hampshire	1921
135*	M Newell	Derbyshire	1998
133*	PGH Fender	Oxford University	1912
133	MJ Prior	Nottinghamshire	2003
130	EH Bowley	Glamorgan	1929
127	G Cox	Warwickshire	1953
127*	CM Wells	Northamptonshire	1984
127	MG Bevan	Derbyshire	1998
126	John Langridge	Cambridge University	1954
125	WG Khan	Derbyshire	1998
122	JH Parks	Surrey	1934
122*	RR Montgomerie	Leicestershire	2002
120	EH Bowley	Glamorgan	1923
120	AF Wensley	Derbyshire	1930
120	KG Suttle	Cambridge University	1971
118	NJ Lenham	Durham	1992
116	KS Duleepsinhji	Worcestershire	1932
114	JH Parks	Gloucestershire	1932
113	RSG Scott	Hampshire	1933
112	KG Suttle	Cambridge University	1971
112	K Newell	Kent	1997
112	RR Montgomerie	Worcestershire	2001
111	C Oakes	Surrey	1938
109	JH Parks	Nottinghamshire	1931
109	KS Duleepsinhji	Nottinghamshire	1931
109	MW Goodwin	Worcestershire	2001
107	GD Mendis	Northamptonshire	1984

107	FD Stephenson	Lancashire	1994
106	HS Malik	Leicestershire	1921
106*	SC Griffith	Northamptonshire	1948
106	DV Smith	Essex	1950
106	AM Green	Surrey	1985
105	PWG Parker	Surrey	1985
105	RR Montgomerie	Nottinghamshire	2003
104	JH Parks	Nottinghamshire	1934
103*	KS Innes	Nottinghamshire	2003
102	John Langridge	Derbyshire	1937
102*	JRT Barclay	Sri Lanka	1979
102	NJ Lenham	Lancashire	1994
100	RR Relf	Surrey	1909
100	EH Bowley	Essex	1929

ii) Against

262*	IR Bell	Warwickshire	2004
224	CP Mead	Hampshire	1921
179	D Brookes	Northamptonshire	1948
166	RJ Gregory	Surrey	1936
166	KP Pietersen	Nottinghamshire	2003
162	KJ Barnett	Derbyshire	1998
160	WR Hammond	Gloucestershire	1937
157*	MK Foster	Worcestershire	1924
150	AJ Stewart	Surrey	1995
149	FC Hayes	Lancashire	1983
147	MCJ Nicholas	Hampshire	1987
142	SA Marsh	Kent	1997
139*	FE Woolley	Kent	1920
135*	T Frost	Warwickshire	2004
134	GA Hick	Worcestershire	1999
133*	TS Worthington	Derbyshire	1937
128	A Sandham	Surrey	1922
126	OA Shah	Middlesex	2006
121	ME Cassar	Derbyshire	1998
119	NH Rogers	Hampshire	1952
117	AE Dipper	Gloucestershire	1922
117	JA Cutmore	Essex	1933
115*	JF Pretlove	Cambridge University	1954
114	HAW Bowell	Hampshire	1914

113	CP Mead	Hampshire	1921
111	W Place	Lancashire	1948
110	TH Barling	Surrey	1936
110	GP Thorpe	Surrey	1995
107	JT Tyldesley	Lancashire	1913
107	CB Harris	Nottinghamshire	1934
107*	LB Fishlock	Surrey	1939
107*	NA Foster	Essex	1991
106	WE Davis	Surrey	1910
105	HTW Hardinge	Kent	1927
105	RE Bird	Worcestershire	1947
105	L Livingston	Northamptonshire	1952
104*	FR Santall	Warwickshire	1936
103	AE Dipper	Gloucestershire	1922
103	AE Alderman	Derbyshire	1937
102*	DG Cork	Derbyshire	1998
101*	A Ducat	Surrey	1928

FIELDING: FIRST CLASS MATCHES

Most catches in an innings
For:	5	AF Wensley	v. Surrey, 1934
Against:	4	Majid Khan	Cambridge University, 1971

Most catches in a match
For:	7	AF Wensley	v. Surrey, 1934
Against:	4	10 players	

Most wicket-keeper dismissals in an innings
For:	5	GB Street	v. Gloucestershire, 1922
	5	WL Cornford	v. Hampshire, 1925
Against:	5	EA Meads	Nottinghamshire, 1951

Most wicket-keeper dismissals in a match
For:	7	WL Cornford	v. Hampshire, 1925
	7	WL Cornford	v. Worcestershire, 1932
	7	IJ Gould	v. Derbyshire, 1988
	7	TR Ambrose	v. Nottinghamshire, 2003
Against:	7	BJM Maher	Derbyshire, 1988

C) - SUSSEX'S PLAYING RECORD AT HORSHAM
(ONE-DAY MATCHES)

Played   26
Won   12
Lost   14

(the matches in 1990, 1991 and 1996 were all abandoned without a ball being bowled)

RESULTS

1971   **Leics** (200/8) beat Sussex (171/8) by 29 runs
1972-1976   No Matches
1977   Lancashire (195/4) lost to **Sussex** (196/8) by 2 wkts
1978   Somerset (136/8) lost to **Sussex** (137/4) by 6 wkts
1979   **Surrey** (185/6) beat Sussex (72/2) on faster scoring rate
1980   **Sussex** (293/4) beat Worcs (261) by 32 runs
1981   Sussex (198/9) lost to **Warwicks** (200/3) by 7 wkts
1982   Sussex (206/8) lost to **Worcs** (208/7) by 3 wkts
1983   **Sussex** (202/8) beat Lancashire (200) by 2 runs
1984   **Sussex** (236/8) beat Northants (165) by 71 runs
1985   Sussex (196/7) lost to **Notts** (197/8) by 2 wkts
1986   Sussex (108/9) lost to **Somerset** (111/2) by 8 wkts
1987   Hampshire (216/7) lost to **Sussex** (218/9) by 1 wkt
1988   **Derbyshire** (213/8) beat Sussex (208/8) by 5 runs
1989   Sussex (154/7) lost to **Essex** (157/4) by 6 wkts
1990   Sussex v. Lancashire – Abandoned
1991   Sussex v. Essex – Abandoned
1992   **Durham** (275/4) beat Sussex (270/9) by 5 runs
1993   **Sussex** (283/8) beat Leics (220/7) by 63 runs
1994   Sussex (229/9) lost to **Lancashire** (232/3) by 7 wkts
1995   **Sussex** (222/7) beat Surrey (212) by 10 runs
1996   Sussex v. Middlesex – Abandoned
1997   Kent (220/9) lost to **Sussex** (224/6) by 4 wkts
1998   Sussex (148) lost to **Derbyshire** (150/4) by 6 wkts
1999   No Match
2000   **Sussex** (219) beat Leics (208) by 11 runs
2001   **Worcs** (210/6) beat Sussex (140) by 70 runs
2002   **Sussex** (240) beat Essex (208) by 32 runs
2003   **Notts** (258/6) beat Sussex (150) by 97 runs
        (Duckworth/Lewis method)
2004   **Leics** (324/4) beat Sussex (323/5 by 1 run

2005   Scheduled match against Warwicks transferred to Hove

2006   Somerset (158/7) lost to **Sussex** 123/5) by 5 wkts
(Duckworth/Lewis)

2007   No Game

1971-1992	40 overs per innings
1993	50 overs per innings
1994-1998	40 overs per innings
2000-2004	45 overs per innings
2006	50 overs per innings

OTHER MATCH

2001   **Gloucs** (238/9) beat Sussex Cricket Board (143) by 95 runs

D) - GENERAL PLAYING RECORDS (ONE-DAY MATCHES)
HIGHEST INNINGS TOTALS

For: 323/5 v. Leicestershire, 2004

Against: 324/4 by Leicestershire, 2004

HIGHEST INDIVIDUAL SCORES

For: 136   IJ Ward v. Leicestershire, 2004

Against: 154*   BJ Hodge, Leicestershire, 2004

RECORD WICKET STANDS

i) For

1st	96	KC Wessels & JA Snow	Lancashire	1977
2nd	143	IJ Ward & MW Goodwin	Leicestershire	2004
3rd	156	PWG Parker & Imran Khan	Worcestershire	1980
4th	89	PWG Parker & AP Wells	Northants	1984
5th	55	Imran Khan & CM Wells	Nottinghamshire	1985
6th	79	DR Law & P Moores	Surrey	1995
7th	51	PWG Parker & CP Phillipson	Worcestershire	1982
8th	57	ACS Pigott & NJ Lenham	Derbyshire	1988
9th	39	JRT Barclay & GG Arnold	Warwickshire	1981
10th	16	RJ Kirtley & MA Robinson	Derbyshire	1998

ii) Against

1st	107	W Larkins & JD Glendenen	Durham	1992
2nd	165	DL Maddy & BJ Hodge	Leicestershire	2004
3rd	101	GR Napier & A Flower	Essex	2002
4th	121*	MA Atherton & JER Gallian	Lancashire	1994

5th	89	GP Thorpe & AJ Hollioake	Surrey	1995
6th	59	VJ Wells & PA Nixon	Leicestershire	1993
7th	24	CC Lewis & JM Dakin	Leicestershire	2000
		JE Morris & BJM Maher	Derbyshire	1988
8th	61*	VJ Wells & JM Dakin	Leicestershire	1993
9th	30	J Abrahams & NH Fairbrother	Lancashire	1983
10th	26	ACS Pigott & CG Rackemann	Surrey	1995

MOST ECONOMICAL BOWLING ANALYSES

i) For

8-2-8-2	Imran Khan	Somerset	1978
8-2-14-1	MA Buss	Lancashire	1977

ii) Against

8-5-9-2	KF Jennings	Somerset	1978
8-0-11-2	TD Topley	Essex	1989
8-1-12-3	A Walker	Northamptonshire	1984

MOST EXPENSIVE BOWLING ANALYSES

i) For:

8-0-75-1	RJ Kirtley	Leicestershire	2004
10-0-69-0	ACS Pigott	Leicestershire	1993
8-0-65-1	ACS Pigott	Durham	1992
9-0-63-0	Mohammad Akram	Leics	2004
7-0-62-1	ACS Pigott	Worcestershire	1982
8-0-60-2	J Spencer	Worcestershire	1980

ii) Against:

10-0-72-2	GJ Parsons	Leicestershire	1993
9-0-66-0	PAJ DeFreitas	Leicestershire	2004
10-1-62-1	J Dakin	Leicestershire	1993
8-0-61-4	DJ Capel	Northamptonshire	1984
8-0-60-0	PW Henderson	Durham	1992
9-0-60-2	DS Brignull	Leicestershire	2004
6-0-54-2	CW Henderson	Leicestershire	2004
5-0-53-2	B Roberts	Derbyshire	1988

CENTURIES SCORED

i) For

136	IJ Ward	v. Leicestershire	2004
109*	CWJ Athey	v. Kent	1997
106*	PWG Parker	v. Worcestershire	1980

ii) Against

154*	BJ Hodge	Leicestershire	2004
147	GM Turner	Worcestershire	1980
117*	DL Amiss	Warwickshire	1981
101*	MA Atherton	Lancashire	1994

E) INDIVIDUAL PLAYING RECORDS AT HORSHAM, FIRST CLASS MATCHES

i) SUSSEX, BATTING & FIELDING

Name	App	Inns	N/O	Runs	H/S	Aver	50s	100s	catches
Adams, CJ	6	7	0	511	193	73.00	1	2	6
Alikhan, RI	1	2	0	57	56	28.50	1	0	0
Ambrose, TR	3	3	0	56	55	18.66	1	0	5+3 st
Arnold, GG	1	2	1	12	12*	12.00	0	0	0
Athey, CWJ	3	5	0	115	37	23.00	0	0	2
Babington, AM	2	4	1	6	5	2.00	0	0	0
Barclay, JRT	4	7	1	189	102*	31.50	0	1	5
Bartlett, HT	6	12	0	308	74	25.66	3	0	3
Bates, DL	3	1	0	8	8	8.00	0	0	2
Bates, JJ	1	1	0	1	1	1.00	0	0	3
Bevan, MG	2	3	0	204	127	68.00	1	1	3
Blake, PDS	2	4	0	102	77	25.50	1	0	2
Bowley, EH	29	47	2	1543	176	34.33	10	4	18
Browne, FBR	2	2	0	0	0	-	0	0	3
Bunting, RA	1	2	1	10	10*	10.00	0	0	0
Buss, A	1	1	0	15	15	15.00	0	0	0
Buss, MA	1			Did Not Bat			0	0	1
Butt, HR	3	4	3	35	33	35.00	0	0	4+1 st
Carey, PAH	6	11	0	52	12	4.70	0	0	4
Carpenter, JR	1	2	0	20	19	10.00	0	0	1
Cartwright, P	4	8	0	102	46	12.75	0	0	1
Chaplin, HP	8	14	1	264	62	20.33	1	0	2
Clapp, DA	1	1	0	6	6	6.00	0	0	0
Clarke, AR	1	2	1	3	3*	3.00	0	0	0
Collins, GAK	1	2	0	17	14	8.50	0	0	1
Cook, TER	29	45	5	1137	95	28.40	8	0	11
Cornford, JH	22	32	14	88	11	4.88	0	0	9
Cornford, WL	30	40	13	402	50	14.88	1	0	45+29 st
Cottey, PA	4	4	0	100	58	25.00	1	0	3

Name									
Cox, G (jnr)	27	48	3	1274	127	28.33	9	1	12
Cox, GR (sen)	22	33	6	369	35	13.66	0	0	14
Davis, MJG	4	5	2	171	43*	57.00	0	0	0
Denman, J	1	1	0	42	42	42.00	0	0	0
Di Venuto, MJ	1	1	0	64	64	64.00	1	0	3
Dodemaide, AIC	4	5	1	146	70	36.50	1	0	2
Doggart, AP	3	6	1	77	34	15.40	0	0	0
Doggart, GHG	2	3	0	38	21	12.66	0	0	3
Donelan, BTP	2	3	1	8	8*	4.00	0	0	1
Drakes, VC	1	2	0	1	1*	0.50	0	0	0
Duffield, J	1	2	1	3	3	3.00	0	0	0
Duleepsinhji, KS	6	8	0	370	116	46.25	2	1	10
Eaton, VJ	1	2	0	5	3	2.50	0	0	2+1 st
Faber, MJJ	1	2	1	31	20	15.50	0	0	0
Fender, PGH	4	7	1	209	133*	34.80	0	1	2
Foreman, DJ	3	5	1	113	65	28.25	1	0	3
Gibson, CH	1	1	0	15	15	15.00	0	0	0
Giddins, ESH	3	4	1	6	6*	2.00	0	0	1
Gilligan, AER	11	15	2	307	54*	23.66	1	0	10
Gilligan, AHH	18	29	3	544	78	20.90	3	0	8
Goodwin, MW	6	9	1	358	109	44.75	2	1	1
Gould, IJ	5	6	2	193	58*	48.25	2	0	10
Graves, PJ	2	4	1	155	76	51.66	1	0	1
Green, AM	6	11	1	334	106	33.40	1	1	6
Greenfield, K	2	4	0	121	37	30.25	0	0	3
Greenidge, GA	2	4	0	59	51	14.75	1	0	0
Greig, IA	2	2	1	77	43	77.00	0	0	2
Griffith, MG	1	2	0	28	25	14.00	0	0	0
Griffith, SC	9	16	1	251	106*	16.70	0	1	14+2 st
Grimston, GS	1	2	0	5	5	2.50	0	0	0
Groome, JJ	1	2	0	19	19	9.50	0	0	1
Hall, JW	5	9	0	303	82	33.60	3	0	0
Hammond, HE	8	12	2	140	60	14.00	1	0	7
Harris, ELJ	3	4	0	62	41	15.50	0	0	2
Head, TJ	1	2	1	11	6*	11.00	0	0	1
Hemmings, EE	3	5	3	28	9	14.00	0	0	2
Heseltine, PAW	1			Did Not Bat				0	
Heygate, RB	2	4	1	115	74	38.33	1	0	2
Higgs, KA	9	13	1	254	85	21.20	2	0	5

Name									
Hodd, AJ	1	1	0	72	72	72.00	1	0	0
Hollingdale, RA	5	6	1	76	34*	15.20	0	0	1
Holloway, NJ	4	7	4	26	7*	8.66	0	0	1
Holmes, AJ	13	22	3	495	93	26.10	2	0	8
Hopkinson, CD	1	2	0	66	62	33.00	1	0	0
House, WJ	1	2	0	34	21	17.00	0	0	1
Humphries, S	2	3	0	16	16	5.33	0	0	2
Innes, KJ	1	1	1	103	103*	-	0	1	0
Isherwood, LCR	1	2	0	36	31	18.00	0	0	0
James, AE	15	22	8	142	27	10.10	0	0	3
Jarvis, PW	3	6	0	146	55	24.33	1	0	3
Javed Miandad	1	2	0	9	9	4.50	0	0	0
Jenner, FD	1	1	0	5	5	5.00	0	0	1
Jones, AN	3	1	1	10	10*	-	0	0	0
Jupp, VWC	8	10	1	362	151	40.20	2	1	2
Khan, AA	2	4	1	56	29	18.66	0	0	3
Khan, WG	2	3	0	203	125	67.66	1	1	0
Killick, EH	4	7	0	151	48	21.60	0	0	1
Kimber, SJS	1	2	0	13	8	6.50	0	0	0
Kirtley, RJ	7	8	3	61	17*	12.20	0	0	1
Lang, AH	3	6	0	129	71	21.50	1	0	1+2 st
Langridge, Jas	39	62	10	1477	87	28.40	12	0	18
Langridge, John	37	68	1	1878	160	28.00	10	3	44
Langridge, RJ	1	2	0	18	17	9.00	0	0	1
Law, DR	1	1	0	3	3	3.00	0	0	0
Lawrence, AAK	3	5	1	34	15	8.50	0	0	2
Leach, G	3	5	1	100	43	25.00	0	0	3
Lenham, NJ	9	16	0	607	118	35.70	3	2	3
Le Roux, GS	3	2	0	81	49	40.50	0	0	0
Lewry, JD	8	11	3	79	31*	9.90	0	0	6
Malden, WJ	4	5	0	42	26	8.40	0	0	3
Malik, HS	2	2	0	118	106	59.00	0	1	0
Mansell, AW	2	2	1	14	14*	14.00	0	0	4
Mantell, DN	2	1	0	2	2	2.00	0	0	0
Manville, DW	1	2	0	2	2	1.00	0	0	1
Marlar, RG	4	6	2	33	26	8.25	0	0	5
Martin-Jenkins, RCS									
	7	8	1	229	49	32.70	0	0	3
Melville, A	3	3	0	37	35	12.33	0	0	2

Mendis, GD	4	8	1	210	107	30.00	0	1	1
Mercer, J	2	3	0	14	10	4.66	0	0	1
Mohammad Akram									
	1	1	0	34	34	34.00	0	0	0
Montgomerie, RR									
	8	11	1	660	122	66.00	3	3	11
Moores, P	9	15	2	191	39	13.60	0	0	27+2 st
Morley, JD	2	4	1	86	50	28.66	1	0	3
Mushtaq Ahmed	4	4	2	104	62	52.00	1	0	1
Myles, SD	1	1	1	18	18*	-	0	0	1
Nash, CD	1	1	0	63	63	63.00	1	0	0
Naumann, JH	1	2	0	7	7	3.50	0	0	0
Naved-ul-Hasan, R									
	2	3	0	67	64	22.33	1	0	0
Newell, K	3	6	0	228	112	38.00	1	1	1
Newell, M	2	4	1	255	135*	85.00	1	2	2
Nye, JK	3	5	1	23	12*	5.75	0	0	0
Oakes, C	20	37	3	743	111	21.90	3	1	8
Oakes, JY	11	21	0	385	95	18.33	2	0	4
Oakman, ASM	12	21	1	399	90	19.95	2	0	14
Parker, PWG	6	8	0	291	76	36.40	2	0	9
Parks, HW	31	51	4	1026	170	21.80	4	1	11
Parks, JH	30	50	4	1375	122	29.90	3	4	24
Parks, JM	12	22	4	493	175*	27.40	0	1	4
Patterson, AD	1	1	0	8	8	8.00	0	0	1
Pearce, GS	4	6	1	60	26	12.00	0	0	3
Pelham, AG	1	1	0	0	0	0.00	0	0	1
Pheasant, ST	1	2	1	2	2*	2.00	0	0	2
Phillipson, CP	2	3	0	20	14	6.66	0	0	1
Pierce, MTE	3	4	0	107	75	26.75	1	0	1
Pigott, ACS	8	11	1	206	45*	20.60	0	0	9
Potter, G	3	5	0	83	35	16.60	0	0	2
Prior, MJ	5	7	0	304	133	43.40	1	1	11+2 st
Radford, TA	1	2	0	4	4	2.00	0	0	2
Ranjitsinhji, KS	1	1	0	8	8	8.00	0	0	0
Rashid, UBA	2	3	1	90	51*	45.00	1	0	1
Rayner, OP	1	2	0	4	4	2.00	0	0	2
Relf, AE	10	16	2	530	153	37.86	2	1	9
Relf, RR	9	15	1	531	100*	37.93	5	1	4

Name	M	I	NO	Runs	HS	Avg	100	50	Ct/St
Reeve, DA	4	3	2	72	42*	72.00	0	0	3
Richards, DS	1	1	0	3	3	3.00	0	0	1
Ricketts, CIO	1			Did Not Bat					0
Roberts, HE	7	12	6	130	62	21.66	1	0	2
Robinson, MA	3	5	3	8	4	4.00	0	0	2
Robson, AG	1			Did Not Bat					
Salisbury, IDK	6	10	3	111	37	15.80	0	0	6
Scott, RSG	5	7	1	206	113	34.33	0	1	2
Sheppard, DS	4	7	1	244	174*	40.66	0	1	4
Simms, HL	3	4	0	60	53	15.00	1	0	1
Simms, RK	1	1	0	4	4	4.00	0	0	0
Smith, CLA	2	2	0	16	12	8.00	0	0	1
Smith, DJ	1	2	1	6	6	6.00	0	0	3
Smith, David M	3	5	0	207	71	41.40	2	0	6
Smith, Douglas M	2	4	1	11	9	3.66	0	0	1
Smith, DV	12	22	0	518	106	23.50	2	1	1
Snow, JA	1	1	0	17	17	17.00	0	0	0
Speight, MP	5	8	0	243	49	27.00	0	0	5
Stainton, RG	2	4	0	67	32	16.75	0	0	2
Standing, DK	2	3	0	10	7	3.33	0	0	0
Stannard, GA	2	3	1	28	20*	14.00	0	0	1
Street, GB	11	15	5	313	87	31.30	1	0	23+12 st
Stephenson, FD	4	6	1	252	107	50.40	1	1	2
Stripp, DA	2	4	0	29	21	7.25	0	0	1
Suttle, KG	11	20	2	726	120	40.33	3	2	6
Tate, MW	29	42	4	965	142	25.40	4	1	12
Taylor, BV	1			Did Not Bat				0	
Thomson, NI	9	15	3	149	43	12.40	0	0	4
Tuppin, AG	1	2	0	9	9	9.00	0	0	0
Upton, M	1	1	1	2	2*	-	0	0	0
Vincett, JH	9	11	1	157	55	15.70	1	0	10
Vine, J	9	15	0	456	83	30.40	4	0	3
Waller, CE	5	4	0	11	5	2.75	0	0	1
Ward, IJ	1	1	0	160	160	160.00	0	1	0
Watson, AC	9	13	0	212	39	16.30	0	0	7
Webb, RT	10	13	6	139	26*	19.85	0	0	16+6 st
Wells, AP	12	19	0	546	92	28.70	3	0	12
Wells, CM	8	13	2	289	127*	26.30	1	1	0

Wensley, AF	27	40	3	872	120	23.60	4	1	25
Wessels, KC	1	2	0	94	66	47.00	1	0	1
Williams, L	2	4	0	60	34	15.00	0	0	0
Willson, RH	1	2	0	1	1	0.50	0	0	1
Wilson, AK	2	4	0	17	6	4.25	0	0	1
Wilson, HL	7	12	0	242	58	20.20	2	0	4
Wisdom, N	1	1	1	31	31*	-	0	0	0
Wood, DJ	14	19	3	89	30*	5.60	0	0	6
Wright, LJ	2	3	0	87	59	29.00	1	0	0
Yardy, MH	3	4	0	28	14	7.00	0	0	5
Zuiderent, B	1	2	0	10	8	5.00	0	0	1

F) INDIVIDUAL PLAYING RECORDS AT HORSHAM
FIRST-CLASS MATCHES
ii) SUSSEX, BOWLING

Name	Mtchs	Ovrs	Mdns	Runs	Wkts	Aver	BB	5/i	10/m	SR	ER
Adams, CJ	6	8	2	20	1	20.00	1-5	0	0	8.	2.5
Arnold, GG	1	13	3	50	2	25.00	2-46	0	0	6.5	3.8
Athey, CWJ	3	1	0	4	0	-	0-4	0	0	-	4.0
Babington, AM	2	20.3	2	82	2	41.00	1-27	0	0	10.1	4.1
Barclay, JTR	4	120	41	250	19	13.20	6-61	1	0	6.3	2.1
Bates, DL	3	94.5	25	227	7	32.40	4-50	0	0	13.6	2.4
Bates, JJ	1	44	7	136	2	68.00	2-85	0	0	22.0	3.1
Bevan, MG	2	42.4	3	179	2	89.50	1-40	0	0	8.0	5.1
Bowley, EH	29	448	105	1143	64	17.85	7-28	3	0	7.0	2.6
Browne, FBR	2	104	28	184	10	18.40	6-50	1	0	10.4	1.8
Bunting, RA	1	16	1	81	2	40.00	1-20	0	0	8.0	5.1
Buss, A	1	24	12	30	2	15.00	2-27	0	0	6.3	2.1
Buss, MA	1	9	3	12	2	6.00	2-12	0	0	4.5	1.33
Carey, PAH	6	210.1	44	591	22	26.90	4-99	0	0	9.5	2.8
Cartwright, P	4	1	0	8	0	-	0-8	0	0	-	8.0
Clarke, AR	1	18.3	5	52	1	52.00	1-22	0	0	18.3	2.8
Cook, TER	29	61	9	167	3	55.66	1-9	0	0	20.33	2.7
Cornford, JH	22	775.2	163	2023	93	21.50	6-54	7	1	8.3	2.6
Cox, G (jnr)	27	58.2	17	120	4	30.00	2-39	0	0	14.6	2.1
Cox, GR (snr)	22	611.3	190	1371	83	16.50	9-50	7	1	7.4	2.2
Davis, MJG	4	118	14	405	8	50.60	6-116	1	0	14.75	3.4
Denman, J	1	35.3	7	121	2	60.60	2-53	0	0	17.5	3.4
Dodemaide, AIC	4	141.5	22	414	16	25.90	6-106	1	0	8.9	2.9
Doggart, AP	3	6.5	0	41	2	20.50	2-8	0	0	3.5	5.8
Doggart, GHG	2	27	4	93	1	93.00	1-88	0	0	27.0	3.4

Name											
Donelan, BTP	2	47.4	6	177	1	177.00	1-102	0	0	47.4	3.7
Drakes, VC	1	69	9	257	8	32.10	4-152	0	0	8.6	3.7
Duffield, J	1	26	6	40	2	20.00	1-17	0	0	13.0	1.5
Fender, PGH	4	43	14	118	9	13.10	5-42	1	0	4.8	2.7
Foreman, DJ	3	3	0	22	0	-	0-22	0	0	-	7.33
Gibson, CH	1	35	13	49	3	16.33	2-15	0	0	11.66	1.4
Giddins, ESH	3	102.2	18	379	16	23.70	5-81	1	0	6.	3.7
Gilligan, AER	11	267.3	5	820	35	23.40	4-31	0	0	7.6	3.1
Gilligan, AHH	18	71	11	220	5	44.00	2-61	0	0	14.2	3.1
Graves, PJ	2	2	0	10	0	-	0-10	0	0	-	5.0
Green, AM	6	2	0	8	0	-	0-8	0	0	-	4.0
Greenidge, GA	2	5	0	31	0	-	0-31	0	0	-	4.0
Greig, IA	2	46	9	147	4	36.75	2-41	0	0	11.5	3.2
Grimston, GS	1	2	0	2	0	-	0-2	0	0	-	1.0
Hammond, HE	8	191.1	36	598	20	29.90	6-78	2	0	9.6	3.1
Harris, ELJ	3	6	2	10	0	-	0-10	0	0	-	1.66
Hemmings, EE	3	106.4	36	275	15	18.33	7-31	2	1	7.1	2.6
Heseltine, PAW	1	13	2	47	0	-	0-47	0	0	-	3.6
Higgs, KA	9	7	1	36	0	-	0-6	0	0	-	5.1
Hollingdale, RA	5	53	10	124	3	41.33	1-11	0	0	17.66	2.3
Holloway, NJ	4	110.1	27	278	17	16.30	6-39	1	0	6.5	2.5
Holmes, AJ	13	1	0	1	0	-	0-1	0	0	-	1.0
James, AE	15	514.4	171	1147	49	23.40	5-31	2	0	10.5	2.2
Jarvis, PW	3	125.4	27	398	13	30.60	3-26	0	0	9.7	3.2
Javed Miandad	1	7	1	30	0	-	0-30	0	0	-	4.3
Jones, AN	3	42	2	245	3	81.66	2-110	0	0	14.0	5.8
Jupp, VWC	8	108.3	20	350	11	31.80	3-59	0	0	9.9	3.2
Khan, AA	2	93	21	271	5	54.20	2-24	0	0	18.6	2.9
Killick, EH	4	22	5	94	1	94.00	1-21	0	0	22.0	4.3
Kimber, SJS	1	28	7	70	5	14.00	3-44	0	0	5.6	2.5
Kirtley, RJ	7	234.5	51	756	19	39.80	5-60	1	0	12.4	3.2
Langridge, Jas	39	753.4	198	1583	68	23.30	5-12	3	0	11.1	2.1
Langridge, John	37	20	1	91	2	45.50	1-8	0	0	10.0	4.6
Law, DR	1	4	0	14	3	4.66	3-14	0	0	1.33	3.5
Lawrence, AAK	3	0.2	0	3	0	-	0-3	0	0	-	9.0
Leach, G	3	57	10	160	5	32.00	3-88	0	0	11.4	2.8
Lenham, NJ	9	2	0	3	0	-	0-3	0	0	-	1.5
Le Roux, GS	3	68	16	198	4	49.50	2-66	0	0	17.0	2.9
Lewry, JD	8	245.2	55	820	36	22.80	6-63	3	0	6.8	3.3
Marlar, RG	4	178.4	59	386	24	16.10	7-53	3	1	7.4	2.2
Martin-Jenkins, RCS	7	151.4	34	498	19	26.20	7-51	1	0	7.9	3.3

Melville, A	3	19.2	4	55	9	6.11	5-37	1	0	2.2	2.8
Mercer, J	2	29	4	89	4	22.25	4-46	0	0	7.2	3.0
Mohammad Akram											
	1	29	2	94	2	47.00	2-94	0	0	14.5	3.2
Mushtaq Ahmed	4	217.2	36	808	35	23.10	6-81	4	2	6.2	3.7
Myles,SD	1	2	0	14	0	-	0-14	0	0	-	7.0
Naved-ul-Hasan	2	41	6	181	5	36.20	2-52	0	0	8.2	4.4
Newell, K	3	38.1	9	130	5	26.00	4-61	0	0	7.6	3.4
Nye, JK	3	83.1	12	330	9	36.66	4-103	0	0	9.2	4.0
Oakes, C	20	218	53	671	17	39.50	3-11	0	0	12.5	2.0
Oakes, JY	11	118	32	306	13	23.50	5-33	1	0	12.8	3.1
Oakman, ASM	12	172	66	368	20	18.40	6-91	1	0	8.6	2.1
Parker, PWG	6	4	0	25	0	-	0-25	0	0	-	6.25
Parks, HW	31	16	3	48	1	48.00	1-12	0	0	16.0	3.0
Parks, JH	30	749.5	256	1507	60	25.10	7-17	2	0	12.5	2.0
Parks, JM	12	34.5	11	77	5	15.40	3-23	0	0	7.0	2.2
Pearce, GS	4	32	4	121	3	40.33	2-51	0	0	10.66	3.8
Pelham, AG	1	8	0	28	1	28.00	1-28	0	0	8.0	3.5
Pheasant, ST	1	50	14	121	4	30.25	4-88	0	0	12.5	2.4
Phillipson, CP	2	39	18	50	5	10.00	5-30	1	0	7.8	1.3
Pierce, MTE	3	1	0	13	0	-	0-13	0	0	-	13.0
Pigott, ACS	8	184.1	29	680	27	25.20	5-55	1	0	6.8	3.7
Potter, G	3	32	8	97	0	-	0-28	0	0	-	3.0
Rashid, UBA	2	51	13	179	3	59.66	1-7	0	0	17.0	3.5
Rayner, OP	1	6	0	24	0	-	0-10	0	0	-	4.0
Reeve, DA	4	104.2	33	237	11	21.50	3-23	0	0	9.5	2.3
Relf, AE	10	355.1	112	773	46	16.80	6-36	6	1	7.7	2.2
Relf, RR	9	42	12	116	6	19.30	3-6	0	0	7.0	2.8
Richards, DS	1	6	4	4	0	-	0-4	0	0	-	1.5
Ricketts, CIO	1	17	2	50	1	50.00	1-50	0	0	17.0	2.9
Roberts, HE	7	169	28	438	13	33.70	5-66	1	0	13.0	2.6
Robinson, MA	3	106	36	251	9	27.90	3-25	0	0	11.8	2.4
Robson, AG	1	16	1	49	0	-	0-20	0	0	-	3.1
Salisbury, IDK	6	132	36	420	9	46.66	5-109	1	0	14.66	3.2
Scott, RSG	5	110	31	214	10	21.40	4-70	0	0	11.0	1.9
Simms, HL	3	58	18	123	9	13.66	4-51	0	0	6.4	2.1
Simms, RK	1	14	1	41	1	41.00	1-41	0	0	14.0	2.9
Smith, Douglas M											
	2	52.2	2	191	9	21.22	5-25	1	0	5.8	3.6
Smith, DV	12	77	27	191	8	23.90	3-69	0	0	9.6	2.5
Snow, JA	1	6	0	19	0	-	0-19	0	0	-	3.2

Stephenson, FD	4	89.3	16	314	13	24.20	4-45	0	0	6.9	3.5
Stripp, DA	2	10	3	24	0	-	0-24	0	0	-	2.4
Suttle, KG	11	30	6	107	4	26.75	2-46	0	0	7.5	3.6
Tate, MW	29	1244	397	2396	150	15.90	8-18	9	4	8.3	1.9
Taylor, BV	1	24	6	68	1	68.00	1-32	0	0	24.0	2.8
Thomson, NI	9	267	70	568	23	24.70	4-55	0	0	11.6	2.1
Tuppin, AG	1	15	2	48	0	-	0-48	0	0	-	3.2
Upton, M	1	30	8	120	1	120.00	1-72	0	0	30.0	4.0
Vincett, JH	9	163.2	30	478	21	22.80	5-25	1	0	7.8	2.9
Vine, J	9	102.2	23	305	20	15.25	4-17	0	0	5.1	3.0
Waller, CE	5	215.5	89	411	13	31.60	5-69	1	0	16.6	1.9
Watson, AC	9	1	1	0	0	-	0-0	0	0	-	-
Wells, AP	12	3	0	18	0	-	0-18	0	0	-	6.0
Wells, CM	8	167.4	42	430	17	25.30	4-33	0	0	9.9	2.6
Wensley, AF	27	861.1	230	2014	69	29.20	5-49	1	0	12.5	2.3
Wilson, HL	7	13	1	79	2	39.50	1-8	0	0	6.5	6.1
Wisdom, N	1	12.5	3	28	2	14.00	1-0	0	0	6.5	2.2
Wood, DJ	14	481.3	124	1179	66	17.90	7-52	4	0	7.3	2.4
Wright, LJ	2	35	3	133	6	22.20	3-39	0	0	5.8	3.8
Yardy, MH	3	10	1	46	1	46.00	1-36	0	0	10.	4.6

G) INDIVIDUAL PLAYING RECORDS AT HORSHAM
ONE-DAY MATCHES
SUSSEX

Name	Mtchs	Inns	N/O	Runs	HS	Aver	Overs	Runs	Wkts	Avr	Ctchs
Adams, CJ	5	5	0	135	52	27.00	2	12	1	12.00	1
Alikhan, RI	1	1	1	0	0*	-	8	42	0	-	0
Ambrose, TR	1	1	0	16	16	16.00		DNB			0
Arnold, GG	3	1	1	19	19*	19.00	15	85	1	85.00	0
Athey, CWJ	2	2	1	128	109*	128.00		DNB			1
Babington, AM	3	1	1	0	0*	0.00	22	113	2	56.50	0
Barclay, JRT	8	7	1	95	47	15.80	24.5	152	3	50.66	2
Bevan, MG	2	2	0	7	7	3.50	3.2	21	1	21.00	2
Booth-Jones, TD	1	1	0	30	30	30.00		DNB			0
Buss, A	1	1	0	10	10	10.00	3	17	0	-	0
Buss, MA	3	3	0	87	45	29.00	22	76	5	15.20	3
Carpenter, JR	1	1	0	26	26	26.00		DNB			1
Cheatle, RGL	2	1	1	5*	5	-	11	33	2	16.50	2
Clarke, AR	1			DNB			6	18	2	9.00	0
Cottey, PA	1	1	0	10	10	10.00		DNB			0
Davis, MJG	4	3	0	35	18	11.66	33	173	4	43.25	2

	M	I	NO	Runs	HS	Avg	O	R	W	Avg	Ct
Dexter, ER	1			DNB				DNB			1
Dodemaide, AIC	1	1	1	38	38*	-	7	43	0	-	1
Drakes, VC	1	1	1	6	6*	-	8	48	1	48.00	-
Edwards, AD	1	1	0	9	9	9.00		DNB			-
Giddins, ESH	3			DNB			24.4	116	2	58.00	-
Goodwin, MW	5	5	0	89	66	17.80		DNB			-
Gould, IJ	8	8	0	124	63	15.50		DNB			4
Graves, PJ	2	1	0	10	10	10.00		DNB			-
Green, AM	5	5	0	44	17	8.80		DNB			3
Greenfield, K	5	5	0	84	35	16.80	14	85	2	42.50	1
Greig, AW	2	2	0	70	40	35.00	16	105	1	105.00	1
Greig, IA	4	4	0	87	43	21.75	22.4	120	2	60.00	-
Griffith, MG	1	1	0	9	9	9.00		DNB			-
Groome, JJ	1			DNB				DNB			-
Hall, JW	3	3	0	106	69	35.33		DNB			1
Hansford, AR	2	1	1	5	5	5.00	14	80	1	80.00	-
Hopkinson, CD	2	2	0	31	31	15.50		DNB			1
House, WJ	3	3	0	88	34	29.33	4	21	0	-	-
Humphries, S	1	1	0	9	9	9.00		DNB			0+1st
Imran Khan	8	8	0	182	73	22.75	56	209	10	20.90	2
Innes, KJ	2	2	1	59	41*	59.00	12	93	1	93.00	1
Jarvis, PW	2	2	0	12	6	6.00	14	64	3	21.33	1
Javed Miandad	2	2	0	39	33	19.50		DNB			1
Jones, AN	1	1	1	1	1*	-	5	29	2	14.50	-
Khan, AA	1			DNB			8	40	5	8.00	-
Kimber, SJS	1	1	0	15	15	15.00	8	49	1	49.00	-
Kirtley, RJ	7	5	3	38	15*	19.00	52	307	7	43.90	2
Knight, RDV	1	1	0	12	12	12.00		DNB			-
Law, DR	1	1	1	39	39*	-		DNB			2
Lenham, NJ	4	4	2	88	43	44.00	4	21	1	21.00	1
Le Roux, GS	7	6	1	118	83*	23.60	43.1	220	8	26.50	2
Lewry, JD	4	3	1	2	1	1.00	30.3	157	4	39.25	2
Long, A	4	1	0	2	2	2.00		DNB			2+1st
Martin-Jenkins, RSC	6	6	2	47	34*	11.75	46	238	7	34.00	2
Mendis, GD	8	7	0	126	64	18.00		DNB			2
Moh'd Akram	1			DNB			9	63	1	63.00	-
Montgomerie, RR	6	6	0	148	42	24.66		DNB			1
Moores, P	8	8	0	134	42	16.75		DNB			9+1st
Mushtaq Ahmed	2			DNB			12	95	4	23.75	-
Myles, SD	1	1	0	4	4	4.00		DNB			-

Name	M	I	NO	Runs	HS	Avg	Balls	Runs	Wkts	Avg	Ct
Naved-ul-Hasan	1			DNB			5	24	1	24.00	-
Newell, K	3	3	0	88	42	29.33	13	43	1	43.00	1
Newell, M	2	2	0	19	16	9.50	DNB				2
North, JA	2	2	0	60	56	30.00	1	13	0	-	-
Parker, PWG	10	10	3	501	106*	71.6	DNB				4
Parks, JM	1	1	0	20	20	20.00	DNB				1
Patterson, AD	1	1	0	20	20	20.00	DNB				-
Phillips, NC	1			DNB			DNB				-
Phillipson, CP	9	8	4	95	36*	23.75	17	86	2	43.00	3
Pierce, MTE	1	1	0	25	25	25.00	DNB				-
Pigott, ACS	9	5	3	81	40	40.50	62	404	12	33.66	4
Prideaux, RM	1	1	0	9	9	9.00	DNB				-
Prior, MJ	4	4	0	132	73	33.00	DNB				1+1st
Rao, RK	1	1	0	15	15	15.00	DNB				1
Rashid, UBA	2	2	0	35	34	17.50	14	73	1	73.00	1
Reeve, DA	5	5	2	23	14*	7.66	32	158	8	19.75	2
Remy, CC	1	1	0	0	0	-	8	51	1	51.00	-
Ricketts, CIO	1	1	0	9	9	9.00	2	17	0	-	-
Robinson, MA	4	3	0	5	3	1.66	34	141	3	47.00	1
Robson, AG	1	1	1	1	1*	-	6	34	0	-	-
Salisbury, IDK	2	2	0	8	8	4.00	17	73	4	18.25	1
Smith, DJ	1	1	1	5	5*	-	DNB				1
Smith, DM	1	1	0	75	75	75.00	DNB				-
Snow, JA	2	2	0	71	57	35.50	16	69	4	17.25	1
Speight, MP	4	4	0	135	52	33.75	DNB				-
Spencer, J	4	1	1	10	10*	-	28	152	6	25.33	-
Stephenson, FD	4	4	0	101	35	25.25	34	157	5	31.40	-
Taylor, BV	3	3	1	4	4*	2.00	24	102	5	20.40	1
Thomson, NI	1	1	1	6	6*	-	8	42	1	42.00	-
Waller, CE	5	1	1	1	1*	-	21	95	3	31.66	-
Ward, IJ	1	1	0	136	136	136.00	DNB				1
Waring, IC	2	1	0	8	8	8.00	15	71	1	71.00	1
Wells, AP	11	11	0	221	49	20.09	0.1	4	0	-	1
Wells, CM	9	9	1	226	70	28.25	55	224	12	18.66	-
Wessels, KC	1	1	0	40	40	40.00	DNB				-
Wright, LJ	1	1	1	32	32*	-	5	37	0	-	-
Yardy, MH	4	3	1	36	18	18.00	9	47	1	47.00	2
Zuiderent, B	2	2	0	14	14	7.00	DNB				1

H) OPPONENTS APPEARANCES AT HORSHAM
FIRST-CLASS MATCHES

Abel, WJ	Surrey, 1910, 1912, 1922
Abrahams, J	Lancashire, 1983
Afzaal, U	Notts, 2003
Ahl, FD	Worcs, 1932
Aird, R	Hampshire, 1925
Alderman, AE	Derbyshire, 1930, 1937, 1947
Ali, K	Worcs, 2001
Allen, BO	Gloucs, 1937
Allott, PJW	Lancashire, 1990
Altham, HS	Oxford University, 1912
Ames, LEG	Kent, 1927
Andrew, KV	Northants, 1955, 1956
Andrew, SJW	Hampshire, 1987; Essex, 1991
Andrews, WHR	Somerset, 1946
Angell, FL	Somerset, 1951
Armstrong, NF	Leics, 1930
Arnold, ACP	Hampshire, 1914
Arnold, AP	Northants, 1955, 1956
Arnold, J	Hampshire, 1933, 1935, 1938
Arnott, T	Glamorgan, 1929
Ashdown, WH	Kent, 1927
Astill, WE	Leics, 1921, 1924, 1930
Atherton, MA	Lancashire, 1990, 1994
Avery, AV	Essex, 1950
Bailey, J	Hampshire, 1933
Bailey, RJ	Northants, 1984
Baker, EC	Cambridge University, 1914
Bakewell, AH	Northants, 1935
Bale, F	Leics, 1924
Bannister, JD	Warwicks, 1956
Bardsley, RV	Oxford University, 1912
Barford, MT	Cambridge University, 1971
Barling, HT	Surrey, 1928, 1934, 1936, 1938, 1939
Barnett, CJ	Gloucs, 1932, 1937
Barnett, CS	Gloucs, 1926
Barnett, KJ	Derbyshire, 1988, 1998
Barnwell, CJP	Somerset, 1946

Barratt, F	Notts, 1923, 1931
Barrick, DW	Northants, 1952, 1955
Barron, W	Northants, 1948
Bass, JG	Northants, 1935
Bates, LTA	Warwicks, 1926, 1927
Bates, WE	Glamorgan, 1923, 1929
Batt, CJ	Middlesex, 2000
Beeching, THP	Kent, 1920
Bell, IR	Warwicks, 2004
Bell, JT	Glamorgan, 1929
Bellamy, BW	Northants, 1935
Benham, CE	Essex, 1908
Benjamin, JE	Surrey, 1995
Benjamin, WKM	Leics, 1993
Benkenstein, DM	Durham, 2007
Benskin, WE	Leics, 1921, 1924
Berridge, WCM	Leics, 1921
Berry, F	Surrey, 1939
Berry, GL	Leics, 1930
Beslee, GP	Kent, 1927
Bessant, JGWT	loucs, 1922
Bevan, MG =	Leics, 2002
Bichel, AJ	Worcs, 2001
Bicknell, DJ	Notts, 2003
Bird, MC	Surrey, 1910, 1912
Bird, RE	Worcs, 1947
Blackwell, ID	Derbyshire, 1998
Blake, DE	Hampshire, 1952
Bland, RDF	Notts, 1931
Bligh, AS	Somerset, 1925
Bloodworth, BS	Gloucs, 1920, 1926, 1932
Boddington, RA	Lancashire, 1913
Boon, TJ	Leics, 1993
Botton, ND	Oxford University, 1974
Bowden, J	Derbyshire, 1930
Bowell, HAW	Hampshire, 1914, 1921, 1925
Bowler, PD	Derbyshire, 1988
Boyes, GS	Hampshire, 1925, 1928, 1933, 1938
Bradshaw, JC	Leics, 1924, 1930

Bray, C		Essex, 1929
Brierley, TL		Lancashire, 1948
Briers, MP		Durham, 1992
Briers, NE		Leics, 1993
Broderick, V		Northants, 1948, 1955
Brook, GW		Worcs, 1932
Brookes, D		Northants, 1948, 1952, 1955, 1956
Brooks, EWJ		Surrey, 1928, 1931, 1934, 1936, 1938, 1939
Brown, AD		Surrey, 1995
Brown, DR		Warwicks, 2004
Brown, FR		Surrey, 1934; Northants, 1952
Brown, G	#	Hampshire, 1914, 1921, 1925, 1928, 1933
Brown, KR		Middlesex, 1996
Brutton, CP		Hampshire, 1921
Bryan, JL		Kent, 1920
Bryant, EH		Worcs, 1924
Buckenham, CB		Essex, 1908
Buckingham, J		Warwicks, 1939
Buckston, RHR		Derbyshire, 1937
Budd, WL		Hampshire, 1935, 1938
Burnett, AC		Cambridge University, 1949
Burns, ND		Leics, 2002
Buse, HFT		Somerset, 1946, 1951
Bush, HS		Surrey, 1912
Bushby, MH		Cambridge University, 1954
Buswell, WA	#	Northants, 1913
Butcher, AR		Surrey, 1985
Butcher, MA		Surrey, 1995
Butler, HJ		Notts, 1934, 1950, 1951
Caesar, WC		Somerset, 1946
Calthorpe, FSG		Cambridge University, 1914; Warwicks, 1927
Campbell, IPF		Oxford University, 1912
Cannings, VHD		Hampshire, 1952
Capel, DJ		Northants, 1984
Carr, AW		Notts, 1923, 1931
Carr, DB		Derbyshire, 1954
Carr, JD		Middlesex, 1996
Carter, NM		Warwicks, 2004
Case, CCC		Somerset, 1925

Cassar, ME	Derbyshire, 1998
Childs, JH	Essex, 1989, 1991
Childs-Clarke, AW	Northants, 1948
Clark, EW	Northants, 1935
Clarke, RW	Northants, 1948, 1952, 1955, 1956
Clay, JC	Glamorgan, 1923, 1946
Clay, JD	Notts, 1950
Clift, PB	Glamorgan, 1953
Clinton, GS	Surrey, 1985
Cockbain, I	Lancashire, 1983
Coe, S	Leics, 1921
Coetzer, KJ	Durham, 2007
Collin, T	Warwicks, 1936
Collins, GC	Kent, 1920
Compton, NRD	Middlesex, 2006
Cook, G	Northants, 1984
Cooper, E	Worcs, 1947
Cooper, F	Worcs, 1947
Copson, WH	Derbyshire, 1937
Corbett, LJ	Gloucs, 1920, 1922
Cork, DG	Derbyshire, 1998
Coventry, JB	Worcs, 1924
Cowdrey, GR	Kent, 1997
Cox, AL	Northants, 1935
Cranmer, P	Warwicks, 1939
Cranston, K	Lancashire, 1948
Crapp, JF	Gloucs, 1937
Crawford, JN	Surrey, 1909
Crawley, JP	Lancashire, 1994
Cray, SJ	Essex, 1950
Creese, WLC	Hampshire, 1933, 1935, 1938
Croft, PD	Cambridge University, 1955
Croom, AJW	Warwicks, 1926, 1927, 1936, 1939
Crowe, CD	Leics, 2002
Crutchley, GEV	Oxford University, 1912
Cuthbertson, GB	Northants, 1935
Cutmore, JA	Essex, 1929, 1933
Dacre, CCR	Gloucs, 1932
Daer, AG	Essex, 1933

Dagnall, CE		Leics, 2002
Daley, JV		Surrey, 1938
Dalrymple, JWM		Middlesex, 2006
Dare, RA		Hampshire, 1952
Davies, D	#	Glamorgan, 1923, 1929
Davies, DE		Glamorgan, 1929, 1946, 1953
Davies, GB		Cambridge University, 1914
Davies, HG		Glamorgan, 1946, 1953
Davis, CP		Northants, 1948
Davis, WE		Surrey, 1909, 1910
Dawkes, GO		Derbyshire, 1954
DeFreitas, PAJ		Lancashire, 1990; Derbyshire, 1998; Leics, 2002
De Lisle, JAFMP		Leics, 1930
De Silva, GRA		Sri Lanka, 1979
De Silva, DS		Sri Lanka, 1979
Dean, H		Lancashire, 1913
Dean, KJ		Derbyshire, 1998
Dennett, EG		Gloucs, 1922
Denton, JS		Northants, 1913
Denton, WH		Northants, 1913
Dewes, JG		Cambridge University, 1949
Dias, RL		Sri Lanka, 1979
Dipper, AE		Gloucs, 1920, 1922, 1926, 1932
Dodds, TC		Essex, 1950
Doggart, GHG	=	Cambridge University, 1949
Dollery, HE		Warwicks, 1936, 1939, 1953
Dollery, KR		Warwicks, 1953
Douglas, JWHT		Essex, 1908
Down, JH		Hampshire, 1914
Ducat, A		Surrey, 1909, 1910, 1912, 1922, 1928, 1931
Dyson, AH		Glamorgan, 1946
Eagar, EDR		Hampshire, 1952
Earle, GF		Somerset, 1925
Eastman, GF		Essex, 1929
Eastman, LC		Essex, 1929, 1933
Eato, A		Derbyshire, 1954
Edmonds, PH		Middlesex, 1996
Edrich, EH		Lancashire, 1948

Edrich, GA		Lancashire, 1948
Elliott, CS		Derbyshire, 1937, 1947
Elliott, H	#	Derbyshire, 1930, 1937
Elworthy, S		Notts, 2003
Estcourt, NSD		Cambridge University, 1954
Evans, AJ		Kent, 1927
Evans, VJ		Essex, 1933
Eve, SC		Essex, 1950
Every, T		Glamorgan, 1929
Ewens, PC		Somerset, 1925
Fairbairn, GA		Cambridge University, 1914
Fairbrother, NH		Lancashire, 1983, 1990, 1994
Fairservice, WJ		Kent, 1920
Fane, FL		Essex, 1908
Faviell, WFO		Essex, 1908
Fender, PGH	=	Surrey, 1922, 1928, 1931, 1934
Fenley, S		Surrey, 1928
Fiddling, K		Northants, 1948, 1952
Fishlock, LB		Surrey, 1934, 1936, 1938, 1939
Fitton, JD		Lancashire, 1990
Fleming, MV		Kent, 1997
Flint, WA		Notts, 1923
Follett, D		Middlesex, 1996
Foster, MK		Worcs, 1924
Foster, NA		Essex, 1989, 1991
Fowke, GHS		Leics, 1924
Fowler, G		Lancashire, 1990
Fox, J		Warwicks, 1927; Worcs, 1932
Fraser, AGJ		Essex, 1991
Fraser, ARC		Middlesex, 1996, 2000
Fraser, JN		Oxford University, 1912
Freeman, AP		Kent, 1920, 1927
Freeman, E		Northants, 1913
Freeman, EJ		Essex, 1908
Frost, T		Warwicks, 2004
Fulton, DP		Kent, 1997
Fursdon, ED		Oxford University, 1974
Gallian, JER		Lancashire, 1994; Notts, 2003
Gange, TH		Gloucs, 1920

Gardner, FC	Warwicks, 1953, 1956
Garland-Wells, HM	Surrey, 1936, 1938, 1939
Garlick, RG	Northants, 1948
Garnham, MA	Essex, 1989, 1991
Gatting, MW	Middlesex, 1996
Geary, G	Leics, 1930
Gemmill, WN	Glamorgan, 1923
Gibbons, HHIH	Worcs, 1932
Gibson, OD	Durham, 2007
Giles, RJ	Notts, 1950, 1951
Gillingham, FH	Essex, 1908
Gimblett, H	Somerset, 1946, 1951
Gimson, C	Leics, 1921
Gladwin, C	Derbyshire, 1947, 1954
Glover, TR	Oxford University, 1974
Goddard, TWJ	Gloucs, 1926, 1932, 1937
Goldsmith, SC	Derbyshire, 1988
Gooch, GA	Essex, 1989
Goonesena, G	Cambridge University, 1954, 1955
Gothard, EJ	Derbyshire, 1947
Gouldsworthy, WR	Gloucs, 1926
Gover, AR	Surrey, 1928, 1931, 1934, 1938, 1939
Graveney, DA	Durham, 1992
Gray, JR	Hampshire, 1952
Green, MA	Gloucs, 1922
Gregory, RJ	Surrey, 1928, 1931, 1934, 1936, 1938, 1939
Greig, JG	Hampshire, 1914, 1921
Griffiths, BJ	Northants, 1984
Grimshaw, N	Northants, 1935
Grove, CW	Warwicks, 1939, 1953
Gunatilleke, FRMD	Sri Lanka, 1979
Gunn, G	Notts, 1923, 1931
Gunn, GV	Notts, 1934
Gunn, JR	Notts, 1923
Hacker, WS	Glamorgan, 1923
Hadley, RJ	Cambridge University, 1971
Hall, CG	Hampshire, 1935
Hall, PJ	Cambridge University, 1949
Hamer, A	Derbyshire, 1954

Hammond, WR		Gloucs, 1932, 1937
Hanley, RW		Northants, 1984
Hardinge, HTW		Kent, 1920, 1927
Hardstaff, J (jnr)		Notts, 1931, 1934, 1950, 1951
Harfield, L		Hampshire, 1928
Harmison, BW		Durham, 2007
Harmison, SJ		Durham, 2007
Harris, AJ		Notts, 2003
Harris, CB		Notts, 1934, 1950, 1951
Harrison, HS		Surrey, 1909, 1910
Harvey, PF		Notts, 1951
Hayes, EG		Surrey, 1909, 1912
Hayes, FC		Lancashire, 1983
Haynes, RW		Gloucs, 1937
Hayward, TW		Surrey, 1910, 1912
Haywood, ETLR		Somerset, 1925
Haywood, RA		Northants, 1913
Hazell, HL		Somerset, 1946
Heap, JS		Lancashire, 1913
Heath, DMW		Warwicks, 1953
Heath, GEM		Hampshire, 1938
Hegg, WK		Lancashire, 1990, 1994
Herman, OW		Hampshire, 1933, 1935, 1938
Hewitt, JP		Middlesex, 1996
Hick, GA		Worcs, 1999, 2001
Hill, E		Somerset, 1951
Hill, G		Hampshire, 1935, 1938, 1952
Hill, ML		Somerset, 1925
Hill, WA		Warwicks, 1936, 1939
Hills, JJ	#	Glamorgan, 1929
Hilton, MJ		Lancashire, 1948
Hipkin, AB		Essex, 1929
Hitch, JW		Surrey, 1909, 1910, 1922
Hitchcock, RE		Warwicks, 1956
Hobbs, JB		Surrey, 1909, 1910, 1912, 1922, 1931, 1934
Hogg, GB		Warwicks, 2004
Hollies, WE		Warwicks, 1936, 1939, 1953, 1956
Hollioake, AJ		Surrey, 1995
Holmes, ERT		Surrey, 1934, 1936, 1938

Hopkins, V		Gloucs, 1937
Hornby, AH		Lancashire, 1913
Horner, NF		Warwicks, 1953, 1956
Horsfall, R		Essex, 1950
Hosie, AL		Hampshire, 1925, 1928, 1935
Hough, GD		Kent, 1920
Howard, A		Leics, 1921
Howard, ND		Lancashire, 1948
Howorth, R		Worcs, 1947
Hubble, JC		Kent, 1920, 1927
Huddleston, W		Lancashire, 1913
Hughes, DP		Lancashire, 1983, 1990
Hughes, SP		Durham, 1992
Hunt, GE		Somerset, 1925
Hussain, N		Essex, 1989, 1991
Hutchinson, JM		Derbyshire, 1930
Hutton, BL		Middlesex, 2006
Hutton, S		Durham, 1992
Ikin, JT		Lancashire, 1948
Illingworth, RK	#	Worcs, 1999
Imran Khan	=	Oxford University, 1974
Insole, DJ		Cambridge University, 1949; Essex, 1950
Isherwood, LCR	=	Hampshire, 1921
Jackson, GR		Derbyshire, 1930
Jackson, HL		Derbyshire, 1954
Jackson, PF		Worcs, 1947
Jakeman, F		Northants, 1952
James, KD		Hampshire, 1987
Jameson, TO		Hampshire, 1925
Jaques, A		Hampshire, 1914
Jardine, DR		Surrey, 1931
Jayasinghe, SA		Sri Lanka, 1979
Jeacocke, A		Surrey, 1922, 1928
Jefferies, ST		Lancashire, 1983
Jenkins, RO		Worcs, 1947
Jepson, A	#	Notts, 1950, 1951
Jessop, GLO		Hampshire, 1933
Jessop, WH		Gloucs, 1920
Jesty, TE	#	Surrey, 1985

Jewell, MFS		Worcs, 1924
Johnson, PD		Cambridge University, 1971
Johnson, RL		Middlesex, 2000
Jones, ATM		Somerset, 1946
Jones, DM		Durham, 1992
Jones, EC		Glamorgan, 1946
Jones, WE		Glamorgan, 1946, 1953
Joyce, EC		Middlesex, 2006
Judd, AK		Hampshire, 1935
Judge, PF		Glamorgan, 1946
Keegan, CB		Middlesex, 2006
Keeton, WW		Notts, 1931, 1934
Kelleher, HRA		Northants, 1956
Kelly, JM		Derbyshire, 1954
Kennedy, AS		Hampshire, 1914, 1921, 1925, 1928, 1933
Kenyon, D		Worcs, 1947
Kersey, GJ		Surrey, 1995
Kilner, N	#	Warwicks, 1926, 1927, 1936
King, JH	#	Leics, 1921, 1924
Kirk, EC		Surrey, 1912
Knight, NV		Warwicks, 2004
Knightley-Smith, W		Cambridge University, 1955
Knott, FH		Oxford University, 1912
Krikken, KM		Derbyshire, 1998
Lacey, SJ		Derbyshire, 1998
Lagden, RB		Cambridge University, 1914
Lamb, TM		Oxford University, 1974
Lampitt, SR		Worcs, 1999, 2001
Langer, JL		Middlesex, 2000
Larkins, W		Northants, 1984; Durham, 1992
Larwood, H		Notts, 1934
Lavis, G		Glamorgan, 1946
Lawrence, J		Somerset, 1946, 1951
Lawrie, PE		Hampshire, 1928
Leach, CW		Warwicks, 1956
Leatherdale, DA		Worcs, 1999, 2001
Lee, FS	#	Somerset, 1946
Lee, RJ		Oxford University, 1974
Lees, WS		Surrey, 1909, 1910

Legge, GB	Kent, 1927
Leveson Gower, HDG	Surrey, 1909
Lightfoot, A	Northants, 1955
Lilley, B	Notts, 1923, 1924
Liptrot, CG	Worcs, 1999
Lister-Kaye, KA	Oxford University, 1912
Livingston, L	Northants, 1952, 1955, 1956
Livsey, WH	Hampshire, 1921, 1925, 1928
Llong, NJ #	Kent, 1997
Lloyd, GD	Lancashire, 1994
Lloyd, MFD	Oxford University, 1974
Longrigg, EF	Somerset, 1946
Lord, A	Leics, 1924
Lord, WF	Oxford University, 1912
Louw, J	Middlesex, 2006
Lowndes, WGLF	Hampshire, 1935
Luckes, WT	Somerset, 1946
Lumsden, VR	Cambridge University, 1954, 1955
Lynch, MA	Surrey, 1985
MacGill, SCG	Notts, 2003
MacLeod, KG	Lancashire, 1913
Maddy, DL	Leics, 2002
Madugalle, RS	Sri Lanka, 1979
Maher, BJM	Derbyshire, 1988
Majid Khan	Cambridge University, 1971
Makepeace, JWH	Lancashire, 1913
Malcolm, DE	Derbyshire, 1988: Leics, 2002
Manning, JS	Northants, 1956
Marsh, FE	Derbyshire, 1947
Marsh, SA	Kent, 1997
Marshal, A	Surrey, 1909
Marshall, MD	Hampshire, 1987
Martin, EJ	Notts, 1951
Martin, PJ	Lancashire, 1994
Martin, SH	Worcs, 1932
Maru, RJ	Hampshire, 1987
Mathias, FW	Glamorgan, 1923, 1929
Matthews, ADG	Glamorgan, 1946
Matthews, CS	Notts, 1950

Matthews, FCL		Notts, 1923
Mayer, JH		Warwicks, 1926, 1927, 1936, 1939
Maynard, C		Lancashire, 1983
McCague, MJ		Kent, 1997
McClintock, WK		Gloucs, 1920
McConnon, JE		Glamorgan, 1953
McCorkell, NT		Hampshire, 1933, 1935, 1938
McEwan, SM		Durham, 1992
McGahey, CP		Essex, 1908
McIntyre, AJW		Surrey, 1939
Mead, CP		Hampshire, 1921, 1925, 1928, 1933, 1935
Meads, EA		Notts, 1950, 1951
Melluish, MEL		Cambridge University, 1954, 1955
Mendis, GD	=	Lancashire, 1990
Mendis, LRD		Sri Lanka, 1979
Mercer, J	=	Glamorgan, 1929
Middleton, JW		Leics, 1921
Middleton, TC		Hampshire, 1987
Miller, G		Essex, 1989
Mills, PT		Gloucs, 1920, 1922
Mitchell, TB		Derbyshire, 1930, 1937
Mobey, GS		Surrey, 1936
Mohammad Ali		Middlesex, 2006
Monks, CI		Gloucs, 1937
Morgan, DC		Derbyshire, 1954
Morgan, MN		Cambridge University, 1954
Morgan, TR		Glamorgan, 1923
Morgan, WG		Glamorgan, 1929
Morris, HM		Essex, 1929
Morris, JE		Derbyshire, 1988
Morris, RJ		Cambridge University, 1949
Morrison, EG		Gloucs, 1926
Morrison, JSF		Cambridge University, 1914
Mortensen, OH		Derbyshire, 1988
Mounteney, A		Leics, 1921, 1924
Mullally, AD		Leics, 1993
Muncer, BL		Glamorgan, 1953
Mustard, P		Durham, 2007
Nash, DC		Middlesex, 2000

Nash, DJ		Middlesex, 1996
Nasir Zaidi, SM		Lancashire, 1983
Naumann, FCG		Oxford University, 1912
Neale, WL		Gloucs, 1932, 1937
Needham, A		Surrey, 1985
Newman, JA	#	Hampshire, 1914, 1921, 1925, 1928
Newport, PJ		Worcs, 1999
Nichol, M		Worcs, 1932
Nicholas, MCJ		Hampshire, 1987
Nichols, MS		Essex, 1929, 1933
Nixon, PA		Leics, 1993
Norman, MEJC		Northants, 1956
Nowell, RW		Surrey, 1995
Nutter, AE		Northants, 1948, 1952
O'Brien, R		Cambridge University, 1955
O'Connor, J		Essex, 1929, 1933
O'Shaughnessy, SJ		Lancashire, 1983
Oldfield, N		Northants, 1948, 1952
Opatha, ARM		Sri Lanka, 1979
Ord, JS		Warwicks, 1936
Owen-Thomas, DR		Cambridge University, 1971
Paine, GAE		Warwicks, 1936
Paris, CGA		Hampshire, 1938
Parker, CWL		Gloucs, 1920, 1922, 1926, 1932
Parker, JF		Surrey, 1936, 1938, 1939
Parker, PWG	=	Durham, 1992
Parkhouse, WGA		Glamorgan, 1953
Parks, RJ		Hampshire, 1987
Parsons, ABD		Cambridge University, 1954, 1955
Parsons, JH		Warwicks, 1926, 1927
Partridge, NE		Warwicks, 1926
Pasqual, SP		Sri Lanka, 1979
Patterson, BP		Lancashire, 1990
Paver, RGL		Oxford University, 1974
Payton, WRD		Notts, 1923
Peach, HA		Surrey, 1922, 1928, 1931
Pearce, TN		Essex, 1933
Peare, WG		Warwicks, 1926
Pearson, FA		Worcs, 1924

Perkins, GC		Northants, 1935
Perks, RTD		Worcs, 1932, 1947
Perrin, PA		Essex, 1908
Phillips, BJ		Kent, 1997
Pierson, ARK		Leics, 1993
Pietersen, KP		Notts, 2003
Pitt, TA		Northants, 1935
Place, W		Lancashire, 1948
Pleass, JE		Glamorgan, 1953
Plunkett, LE		Durham, 2007
Pocock, PI		Surrey, 1985
Pollard, PR		Worcs, 1999
Pollard, R		Lancashire, 1948
Poole, CJ		Notts, 1951
Pooley, JC		Middlesex, 1996
Pope, AV		Derbyshire, 1937
Pope, DF		Essex, 1933
Pope, GH	#	Derbyshire, 1937, 1947
Popplewell, OB		Cambridge University, 1949
Porter, A		Glamorgan, 1946
Pothecary, AE		Hampshire, 1933, 1938
Potter, L		Leics, 1993
Preece, CR		Worcs, 1924
Pretlove, JF		Cambridge University, 1954
Pretorius, D		Warwicks, 2004
Prichard, PJ		Essex, 1989, 1991
Pringle, DR		Essex, 1989
Prouton, RO		Hampshire, 1952
Pryer, BJK		Cambridge University, 1949
Quaife, BW		Worcs, 1932
Quaife, WG		Warwicks, 1926, 1927
Rackemann, CG		Surrey, 1995
Raison, M		Essex, 1929
Ramprakash, MR		Middlesex, 1996, 2000
Ratcliffe, JD		Surrey, 1995
Rawnsley, MJ		Worcs, 2001
Rayment, AWH		Hampshire, 1952
Read, CMW		Notts, 2003
Redman, J		Somerset, 1951

Reeves, W	Essex, 1908
Remnant, ER	Hampshire, 1914, 1921
Revill, AC	Derbyshire, 1947, 1954
Reynolds, BL	Northants, 1956
Rhodes, AEG	Derbyshire, 1947
Rhodes, SJ	Worcs, 1999, 2001
Richards, CJ	Surrey, 1985
Richardson, A	Notts, 1951
Richardson, A	Warwicks, 2004
Riley, H	Leics, 1930
Riley, WN	Cambridge University, 1914
Rimell, AGJ	Cambridge University, 1949
Roberts, B	Derbyshire, 1988
Roberts, WB	Lancashire, 1948
Robertson-Glasgow, RC	Somerset, 1925
Robinson, DC	Essex, 1908; Gloucs, 1926
Robinson, EP	Somerset, 1951
Robinson, PE	Leics, 1993
Rogers, HO	Worcs, 1924
Rogers, JA	Gloucs, 1932
Rogers, NH	Hampshire, 1952
Rogers, SS	Somerset, 1951
Rollins, AS	Derbyshire, 1998
Root, CF	Worcs, 1924, 1932
Roseberry, MA	Middlesex, 2000
Rowlands, WH	Gloucs, 1920
Rudd, GBF	Leics, 1921
Rushby, T	Surrey, 1912
Russell, CAG	Essex, 1929
Ryan, FP	Glamorgan, 1923, 1929
Saleem Malik	Essex, 1991
Sandham, A	Surrey, 1922, 1928, 1931, 1936
Santall, FR	Warwicks, 1926, 1927, 1936, 1939
Saville, SH	Cambridge University, 1914
Scott, BJM	Middlesex, 2006
Scott, CW	Durham, 1992
Seager, CP	Cambridge University, 1971
Selvey, MWW	Cambridge University, 1971
Seymour, ACH	Essex, 1991

Seymour, J		Northants, 1913
Seymour, J		Kent, 1920
Shackleton, D	#	Hampshire, 1952
Shafayat, BM		Notts, 2003
Shah, AO		Middlesex, 2000, 2006
Shahid, N		Essex, 1991
Sharma, R		Derbyshire, 1988
Sharp, G	#	Northants, 1984
Sharp, J		Lancashire, 1913
Shepherd, DJ		Glamorgan, 1953
Shepherd, TF		Surrey, 1922, 1928, 1931
Sheppard, ECJ		Gloucs, 1922
Sheffield, EJ		Surrey, 1931
Sheffield, JR		Essex, 1933
Sheriyar, A		Worcs, 1999, 2001
Shipman, AW		Leics, 1924, 1930
Shortland, NA		Warwicks, 1939
Sidwell, TE		Leics, 1921, 1924, 1930
Silk, DRW		Cambridge University, 1954, 1955
Silverwood, CEW		Middlesex, 2006
Simmons, J		Lancashire, 1983
Simpson, RT		Notts, 1950
Sinfield, RA		Gloucs, 1926, 1932, 1937
Singh, A		Worcs, 2001
Skelding, A	#	Leics, 1924
Skinner, IJ		Essex, 1950
Slack, JKE		Cambridge University, 1954
Slater, AG		Derbyshire, 1930
Slater, MJ		Derbyshire, 1998
Smart, JA		Warwicks, 1926, 1936
Smith, AW		Surrey, 1995
Smith, BF		Leics, 1993
Smith, CL		Hampshire, 1987
Smith, CS		Cambridge University, 1954, 1955
Smith, D		Derbyshire, 1930, 1937, 1947
Smith, DJ		Cambridge University, 1955
Smith, E		Derbyshire, 1954
Smith, EJ		Warwicks, 1927
Smith, ET		Middlesex, 2006

Smith, GJ		Notts, 2003
Smith, H		Gloucs, 1920, 1922, 1926
Smith, HA		Leics, 1930
Smith, HAH		Hampshire, 1914
Smith, I		Durham, 1992
Smith, R		Essex, 1950
Smith, R		Somerset, 1951
Smith, SG		Northants, 1913
Smith, TPB		Essex, 1933, 1950
Smith, WC		Surrey, 1910, 1912
Smith, WR		Durham, 2007
Snary, HC		Leics, 1930
Snowden, AW		Northants, 1935
Solanki, VS		Worcs, 1999, 2001
Somers, AHT		Worcs, 1924
Speak, NJ		Lancashire, 1994
Spencer, J	=	Cambridge University, 1971
Spiring, KR		Worcs, 1999
Spooner, RT		Warwicks, 1953, 1956
Sprinks, HRJ		Hampshire, 1928
Squires, HS		Surrey, 1934, 1938, 1939
Stallibrass, MJD		Oxford University, 1974
Staples, A		Notts, 1931, 1934
Staples, SJ		Notts, 1923, 1931
Starkie, S		Northants, 1952, 1955, 1956
Steele, HKC		Cambridge University, 1971
Steele, DS		Northants, 1984
Stephens, EJ		Gloucs, 1932, 1937
Stephenson, HW		Somerset, 1951
Stephenson, JP		Essex, 1989, 1991
Stevens, DI		Leics, 2002
Stevenson, MH		Cambridge University, 1949
Stewart, AJ		Surrey, 1985, 1995
Stinchcombe, FW		Notts, 1950
Stocks, FW		Notts, 1950, 1951
Stone, J	#	Hampshire, 1914; Glamorgan, 1923
Stoneman, MD		Durham, 2007
Storer, H		Derbyshire, 1930
Strang, PA		Kent, 1997

Strauss, AJ		Middlesex, 2000
Strudwick, H		Surrey, 1909, 1910, 1912, 1922
Styris, SB		Durham, 2007
Subba Row, R		Northants, 1955
Sutcliffe, IJ		Leics, 2002
Swaranjit Singh		Cambridge University, 1955
Tarbox, CV	#	Worcs, 1924
Taylor, CRV		Cambridge University, 1971
Taylor, NS		Surrey, 1985
Taylor, RA		Notts, 1934
Taylor, RM		Essex, 1933
Tennekoon, APB		Sri Lanka, 1979
Tennyson, LH		Hampshire, 1921, 1925
Terry, VP		Hampshire, 1987
Thackeray, PR		Oxford University, 1974
Thomas, DJ		Surrey, 1985
Thompson, GJ		Northants, 1913
Thompson, RG		Warwicks, 1956
Thorpe, GP		Surrey, 1995
Timms, JE		Northants, 1935, 1948
Todd, LJ		Kent, 1927
Tomlinson, H		Glamorgan, 1923
Topley, TD		Essex, 1989
Townsend, A		Warwicks, 1953, 1956
Townsend, AF		Derbyshire, 1947
Townsend, LF		Derbyshire, 1930, 1937
Tremlett, MF		Somerset, 1951
Tremlett, TM		Hampshire, 1987
Tribe, GE		Northants, 1952, 1955, 1956
Trott, IJL		Warwicks, 2004
Troughton, JO		Warwicks, 2004
Troughton, LHW		Kent, 1920
Tufnell, PCR		Middlesex, 1996, 2000
Turner, DR		Hampshire, 1987
Tweats, TA		Derbyshire, 1998
Twining, RH		Oxford University, 1912
Tyldesley, GE		Lancashire, 1913
Tyldesley, JT		Lancashire, 1913
Utley, RPH		Hampshire, 1928

Vaulkhard, P		Notts, 1934
Vidler, JLS		Oxford University, 1912
Vigar, FH		Essex, 1950
Vincent, HG		Cambridge University, 1914
Voce, W		Notts, 1931, 1934
Wade, TH		Essex, 1929, 1950
Wagh, MA		Warwicks, 2004
Walden, FI		Northants, 1913
Walker, A		Northants, 1984
Walker, C		Hampshire, 1952
Walker, DF		Hampshire, 1938
Walker, MJ		Kent, 1997
Walker, W		Notts, 1923, 1931
Waller, GD		Oxford University, 1974
Walters, CF		Worcs, 1932
Ward, TR		Kent, 1997; Leics, 2002
Warner, AE		Derbyshire, 1988
Warr, JJ		Cambridge University, 1949
Wasim Akram		Lancashire, 1994
Waterman, PA		Surrey, 1985
Watkins, AJ		Glamorgan, 1953
Watkinson, M		Lancashire, 1983, 1990, 1994
Watts, EA		Surrey, 1934, 1938, 1939
Watts, T		Surrey, 1922
Waugh, ME		Essex, 1989
Wedel, G		Gloucs, 1926
Weekes, PN		Middlesex, 1996, 2000
Weeks, RT		Warwicks, 1953, 1956
Wells, AP	=	Kent, 1997
Wells, VJ		Leics, 1993, 2002
Wells, W		Northants, 1913
Welton, GE		Notts, 2003
Weston, WPC		Worcs, 2001
Wettimuny, SRD		Sri Lanka, 1979
Wharton, A		Lancashire, 1948
Wheat, AB		Notts, 1931
Whitaker, JJ		Leics, 1993
White, AFT		Worcs, 1947
White, JC		Somerset, 1925

White, ME		Worcs, 1932
Whitehead, R		Lancashire, 1913
Whittington, TAL		Glamorgan, 1923
Whysall, WW		Notts, 1923
Wild, DJ		Northants, 1984
Willatt, GL		Derbyshire, 1954
Williams, L		Gloucs, 1922
Williams, PFC		Gloucs, 1920, 1922
Williams, RG		Northants, 1984
Wilson, GC		Worcs, 1924
Winter, CA		Somerset, 1925
Wiseman, PJ		Durham, 2007
Wolton, AVG		Warwicks, 1953, 1956
Wood, GEC		Cambridge University, 1914
Wood, J		Durham, 1992
Woodroffe, KHC		Cambridge University, 1914
Wooller, W		Glamorgan, 1946, 1953
Woolley, CN	#	Northants, 1913
Woolley, FE		Kent, 1920, 1927
Worthington, TS		Derbyshire, 1930, 1937, 1947
Wright, AC		Kent, 1927
Wright, JG		Derbyshire, 1988
Wyatt, RES		Warwicks, 1926, 1927, 1939
Yarnold, H		Worcs, 1947
Yates, G		Lancashire, 1994
Young, A		Somerset, 1925
Young, DM		Worcs, 1947

#	Also umpired at Horsham
=	Also played for Sussex at Horsham

I) OPPONENTS APPEARANCES AT HORSHAM
ONE-DAY MATCHES

Abrahams, J		Lancashire 1983
Afzaal, U		Notts, 2003
Aldred, P		Derbyshire, 1998
Ali, K		Worcs, 2001
Alleyne, MW	=	Gloucs, 2001
Amiss, DL		Warwicks, 1981

Asif Din		Warwicks, 1981
Atherton, MA		Lancashire, 1994
Austin, ID		Lancashire, 1994
Averis, JMM	=	Gloucs, 2001
Bailey, RJ		Northants, 1984
Ball, MCJ	=	Gloucs, 2001
Bamber, MJ		Northants, 1984
Barnett, KJ	=	Derbyshire, 1988, 1998; Gloucs, 2001
Benjamin, JE		Surrey, 1995
Bichel, AJ		Worcs, 2001
Birch, JD		Notts, 1985
Birkenshaw, J		Leics, 1971
Boon, TJ		Leics, 1993
Bowler, PD		Derbyshire, 1988
Briers, MP		Durham, 1992
Briers, NE		Leics, 1993
Brignull, DS		Leics, 2004
Broad, BC		Notts, 1985
Brown, AD		Surrey, 1995
Burgess, GI		Somerset, 1978
Burns, ND		Leics, 2000
Butcher, AR		Surrey, 1979
Butcher, MA		Surrey, 1995
Caddick, AR		Somerset, 2006
Cairns, CL		Notts, 2003
Capel, DJ		Northants, 1984
Cassar, ME		Derbyshire, 1998
Cawdron, MJ	=	Gloucs, 2001
Clarke, AJ	*	Essex, 2002
Clarke, ST		Surrey, 1979
Cleary, MF		Leics, 2004
Clough, GD		Notts, 2003
Cockbain, I		Lancashire, 1983
Connor, CA		Hampshire, 1987
Cook, G		Northants, 1984
Cooper, KE		Notts, 1985
Cork, DG		Derbyshire, 1998
Cowan, AP		Essex, 2002
Cowdrey, GR		Kent, 1997

Crawley, JP	Lancashire, 1994
Croft, CEH	Lancashire, 1977
Cross, GF	Leics, 1971
Cullen, DJ	Somerset, 2006
Dakin, JM	Leics, 1993, 2000; Essex 2002
Davison, BF	Leics, 1971
Dean, KJ	Derbyshire, 1998
DeFreitas, PAJ	Derbyshire, 1998; Leics 2000, 2004
Denning, PW	Somerset, 1978
Dredge, CH	Somerset, 1978, 1986
Dudleston, B	Leics, 1971
Durston, WJ	Somerset, 2006
Evans, KP	Notts, 1985
Fairbrother, NH	Lancashire, 1983, 1994
Ferreira, AM	Warwicks, 1981
Fleming, MV	Kent, 1997
Flower, A	Essex, 2002
Folley, I	Lancashire, 1983
Foster, NA	Essex, 1989
Fothergill, AR	Durham, 1992
French, BN	Notts, 1985
Gallian, JER	Lancashire, 1994; Notts, 2003
Gard, T	Somerset, 1986
Garner, J	Somerset, 1986
Garnham, MA	Essex, 1989
Gazzard, CM	Somerset, 2006
Gifford, N	Worcs, 1980, 1982
Glendenen, JD	Durham, 1992
Goldsmith, SC	Derbyshire, 1988
Gooch, GA	Essex, 1989
Graveney, DA	Durham, 1992
Griffiths, BJ	Northants, 1984
Habib, A	Leics, 2000; Essex, 2002
Hadlee, RJ	Notts, 1985
Hancock, THC =	Gloucs, 2001
Hanley, RW	Northants, 1984
Harden, RJ	Somerset, 1986
Hardie, BR	Essex, 1989
Hardinges, MA =	Gloucs, 2001

Hardy, JJE		Somerset, 1986
Harvey, IJ	=	Gloucs, 2001
Harris, AJ		Notts, 2003
Hayes, FC		Lancashire, 1977, 1983
Hegg, WK		Lancashire, 1994
Hemmings, EE	*	Notts, 1985
Hemsley, EJO		Worcs, 1980, 1982
Henderson, CW		Leics, 2004
Henderson, PW		Durham, 1992
Hick, GA		Worcs, 2001
Hildreth, JC		Somerset, 2006
Hodge, BJ		Leics, 2004
Hogg, W		Warwicks, 1981
Holder, VA		Worcs, 1980
Holding, MA		Derbyshire, 1988
Hollioake, AJ		Surrey, 1995
Howarth, GP		Surrey, 1979
Hughes, DP		Lancashire, 1977, 1983
Hughes, SP		Durham, 1992
Humpage, GW		Warwicks, 1981
Humphries, DJ		Worcs, 1980, 1982
Hussain, N		Essex, 1989
Illingworth, R		Leics, 1971
Inchmore, JD		Worcs, 1980, 1982
Inman, CC		Leics, 1971
Irani, RC		Essex, 2002
Jackman, RD		Surrey, 1979
James, KD		Hampshire, 1987
Jefferies, ST		Lancashire, 1983
Jefferson, WI		Essex, 2002
Jennings, KF		Somerset, 1978
Johnson, P		Notts, 1985
Jones, DM		Durham, 1992
Kallicharran, AI		Warwicks, 1981
Kenlock, SG		Surrey, 1995
Kitchen, MJ		Somerset, 1978
Knight, RDV	*	Surrey, 1979
Krikken, KM		Derbyshire, 1998
Lampitt, SR		Worcs, 2001

Larkins, W	Northants, 1984; Durham, 1992
Leatherdale, DA	Worcs, 2001
Lee, PG	Lancashire, 1977
Lever, JK	Essex, 1989
Lewis, CC	Leics, 2000
Llong, NJ	Kent, 1997
Lloyd, CH	Lancashire, 1977
Lloyd, D	Lancashire, 1977
Lloyd, GD	Lancashire, 1994
Lloyd, TA	Warwicks, 1981
Logan, RJ	Notts, 2003
Lynch, MA	Surrey, 1979
Lyon, J	Lancashire, 1977
MacGill, SCG	Notts, 2003
Maddy, DL	Leics, 2000, 2004
Maher, BJM	Derbyshire, 1988
Marks, VJ	Somerset, 1986
Marsh, SA	Kent, 1997
Marshall, MD	Hampshire, 1987
Martin, PJ	Lancashire, 1994
Maru, RJ	Hampshire, 1987
Maynard, C	Lancashire, 1983
McCague, MJ	Kent, 1997
McEwan, SM	Durham, 1992
McKenzie, GD	Leics, 1971
Middlebrook, JD	Essex, 2002
Miller, G	Essex, 1989
Morris, JE	Derbyshire, 1988
Mortensen, OH	Derbyshire, 1988
Moseley, HR	Somerset, 1978
Mullally, AD	Leics, 1993
Napier, GR	Essex, 2002
Neale, PA	Worcs, 1980, 1982
Newman, PG	Derbyshire, 1988
Nicholas, MCJ	Hampshire, 1987
Nixon, PA	Leics, 1993, 2004
Norman, MEJC	Leics, 1971
Ormond, J	Leics, 2000
Ormrod, JA	Worcs, 1980, 1982

O'Shaughnessy, SJ		Lancashire, 1983
Palmer, GV		Somerset, 1986
Parker, PWG	*	Durham, 1992
Parks, RJ		Hampshire, 1987
Parsons, GJ		Leics, 1993
Parsons, KA		Somerset, 2006
Patel, DN		Worcs, 1980, 1982
Perryman, SP		Warwicks, 1981
Phillips, BJ		Kent, 1997
Pietersen, KP		Notts, 2003
Pigott, ACS	*	Surrey, 1995
Pilling, H		Lancashire, 1977
Pocock, PI		Surrey, 1979
Pollard, PR		Worcs, 2001
Potter, L		Leics, 1993
Prichard, PJ		Essex, 1989
Pridgeon, AP		Worcs, 1980, 1982
Rackemann, CG		Surrey, 1995
Randall, DW		Notts, 1985
Ratcliffe, RM		Lancashire, 1977
Rawnsley, MJ		Worcs, 2001
Read, CMW		Notts, 2003
Rhodes, SJ		Worcs, 2001
Rice, CEB		Notts, 1985
Richards, CJ		Surrey, 1979
Richards, IVA		Somerset, 1978, 1986
Roberts, B		Derbyshire, 1988
Roberts, GM		Derbyshire, 1998
Robinson, DDJ		Essex, 2002; Leics, 2004
Robinson, PJ		Somerset, 1978
Robinson, PE		Leics, 1993
Roebuck, PM		Somerset, 1978, 1986
Rollins, AS		Derbyshire, 1998
Roope, GRJ		Surrey, 1979
Rose, BC		Somerset, 1986
Rouse, SJ		Warwicks, 1981
Russell, RC	=	Gloucs, 2001
Sadler, JL		Leics, 2004
Saxelby, K		Notts, 1985

Scott, RJ		Hampshire, 1987
Shafayat, BM		Notts, 2003
Sharma, R		Derbyshire, 1988
Sharp, G		Northants, 1984
Sheriyar, A		Worcs, 2001
Simmons, J		Lancashire, 1977, 1983
Singh, A		Worcs, 2001
Slater, MJ		Derbyshire, 1998
Slocombe, PA		Somerset, 1978
Small, GC		Warwicks, 1981
Smith, AW		Surrey, 1995
Smith, BF		Leics, 1993, 2000
Smith, CL		Hampshire, 1987
Smith, DM		Surrey, 1979
Smith, GJ		Notts, 2003
Snape, JN		Leics, 2004
Solanki, VS		Worcs, 2001
Spencer, CT		Leics, 1971
Stephenson, JP		Essex, 1989, 2002
Stevens, DI		Leics, 2000, 2004
Stewart, AJ		Surrey, 1995
Strang, PA		Kent, 1997
Stringer, PM		Leics, 1971
Suppiah, AV		Somerset, 2006
Taylor, CG	=	Gloucs, 2001
Taylor, DJS		Somerset, 1978
Taylor, NS		Somerset, 1986
Terry, VP		Hampshire, 1987
Thorpe, GP		Surrey, 1995
Tolchard, RW		Leics, 1971
Topley, TD		Essex, 1989
Trego, PD		Somerset, 2006
Tremlett, TM		Hampshire, 1987
Turner, DR		Hampshire, 1987
Turner, GM		Worcs, 1980, 1982
Tweats, TA		Derbyshire, 1998
Walker, A		Northants, 1984
Walker, MJ		Kent, 1997
Ward, DM		Surrey, 1995

Ward, TR	Kent, 1997; Leics, 2000
Warner, AE	Derbyshire, 1988
Wasim Akram	Lancashire, 1994
Watkinson, M	Lancashire, 1983, 1994
Waugh, ME	Essex, 1989
Wells, AP *	Kent, 1997
Wells, VJ	Leics, 1993, 2000
Weston, MJ	Worcs, 1982
Whitaker, JJ	Leics, 1993
White, CL	Somerset, 2006
Wild, DJ	Northants, 1984
Williams, RG	Northants, 1984
Willoughby, CM	Somerset, 2006
Wilson, PHL	Surrey, 1979
Windows, MGN =	Gloucs, 2001
Wood, B	Lancashire, 1977
Wood, J	Durham, 1992
Wood, MJ	Somerset, 2006
Wootton, SH	Warwicks, 1981
Wren, TN	Kent, 1997
Yates, G	Lancashire, 1994
Younis Ahmed	Worcs, 1980, 1982

= played in match v. Sussex Cricket Board rather than Sussex CCC
* Also played for Sussex

J) UMPIRES TO HAVE OFFICIATED AT HORSHAM (FIRST-CLASS CRICKET)

Atfield, AJ	1920, 1923
Attewell, T	1908
Bagshaw, H	1923
Balderstone, JC	1992, 1993
Baldwin, HG	1937, 1947
Barlow, RG	1914
Bartley, TJ	1950
Beet, G	1932
Bird, HD	1991
Blake, J	1921, 1922
Board, JH	1922

Bond, JD		1994
Braund, LC		1935
Brown, G	#	1935, 1936
Brown, TA		1920, 1922
Buller, JS		1952, 1954
Buswell, WA	#	1932
Charlesworth, C		1926
Chester, F		1925, 1929, 1931, 1935, 1939, 1949, 1955
Clarkson, A		1998
Constant, DJ		1989, 1993
Cooke, E		1937
Corrall, P		1956
Cowley, NG		2003
Cruice, H		1939
Cuttell, WR		1927
Davies, D	#	1946
Day, JW		1930
Dudleston, B		1996
Durston, FJ		1939
Elliott, H	#	1954
Field, EF		1930, 1932
Flowers, T		1921
Gray, LH		1954
Hardstaff J (Snr)		1928, 1933, 1936, 1946
Harrison, GP		1909
Hassan, SB		1990
Hendren, D		1934, 1935, 1938, 1947, 1948
Hills, JJ	#	1947, 1949
Holder, JW		1983, 2001
Holder, VA		2002
Illingworth, RK	#	2007
Jameson, JA		1984
Jesty, TE	#	1997, 2006
Jones, AA		1988, 1991, 1997
Julian, R		2000
Kettleborough, RA		2007
Kilner, N	#	1946
King, JH	#	1928, 1929
Langridge, John	#	1974, 1979

Leadbeater, B		1995, 1999, 2004
Lee, FS	#	1950, 1952, 1953
Lee, HW		1938, 1946
Llong, NJ	#	2003
Lyons, KJ		1985
Meyer, BJ		1996
Mills, PT		1947
Morton, A		1933
Newman, JA	#	1934
Oates, TW		1927
Palmer, H		1951
Palmer, KE		1999
Palmer, R		1984, 1987, 2000
Paynter, E		1951
Pepper, CG		1971
Plews, NT		1985, 1998
Pope, GH	#	1971
Price, WFF		1956
Reeves, W	#	1937
Roberts, FG		1914
Robinson, E		1948
Russell, TM		1921, 1924, 1925
Shackleton, D	#	1979
Sharp, G	#	2002
Shepherd, DR		1988, 1989, 1990, 1992, 1994
Skelding, A	#	1933, 1938, 1939, 1953
Smith, EJ	#	1937
Smith, WR		1920
Spencer, CT		1983
Spencer, TW		1955
Steele, JF		2001, 2006
Stone, J	#	1931, 1932
Street, AE		1926, 1927, 1928
Tarbox, CV	#	1938
Thompson, H		1928
Tremlin, B		1923
Trott, AE		1912, 1913
Vining, W		1909, 1910, 1912
Walmsley, H		1910

Webb, G		1912, 1913
Welch, CH		1950
West, WAJ		1908, 1920, 1924, 1925
Whitehead, AGT		1974, 1995
Wight, PB		1987
Willey, P		2004
Woolley, CN	#	1936, 1948
Young, HI		1921, 1926, 1929

K) UMPIRES TO HAVE OFFICIATED AT HORSHAM (ONE-DAY CRICKET)

Alley, WE		1977, 1978
Balderstone, JC		1992, 1993
Bond, JD		1994
Burgess, GI	#	2006
Clarkson, A		1998
Constant, DJ		1989, 1993
Cook, C		1979, 1982
Evans, DGL		1971, 1977
Evans, JH		2004
Gould, IJ	#	2002, 2003
Halfyard, DJ		1980
Hampshire, JH	=	2001
Harris, MJ	=	2001
Holder, JW		1983, 1997, 2001
Holder, VA	#	1997, 2006
Jameson, JA		1984
Jepson, A	#	1981
Jones, AA		1988
Julian, R		2000
Khalid Ibadulla		1982
Langridge, John	#	1980
Leadbeater, B		1995
Llong, NJ	#	2003
Lyons, KJ		1985, 1986
Mallender, NA		2002
Oslear, DO		1981, 1986
Palmer, KE		1979
Palmer, R		1984, 1987, 2000

Plews, NT	1985, 1998
Shepherd, DR	1988, 1989, 1992, 1994
Spencer, CT	1983
Steele, JF	2001
Whitehead, AGT	1995
Wight, PB	1971, 1987
Willey, P	2004
Wilson, RT	1978

| # | Also played at Horsham |
| = | Umpired in Sussex Cricket Board match rather than Sussex CCC |

SELECT BIBLIOGRAPHY

The works consulted most frequently during the preparation of this book were:

- *West Sussex County Times* archives
- Horsham cricket festival programmes, 1931-1956
- Horsham CC minute books, 1907-1990
- Sussex CCC handbooks
- *Wisden Cricketer's Almanack*
- *Cricinfo* website

Of the numerous other books referred to, the following were consulted more frequently than the rest:

Bailey Philip, Thorn Philip & Wynne-Thomas Peter – *Who's Who Of Cricketers*, Newnes Books, 1984

Bannister, Jack – *The History Of Warwickshire CC*, Christopher Helm, 1990

Brooke Robert & Goodyear David – *A Who's Who Of Lancashire Cricket Club*, Breedon Books, 1991

Brooke Robert & Goodyear David – *A Who's Who Of Warwickshire Cricket Club*, Robert Hale, 1989

Brooke Robert & Goodyear David – *A Who's Who Of Worcestershire Cricket Club*, Robert Hale, 1990

Carder Tim & Harris Roger – *A Who's Who Of Brighton & Hove Albion Football Club*, Goldstone Books, 1997

Engel Matthew & Radd Andrew – *The History of Northamptonshire CCC*, Christopher Helm, 1993

Foot, David – *Sunshine, Cider And Sixes*, David & Charles, 1986

Frindall, Bill – *England Test Cricketers*, Collins Willow, 1989

Frindall, Bill – *Wisden Book Of Test Cricket, 1877-1984*, Queen Anne Press, 1985

Gilligan, AER – *Sussex Cricket*, Chapman & Hall, 1933

Gordon, Home – *Sussex County Cricket*, Convoy publications, 1950

Green, Benny (edit) – *Wisden Book Of Obituaries*, Macdonald/ Queen Anne Press, 1986

Green, David – *The History Of Gloucestershire CCC*, Christopher Helm, 1990

Hignell, Andrew – *The History Of Glamorgan CCC*, Christopher Helm, 1988

Hignell, Andrew – *A Who's Who Of Glamorgan CCC*, Breedon Books, 1992

Lambert, Dennis – *The History Of Leicestershire CCC*, Christopher Helm, 1992

Ledbetter, Jim (comp & edit) – *'First Class Cricket, A Complete Record'* series, Limlow Books, various dates

Lee, Christopher – *From The Sea End*, Partridge Press, 1989

Lemmon, David – *The Book Of Essex Cricketers*, Breedon Books, 1994

Lemmon, David – *The History Of Surrey CCC*, Christopher Helm 1989

Lemmon, David - *The History Of Worcestershire CCC*, Christopher Helm, 1989

Marshall, John – *Sussex Cricket, A History*, Heinemann, 1959

Martin-Jenkins, Christopher – *The Complete Who's Who Of Test Cricketers*, Orbis Publishing, 1980

Moore, Dudley – *The History Of Kent CCC*, Christopher Helm, 1988

Northcott, Arthur – *Popular Entertainment in Horsham, 1880-1930* – privately printed, 1988

Robertson-Glasgow, RC – *Cricket Prints*, Werner Laurie, 1943

Robertson-Glasgow, RC – *More Cricket Prints*, Werner Laurie, 1946

Shawcroft, John – *The History Of Derbyshire CCC*, Christopher Helm, 1989

Sproat, Iain (edit) – *Cricketers Who's Who series*, Queen Anne's Press, various dates

Streeton, Richard – *PGH Fender, a biography*, Faber & Faber, 1981

Swanton, EW (gen edit) – *Barclay's World Of Cricket*, Collins, 1980

Turner Dennis & White Alex – *Fulham, A Complete Record 1879-1997*, Breedon Books, 1987

Wallace, John (comp) – *Sussex County Cricket Club* ('Images of Sport' series), Tempus, 2001

Wallace, John – *100 greats, Sussex CCC*, Tempus, 2002

Weaver Paul & Talbot Bruce – *The Longest Journey*, Sutton publications, 2004

Wynne-Thomas, Peter – *The History Of Hampshire CCC*, Christopher Helm, 1988

Wynne-Thomas, Peter – *The History Of Lancashire CCC*, Christopher Helm, 1989

Wynne-Thomas, Peter – *The History Of Nottinghamshire CCC*, Christopher Helm, 1992

Horsham Society Newsletters, July 2001 and June 2004

Horsham Cricket Club Bicentenary Brochure, 1971